Toni Morrison

The Bluest Eye

With Essays in Criticism

Annotated with Critical Introduction

By
Lee, Young-Oak
Sohn, Tae-Soo

Shinasa

Toni Morrison has kindly granted
Professor Young-Oak Lee permission to annotate
the text of *The Bluest Eye* for this edition.

CONTENTS

Critical Introduction

토니 모리슨의 데뷔작 『제일 파란 눈』

—인종과 젠더 문제 연구서—

"*Tell us what it is to be a woman so that we may know what it is to be a man. What moves at the margin. What it is to have no home in this place. To be set adrift from the one you knew. What it is to live at the edge of towns that cannot bear your company.*"

–노벨상 수상 기념연설문(1993) 중에서

토니 모리슨(Toni Morrison 1931-)은 잘 알려진 대로 노벨문학상을 받은 "최초"의 아프리카계 미국 여성작가다. 21세기를 7년 남겨 놓은 시점에, 20세기 말에 와서야 위대한 작가 반열에 흑인 여성이 최초로 오르게 된 것은 암시하는 바가 크다고 생각된다. 출신과 젠더는 작가의 작품 이해에 중요하다. 작가의 관심사나 주제가 곧 그의 경험에 의해서 형성되어 작품으로 표현되어 나오기 때문이다. 첫째로, 백인작가들과 달리 모리슨의 작품에 인종문제가 주요 이슈로 다루어지는 것은 당연하다. 아프리카계 미국인들이 앵글로 색슨계 백인이 주도하는 나라에 노예로 끌려와 살면서 흑인은 곧 노예, 열등한 인종이라는 등식으로 십 수 대(代)에 걸쳐 역사 속에 존재해왔기 때문에 인종문제는 모리슨과 같은 아프리카계 미국인들에게 자신들 존재의 근간이 되는 중요한 문제다. 둘째로, 모리슨은 흑인이면서 여성작가이기 때문에 백인남성작가나 흑인남성작가들과는 달리, 그들이 이해하지 못하고 간과하는 흑인여성들의 삶을 자연스럽게 기술하고 있다. 흑인여성들의 고통은 인종은 물론 젠더의 차원이라는 이중의 억압체계 속에서 가중되었고 그 악순환은 지금도 그들의 삶을 짓누르고 있기 때문이다.

모리슨과 아프리카계 미국문학

모리슨의 문학은 하루 아침에 나온 것이 아니다. 그것은 아프리카에서 팔려 온 선조들이 노예신분이라는 어려운 상황에서도 아프리카계 미국문학의 토대를 쌓아왔기 때문에 가능했던 것이다. 필리스 위틀리(Phyllis Wheatley 1753?—1784)는 18세기 최초의 미국 흑인 시인으로서 백인 주인으로부터 배운 영어로 자신이 암흑의 대륙으로부터 문명의 대륙으로 오게 된 것이 축복이었음을 구사하면서 흑인들도 백인이나 마찬가지로 영혼을 가진 존재임을 노래하였다. 프레드릭 더글라스(Frederick Douglass 1817?—1895)는 노예신세를 간신히 벗어나 일약 노예폐지론의 주요 연사가 되었으며 자신의 노예로서의 삶을 자서전 *Narrative of the Life of Frederick Douglass, an American Slave* (1845)으로 펴냄으로써 <노예 이야기(slave narratives)>의 대표적인 작품이 되었다. 1820년부터 1860년 사이에 나온 수많은 노예 이야기는 미국의 "기이한 제도(a peculiar institution)" 즉 노예제도를 도마 위에 올려놓고 공통적으로 노예로서의 삶의 경험과 자유로의 영웅적인 탈출, 그리고 노예폐지론의 이론과 목표를 제시하고 있다. 그 중에도 해리엇 윌슨(Harriet E. Wilson)의 『우리의 닉(*Our Nig, Or, Sketches from the Life of a Free Black*)』 (1859)은 남북전쟁 이전의 북부인 뉴잉글란드에서의 노예제의 실상을 보인 작품으로, 흑인여성작가에 의해 출간된 최초의 소설작품이다.

본격적인 아프리카계 미국문학 운동은 1910년대, 뉴욕을 중심으로 새로운 세대의 젊은 흑인들이 중산 계층을 이루면서, 미국 문단에 이들의 목소리가 형성되기 시작하였다고 본다. 후일 리차드 라이트(Richard Wright 1908—1960)와 랠프 엘리슨(Ralph Ellison 1914-1994)의 등장은 미국 문단의 주목을 끌기에 충분하였다. 라이트의 『토박이(*Native Son*)』 (1940)는 아프리카계 미국인들의 분노를 담고 있다. 미국사회에서 인정받지 못하고, 가난과 편견과 백인에 대한 두려움 속에서 오히려 범죄로 빠지게 되는 청년의 모습을 통해, 한 인간의 타락이 당사자의 잘못이라기 보다는 사회와 공동체의 그릇된 인식에서 비롯되는 것임을 고발하고 있다. 그와는 대조적으로 엘리슨의 『보이지 않는 인간(*Invisible Man*)』(1952)은 인간과 사회 내면에 자리 잡은 흑인에 대한 편견과 인종의식을 다루면서도 매우 미학적으로, 또한 철학적으로, 인간 존재의 문제로 승화시켰던 것이다. 또한 워커(Alice Walker)에 의해 1960년대에 뒤늦게 발굴된 허스톤(Zora Neale Hurston 1901?—1960)은 『그들의 눈은 신을 쳐다보고 있었다(*Their Eyes Were Watching God*)』(1937)와 같은 대표작에서 흑인 민속 문화를 배경과 재료로 사용하여 당당하게 흑인 여성의 자아 성취문제를 선구적으로 다루고 있다.

20세기 아프리카계 미국문학의 중흥은 1960년대의 흑인 민권운동과 더불어 흑인 작가들과 비평가들의 활동이 두드러지면서 앞당겨진다. 앞에서 언급한 바, 워커가 당시까지 알려지지 않았던 선배 작가 허스톤을 발굴한 것도 흑인정체성 찾기 운동과 무관하지 않으며, 특히 1970년대부터는 백인 부르주아 여성 페미니스트로부터 독립을 선언한 흑인페미니스트 이론의 정립과 운동이 활발해지면서 워커와 모리슨(Toni Morrison)은 그들만의 굳건한 문학전통을 확립한다. 워커의 많은 작품들 중 특히 『컬러 퍼플(*The Color Purple*)』(1982)은 스티븐 스필버그 감독에 의해 영화화되는 등 선풍을 일으켰고, 모리슨은 『빌러비드(*Beloved*)』(1987)로 노벨 문학상을 받기에 이른 것이다. 워커와 모리슨은 여성 주인공들을 통하여 여성의 섹슈얼리티(sexuality)가 착취당하고 있음을 그리고 있으며 동시에 인종문제는 작품 전체에서 큰 그림의 근간을 이루고 있다. 아프리카계 작가들은 법적으로는 인간으로서의 평등과 자유를 획득한지 일 백 오십 년이 가까워오지만, 구체적인 사회활동이나 의식세계에서는 여전히 인종차별이 심각함을 드러내어 이를 문제시하고 있으며, 특히 여성 작가들은 흑인여성들이 인종과 젠더 측면에서 이중적 억압을 받아왔고 아직도 받고 있음을 주요주제로 삼고 있다.

모리슨의 생애와 작품

미국의 퓰리처 상을 수상한 최초의 흑인 여성작가 모리슨(본명 Chloe Anthony Wofford Morrison)의 성장과정은 인종적 전통과 역사의식으로 각인되어 있었다고 해도 과언이 아니다. 1931년 오하이오주 로레인(Lorain) 시에서 태어난 모리슨은 작품 속에서 인종차별적이고 남성 지배적인 사회에서의 흑인 여성의 경험과 역할을 탐구하고 있는데, 그 복합적이고 다층적인 내러티브의 한 가운데에는 아프리카계 미국인들의 특이한 문화적 유산이 깔려있는 것이 특징이다.

모리슨의 부모는 본래 미국의 남부에서 인종차별을 피하여 오하이오로 이사하였으며 노예제도가 없었던 북부에서 더 나은 삶의 기회를 찾고자 하였다. 모리슨의 부친은 근면한 조선공(造船工)으로 일하였는데 배의 측면에 자신이 용접한 증거로 자신의 이름을 새겨 넣을 정도로 자부심이 강하였고, 작가의 모친은 성가대원으로 활약한 신앙인이었다고 한다. 그들은 자기 조상들의 문화적 유산을 자랑스럽게 여겨, 자녀들에게 남부의 흑인 민담이나 노래들을 들려준 것으로 보인다. 인종문제에 있어서 모리슨은 특히 부친의 영향을 받았다. 조지아주에서 어린 시절을 보낸 부친은 백인 어른들로부터의 충격적인 경험으로 인하여 인종차별주의자가 되어 백인들을 노골적으로 멸시했으며, 자기를 멸시하는 백인들을 이해하지도 못했다고 한다.

작가 모리슨은 어려움이 없이 자랐다. 어려서는 발레리나를 꿈꾸었으며 독서를 즐겨서, 톨스토이나 도스토예프스키 같은 러시아 작가들과, 프랑스의 플로베르, 영국의 제인 오스틴을 좋아했다. 1949년에는 로레인 고등학교를 우등으로 졸업하고 워싱턴 D.C.에 있는 흑인 명문인 하워드(Howard) 대학에 입학하여 영문학을 전공하고 고전문학을 부전공으로 공부하였다. 이 때 모리슨은 클로(Chloe)라는 아프리카 이름을 발음하기 어렵다는 이유로 버리고, 가운데 이름인 앤토니(Anthony)를 줄여 중성적 이름인

“Toni”로 개명하였다. 하워드 대학에서 극단에 가입한 모리슨은 극단을 따라 부모가 떠나 온 남부를 여러 차례 돌아 볼 기회를 가질 수 있었다. 1953년 모리슨은 하워드 대학에서 영문학 학사 학위를 받았고, 1955년에는 윌리엄 포크너(William Faulkner)와 버지니어 울프(Virginia Woolf)의 작품 연구로 코넬대에서 석사학위를 받았다.

졸업 후 휴스턴에 있는 텍사스 남부대학에서 영문학 입문을 가르치던 모리슨은 그곳에서, 하워드대와는 달리 "흑인역사 주간"을 정하고 흑인문화를 개인적 혹은 가족적 회상 차원이 아닌 하나의 학문으로 연구하는 것을 보게 되었다. 모리슨은 1957년 교수의 자격으로 하워드대학으로 돌아와 자마이카 출생의 건축가인 해롤드 모리슨(Harold Morrison)을 만나게 되고 이듬해 그와 결혼했다. 당시는 민권운동이 한창이던 시기여서 모리슨은 아미리 바라카(Amiri Baraka, 구 LeRoi Jones)와 후일 마틴 루터 킹을 도왔고, 조지아주 아틀란타의 시장이 된 앤드루 영(Andrew Young) 등 이 투쟁에 가담하는 이들을 만나게 되었다.

1961년, 모리슨 부부의 첫 아들 해롤드 포드(Harold Ford)가 태어나고, 모리슨은 가정을 꾸리면서 계속 가르치는 일에 몰두한다. 그리고는 불행한 결혼생활로부터의 도피 겸 소작가 모임에 참가하기 시작하였다. 문학을 좋아하는 사람들과 만날 필요를 느끼고 있었기 때문이다. 이 모임에서는 각자가 단편이나 시를 들고 와 토론거리를 제공하도록 되어있었는데, 어느 날 아무 것도 가져갈 것이 없게 된 모리슨은, 어릴 적에 알던 어느 여자아이가 하나님에게 파란 눈을 달라고 기도한 내용을 대강 엮어 발표하였다. 이 이야기에 대한 모임 구성원들의 반응은 좋았으나 모리슨은 더 이상 생각하지 않았다고 한다. 모리슨은 결혼생활이 악화되자, 둘째 아이를 임신한 채 남편과 직장을 떠나 아들을 데리고 유럽을 여행하였다. 1964년에 모리슨은 남편과 이혼하고 두 아들을 데리고 로레인의 친정으로 돌아갔다.

1964년 가을, 모리슨은 뉴욕 주 시라큐즈(Syracuse) 시에 있는 랜덤하우스 교과서 자회사에 취직하였고, 1965년 뉴욕 시의 랜덤하우스 편집주간(Senior Editor)으로 전보발령을 받는다. 모리슨이 일하는 동안 아이들은 가정부가 돌보고, 저녁에는 모리슨이 밥을 짓고 아이들과 놀아주다가 재웠다. 아이들이 잠들면, 모리슨은 글을 쓰기 시작하였다. 이 때 모리슨은 작가 소모임에서 전에 발표했던 이야기를 꺼내어 먼지를 털고 그것을 소설로 만들기로 결심했다. 어린 시절 기억을 되살려 상상력으로 확충하고 작중인물들에게 생명을 불어넣었다. 창작은 신나고 도전적인 일이었다. 글 쓰는 일과 아이들을 돌보는 일 외에 다른 일들은 지루하게 생각되었다.

랜덤하우스의 편집인으로 토니 케이드 밤바라(Toni Cade Bambara), 무하마드 알리(Muhammad Ali), 앤드루 영(Andrew Young), 안젤라 데이비스(Angela Davis) 같은 저명한 아프리카계 미국작가들 작품을 편집하면서, 모리슨은 자신의 작품을 여러 출판사에 보내느라 바쁜 나날을 보냈다. 이것이 바로, 불행한 삶에 처한 나머지, 백인들처럼 파란 눈만 가지면 만사가 잘 풀릴 것이라고 생각하는 비극의 흑인 여주인공을 묘사한 『제일 파란 눈(*The Bluest Eye*)』(1970)이다. 그 후로 모리슨은 20여 년간 랜덤하우스에서 일하였고, 다른 한 편으로는 예일대 등에서 가르치며 계속 작품을 발표하였다. 두 흑인여성간의 우정과 사회공동체와의 관계를 그린 1973년의 『술라(*Sula*)』, 헤일리 (Alex Hailey)의 『뿌리(*Roots*)』와 같이 한 흑인 남성의 가계, 내지 정체성을 캐내는 1977년의 『솔로몬의 노래(*Song of Solomon*)』, 카리브 섬을 배경으로 흑인과 백인간의 상호관계를 그린 1981년의 『타르 베이비(*Tar Baby*)』 등이 이때 나왔고, 모리슨은 전국비평가협회상(National Book Critic's Circle Award) 등 각종 상을 받으면서 급기야 그의 사진은 1981년 3월 30일 『뉴스위크(Newsweek)』지 표지를 장식하기도 하였다.

1983년에 모리슨은 랜덤하우스를 그만두고 1984년에는 올버니 뉴욕주립대의 알버트 슈바이처 석좌교수가 되었다. 1987년에 출간된 다음 소설 『빌러비드(*Beloved*)』는 실제로 일어났던 끔찍한 사건에 기초한 작품이다. 마거릿 가너(Margaret Garner)라는 노예는 1851년에 켄터키 주의 백인주인에게서 아이들을 데리고 도망쳐 나왔으나 다시 주인에게 붙잡히게 되었는데, 아이들이 자신처럼 노예로 고통스러운 삶을 살게 될 것을 끔찍하게 여긴 나머지 차라리 아이들이 죽는 게 낫다고 생각하고, 실제로 그 중 한 아기를 죽인 사건이 일어났다. 그러나 가너는 자신의 끔찍한 행동에 대해 조금도 후회하지 않았다고 전하는데 이 이야기를 접한 모리슨은 이를 작품화하는데 성공하여 곧 베스트셀러가 되었다. 이 작품은 계속 관심을 일으켜 1988년에 퓰리처상 수상작이 되었고, 오프라 윈프리(Oprah Winfrey)가 여주인공 세서(Sethe) 역을 맡은 영화로도 제작되었다.

모리슨은 1987년에 프린스톤 대학의 로버트 고힌 석좌교수(Robert F. Goheen Professor)가 됨으로써 아이비리그 대학의 석좌교수가 된 최초의 흑인 여성작가가 되었다. 작품 활동 못지않게 교육에도 관심이 지대한 모리슨은 이곳에서 창작을 가르치면서, 아프리카계 미국연구, 미국학, 여성학 프로그램 등에 관여하였다. 또한 1992년에는 『빌러비드』에 이어 삼부작의 두 번째인 그녀의 여섯 번째 소설 『재즈(*Jazz*)』를 출간하고, 주요 비평서라 할 수 있는 『어둠 속 연주(*Playing in the Dark*)』를 또한 출간하였다. 모리슨은 1993년에 노벨문학상을 수상함으로써 여성으로는 여덟 번째 수상자요, 흑인여성으로는 최초의 수상자가 되었다. 모리슨은 쉬지 않고 작품활동을 하여 현재까지 『패러다이스(*Paradise*)』(1998)와 『사랑 (*Love*)』(2003)을 최근작으로 내어놓고 있다.

인종과 젠더 문제 연구서: 『제일 파란 눈』

『제일 파란 눈』은 모리슨의 첫 소설작품이면서 그녀의 전체적인 창작세계를 잘 드러내는 지표가 되는 작품이다. 모리슨은 작가란 본래부터 정치인이라고 보았다. 작가가 비정치적이라고 생각되는 이유는 어떠한 특정 재앙에 대해 둔감해서 그럴 뿐이라는 것이다. 현대를 사는 흑인작가로서 모리슨은 인종차별을 가장 치명적인 현상이라고 보았으며, 한 인터뷰에서 인종차별주의라면 어떤 형태이든 흥미를 느낀다고 밝힌 바 있다. 사람들이 매일의 생활에서 이 인종차별주의가 얼마나 치명적인지를 잘 의식하지 못한다는 것이다. '인종차별주의' 하면 흑인과 백인간의 관계를 우선 생각하지만, 그보다도 인종차별은 같은 인종집단 내에서도 쉽게 발생한다고 모리슨은 보고 있다. 또한 여성작가로서 여성의 문제를 인종차별주의 못지않게 중요한 문제라고 보았다. 이러한 주제들을 담은 것이 『제일 파란 눈』이다.

여주인공 피콜라(Pecola Breedlove)와 그의 엄마 폴린(Pauline Breedlove)은 백인사회와 백인가치체계의 부산물들이다. 피콜라의 자기평가(self-image)는 사회기준에 비추어 매우 냉혹하다. 즉 스스로를 못생기고 재수 없는 존재라고 여긴다. 피콜라가 이런 생각을 가지게 된 것은 백인 중심의 초등학교 교육과, 주위에 있는 흑인과 백인들의 영향을 받았기 때문이다. 학교 교과서에 나오는 주인공 제인은 온 가족이 화목하게 잘 지내고 부러울 것이 없다. 그런데 제인은 피부가 하얗고, 눈동자는 파랗고, 머리카락은 블론드다. 따라서 피콜라는 자기 집이 난로에 불도 못 피울 정도로 가난하고, 아버지 어머니가 매일 싸우고 폭력이 난무하는 것은 자기 얼굴이 까맣고 머리칼도 꼬불꼬불하게 못생겼기 때문이라고 믿게 되었다는 것이다. 피콜라 뿐 아니라, 피콜라의 어머니 폴린(Pauline)도 새까만 딸이 못생겨서 밉다고 생각한다. 이 모녀의 사례에서 보듯이, 흑인의 노예해방은 2세기 전에 이루어졌으나, 백인주인으로부터의 진정한 해방은 아직도 이루어지지 않은 채 백인사회가 설정한 가치체계를 흑인들은 그대로 답습하고 있다. 모리슨의 메시지는 내면화 된 백인주도의 가치체계가 흑인의 흑인됨을 부인하고 열등한 것으로 치부하고 있음을 지적하는 것이다. 『제일 파란 눈』은 바로 이러한 아프리카계 미국인들의 정신적 식민 상황을 진단하고 있다. 미국은 다인종 사회임에도 불구하고 아름다움과 행복의 기준 등 모든 가치관이 대부분 백인의 시각으로 규정되어 있다. 즉 이 작품에서도 나타나 있듯이, 미국 사회에서 최고의 미인은 하얀 피부에 파란 눈을 한 블론드 머리의 여성이다. 영화와 광고, 신문과 잡지뿐만 아니라 책이나 인형들에서부터 심지어 매일 사용하는 컵에도 하나하나 이러한 요소들이 아름다움과 행복의 기준임을 암시하고 있기 때문에 사람들은 알게 모르게 이러한 가치 기준들을 받아들여 이상적인 미는 자기들의 것이 아니며, 따라서 자기들이 행복해지는 것은 불가능하다는 생각을 부지불식간에 하게 되고 결과적으로 자신들과 동족들을 혐오하게 된다. 피콜라가 동일시할 수 있는 흑인의 미적 조건은 이 작품 그 어디에서도 제시되어 있지 않다. 바로 이 점이 흑인이 어린 나이 때부터 겪는 정신적 식민화의 첫 단계라고 작가는 보고 있는 것이다.

작품 속의 피콜라는 흑인으로서 스스로 못생겼다는 열등의식을 갖고 있을 뿐만 아니라 자신이 속한 사회가 제시한 완벽한 미의 기준 등에 세뇌되어 있기 때문에 식민적 가치가 철저하게 내면화 된 인물이다. 피콜라가 클로디아의 집에 신세를 지면서 무려 1리터나 되는 많은 양의 우유를 밤새 마신 것은 인생을 마음대로 할 수 있는 권력을 휘두르는 흰색에 대한 열망이 반영된 것이고, 또 피콜라가 셜리 템플 잔을 애용하는 것은 셜리 템플이 미인을 대표한다고 여기고 그 기준을 그대로 흠모하는 까닭이다. 피콜라의 이런 터무니 없는 행동이 그녀가 우유를 좋아해서가 아니라 미와 행복의 상징인 셜리 템플이 우유 잔에 그려져 있기 때문이라는 사실은, 내적으로 백인의 가치를 전적으로 수용하고 그 목표를 숭모하는 어린 소녀의 무지와 순수성을 대변해 준다. 부친의 거듭된 성폭행과 모친의 폭행 및 폭언, 방화 사건, 결과적인 가정파괴 등 일련의 절망의 나락에서 무지한 피콜라는 자기의 눈동자가 파래지기만 하다면 교과서에서 본 제인의 행복한 집안처럼 자기 집도 만사형통하게 될 것이라고 믿게 되는 것이고, 그러므로 이 세상에서 "제일 파란 눈"을 달라고 하나님에게 간구하는 것이다. 피콜라의 정신적 질병은 백인사회에서 백인들에게 유리하게 적용되는 것을 거르지 않고 흑인에게 주입한 이데올로기로 인해 생긴 것이다. 여기서 "파란 눈"은 사람을 행복하게 하는 요소들의 상징이 된다. 순진하고 무지한 주인공 흑인 소녀 피콜라는 백인사회의 지배적인 이데올로기를 맹목적으로 추종할 수밖에 없었고, 결국은 비극적 좌절을 맞게 된다.

흑인 여성이 이중 억압 즉 흑인이기 때문에 인종 차별을, 여성이기 때문에 성차별을 받고 시달리는 상황은 사실은 단지 피콜라의 처지에 그치지 않는다. 이 작품에서 피콜라의 어머니인 폴린 브리드러브도 주체성이 결여되고 자아가 텅 비어있는 흑인 여성으로서 기존 사회의 통념에 의해 희생된 식민적 자아다. 폴린은 어린 시절의 사고로 발을 절게 된 것이 평생의 신체적 결함으로 남았다. 걸음걸이가 온전치 못하게 되자 그녀는 매사에 소극적이고 수동적인 아이로 자라나게 되었으며, 피콜라가 그녀 자신과 주변의 불행이 자기의 눈동자가 파랗지 않기 때문이라고 믿듯이 폴린도 자신이 이해할 수 없는 불행한 일들이 생기는 것은 자신이 절름발이이기 때문이라고 믿는다. 다시 말하면 폴린의 신체적 결함은 원죄와 같아서 폴린의 삶을 제약하고 있으며, 결국 폴린은 가족들 가운데 존재감을 박탈당한다. 그녀는 어린 동생들의 학교 뒷바라지를 하며 일하는 부모 대신 살림을 함으로써 자신의 권리를 주장하기보다 양보를 우선시하는 전형적인 여성이 된다. 즉 폴린의 신체적 결함은 이 작품에서 탈식민주의적 여성 정체성의 상징으로 작용한다. 자신이 지니게 된 스티그마(stigma), 즉 못나게도 다리를 절고 또 흑인여성이라는 점이 곧 정상적인 백인과 대등할 수 없게 만드는 극복할 수 없는 열등성임을 의심없이 받아들이고 있다는 점에서 그러하다.

폴린의 자아는 수동적이고 의존적인 식물과 같아서, 그녀는 끊임없는 관심과 사랑을 받지 못하면 금방 자신을 잃어버린다. 그녀는 전적으로 남편에 의존하여 살아간다. 그녀가 남편 찰리

(Cholly Breedlove)와 함께 일자리를 찾아 흑인들이 별로 없는 북부 도시로 이사하는데 압도적인 백인들의 환경 하에서 흑인자아는 더욱 위축된다. 폴린은 낯선 백인들과의 잦은 대면으로 어려움을 겪은 데다가 남편이 예전 같지 않게 되자 시선을 바깥으로 돌려 영화관을 찾게 되고, 수많은 영화를 반복적으로 보는 동안에 그녀는 백인 기득권층이 제시하는 가치관을 고스란히 내면화한다. 영화에서 본 모든 것들은 대조적으로 빈궁한 현실을 더욱 초라하게 보이게 만들고, 초라하고 빈한한 모습은 흑인집단과 동일시되어 그녀로 하여금 흑인으로서의 정체성을 거부하게 만든다. 그녀는 자신의 주체성을 포기하고 백인들이 정한 절대 미, 질서, 청결, 칭찬, 사치에 대한 개념을 가치 기준으로 삼고 자기만의 세계를 구축한다. 즉 백인 기득권층이 설정한 가치를 받아들여 자기 것으로 내면화하며 이 세계에 남편은 물론 자녀들조차 끼어들지 못하게 한다. 폴린 역시 백인 주도의 사회에서 고립된 타자이면서 자신을 백인들과 동일시함으로써 식민적 자아로 변한다.

남편 찰리는 출생의 순간부터 정체성을 박탈당한 남자다. 부모가 쓰레기 더미에 버린 간난 아기로 인생을 시작한 찰리는 정체성을 찾고자 아버지를 찾아 나서지만 인종차별적인 사회는 찰리에게 좌절만을 경험하게 한다. 그의 좌절은 인생의 가장 아름다운 순간인 한 여성과의 데이트 중에 극에 달한다. 이 시골 처녀와의 숲 속 애정 행위 도중, 백인 남자들에게 발각되어 그들이 자신들의 엉덩이에 손전등을 비추는 상황에서 성행위를 계속하도록 강요당한 것이 그것이다. 이러한 수모는 찰리로 하여금 자신의 무능과 인종적 열등의식을 절감하게 하고, 백인에게 향하지 못하는 그의 분노는 인종 차별주의적 경험을 성차별적 경험으로 변형된 형태로 표출된다. 즉 그는 힘이 센 백인 남자보다 같은 흑인이자 약자인 여성에게 분노를 표출하고 또 이들을 경멸하게 된다. 따라서, 폴린과 찰리의 부부관계는 인종 차별의 상흔으로 인해 식민지적 사고를 극복하지 못함으로써 서로에게 더

욱 깊은 상처를 주는 파괴적인 관계로 치닫는다.

모리슨은 피콜라를 성폭행하는 가해자인 부친 촐리를 단순한 동물적 존재로 묘사하지 않음으로써 흑인들의 극한적인 삶의 모습을 복합적으로 조명한다. 촐리는 아버지가 들어온 것도 모르고 부엌에서 설거지를 하고 있는 딸을 보자, 아내 폴린을 처음 만났을 때에 그녀에게 느꼈던 감정이 되살아남을 느끼는 것이다. 어딘가 애틋하고, 희망도 꿈도 없어 보이는 현실에 치인 딸의 모습, 그것은 자신을 향한 비난으로 여겨진다. 딸의 불행한 뒷모습을 보는 촐리는 자신의 무능과 무력함을 떠올리고, 그 순간에 한 다리로 서서 다른 다리의 종아리를 긁는 딸의 모습은 그가 처음 폴린을 만났을 당시를 상기시키면서, 그 연민이 아내 닮은 딸에게 향하는 애틋한 마음과 섞이어 성폭행으로까지 진행됨을 독자는 보게 된다. 백인집단의 희생자가 되어버린 촐리가 이제는 소위 "가장 숭고해야 할 사랑의 행위로" 딸에게 치유하지 못할 상처를 입히는 가해자로 변신하는 것이다.

> The tenderness welled up in him, and he sank to his knees, his eyes on the foot of his daughter. Crawling on all fours toward her, he raised his hand and caught the foot in an upward stroke. . . . The confused mixture of his memories of Pauline and the doing of a wild and forbidden thing excited him . . . Surrounding all of this lust was a border of politeness (195).

작가는 촐리의 짐승 같은 행위를 복합적인 심리적 바탕 위에 탈 자아적인 순간의 숭엄한 자비의 행위로까지 보일 정도로 묘사하고 있다.

『제일 파란 눈』은 작품의 구성과 기교면에서도 관심을 끈다. 백인주도적 가치체계의 메시지를 전하는 초등학교 교과서의 문구를 초두로 하는 묶음들이 작품을 이루고 있는데, 문제는 교과서의 문구들이 처음에는 정식으로 문법에 맞게 대문자와 소문자, 문장 부호를 갖추어 제시되어 있으나, 뒤로 갈수록 띄어쓰기가 사라지고, 대, 소문자가 구분되지 않으며, 부호도 생략되어 있어 피콜라의 의식세계가 갈수록 격화하고 혼란스러워짐을 나타내고 있다.

작품 속의 주요화자는 피콜라(11세) 또래의 맥티어(McTeer) 자매 중 동생 클로디아(Claudia)다. 클로디아는 관찰력이 있고 자부심이 강하며 흑인 정체성에 대한 의식도 지니고 있어 흑인 어른들이 비판의식 없이 수용하는 백인가치체계의 주입에 대항한다. 폴린의 식민적 주체를 그대로 답습한 피콜라는 주어진 환경에 수동적으로 대처하였으나, 어른을 포함하여 모든 여자아이들이 열광하는 인형을 파괴할 정도로, 클로디아는 자기의 주체성을 가지고 강요되는 가치관에 투지를 가지고 대립한다. 클로디아는 사회적 미의 기준을 나타내는 인형을 해체하고 이 인형이 단순한 부속품들의 집합체에 불과하다는 사실을 폭로함으로써 아름다움과 부유함 등 백인과 연상되는 고정관념과 가치관에 도전하고 있다. 그러나 이미 백인들의 미적 기준에 세뇌된 어른들은 클로디아의 행동을 이해하지 못하고 오히려 야단만 친다. 그들은 백인 인형을 높이 평가하고 귀하게 여기는 것이 백인들이 그들에게 심어준 가치관을 그대로 답습하는 식민적인 사고라는 것을 깨닫지 못하기 때문이다. 그들은 클로디아야말로 그들이 도달하지 못했던 자아 인식의 단계를 밟고 있으며 자신의 주체성을 인식하고 자신의 판단에 따라 스스로가 원하는 것이 무엇인지를 생각하고 있음을 이해하지 못한다. 여기서 우리는 내면화된 식민주의적인 가치는 쉽게 극복되지 않는다는 사실을 알 수 있다. 미의 기준을 상징하는 인형은 쉽게 망가뜨릴 수 있지만, 백인 인형으로 표상화 된 예쁜 아이에 대한 어른들의 인식은 바꾸기가 힘들다. 피콜라가 유일한 탈출구인 광증(insanity)으로 도피하였다면, 클로디아는 역경을 디디고 일어서서 폴린이 계승시킨 수동적 패배의식을 차단하는 첫 세대가 될 것이다. 클로디아가 화자인 것은 미래의 흑인의 정체성 확립에 희망의 빛을 던진다. 그가 십대를 대표하여 자신의 부모를 비롯한 어른들에게 던지는 비판적인 시선은 앞으로의 세대가 백인들의 영향에서 벗어나 주체적으로 가치관을 형성해갈 것임을 예시하고 있다.

작품『제일 파란 눈』은 아름다운 눈을 갖고자 하는 피콜라의 이야기이지만, "아름다움"에 국한된 이야기는 아니다. 물론 아름다워지는 것은 만인의 소망이다. 태고적부터, 현대에 이르기까지 미에 대한 여성들의 갈망은 시대를 초월하고 있다. 젊은 여성들에게는 미에 대한 욕구가 고통스러울 정도로 특별할 것이고, 여유로운 사회일수록 남성들도 피부건강과 이목구비 관리에 관심을 보인다. 그러나 모리슨은 아름다움이란 신체적 미에 국한되는 것이 아니라, 인간이 노력하여 성취할 수 있는 모든 것이 아름다움이라고 강조하고 있다. 즉 정직하다거나, 교육을 받는다거나, 절제할 수 있다거나, 건강하다거나, 우아하다거나 하는 등의 덕목들이 그러하다. 따라서 아이들을 볼 때, "너 이쁘구나, 잘 생겼구나" 라고 할 것이 아니라 "너 정직하구나, 너의 생김이 맘에 든다" 와 같이 칭찬을 해주어야 할 것이라고 모리슨은 제안하고 있다.

『제일 파란 눈』을 읽을 때, 다음과 같은 질문을 상정하며 생각해볼 수 있겠다(2002: Lee 1016-1017) .

1. 우리 사회에도 피콜라의 경우와 같은 이야기가 있는가? 반세기 동안 미국은 우리의 동맹국이었고 따라서 우리에게 많은 영향을 끼쳤다. 그렇다면 우리 역시 미국적 가치를 맹목적으로 추종하고 있지는 않은가? 어떤 점에서 그러한가?

2. 한국은 일본으로부터 1945년에 해방되었다. 우리는 한국적 정체성을 되찾았는가? 만일 아직 완전히 되찾지 못했다면, 어느 점에서 우리가 아직 일본의 식민적 잔재를 가지고 있는가?

3. 한국은 숱한 외세의 침략에도 불구하고 혈통의 순수성을 지켜왔다고 자부하고 있다. 이제 다른 인종과 민족, 이데올로기를 가진 사람들과 자주 소통하며 살아야 하는 시대에 직면하고 있는데, 한국인 단일민족사상은 세계화의 시대에 어떻게 이해되어야 하는가?

4. 빈곤은 종종 교육정도와 유관하고 가정폭력상태로 이어진다. 빈곤가정 출신 아동들은 교육을 별로 받지 못하여 후일 직업조차 쉽게 구하지 못한다. 빈곤—교육—가정폭력의 악순환이 한국의 가정과 사회에서 어떻게 벌어지고 있는지 토론하라.

5. 미국의 초등학교 교과서에 비해 한국의 초등 교과서는 어떠한가? 한국의 교과서는 아동들의 사고 형성에 어떤 영향을 끼치는가?

6. 탈식민주의 학자인 가야트리 스피박(Gayatri Spivak)은 다음과 같이 주장하고 있다. 『제일 파란 눈』을 놓고 스피박의 논지를 조명해보라.

"인종차별의 가장 한심한 사실은 주도문화권에 진입한 사람의 행동 하나하나를 이미 주도문화권에 사는 사람의 행동에 연관시켜 해석 한다는 점이다. 마치 후자는 역사에 오염되지 않은 신성한 존재인 것처럼 가정하고 있다."

토니 모리슨 연보

1931년 2월 18일 오하이오(Ohio) 주 로레인(Lorain)에서 워포드 부부(George and Ramah Willis Wofford) 사이에 둘째로 태어남. 본명은 클로 앤서니 워포드(Chloe Anthony Wofford).

1953년 워싱턴, DC 소재 하워드 대학(Howard University)에서 학사 학위를 받고 난 이후 코넬 대학(Cornell University) 대학원 진학. 하워드 대학 시절 이름을 토니(Toni)로 개명.

1955년 코넬 대학(Cornell University) 대학원에서 버지니아 울프(Virginia Woolf)와 윌리엄 포크너(William Faulkner) 작품에 나타난 자살 연구로 석사 학위.

1955-57년 휴스턴(Houston) 소재 텍사스 서던 대학(Texas Southern University)에서 영문과 강사.

1957-64년 하워드 대학에서 교편

1958년 자마이카(Jamaica) 출신 건축가 해롤드 모리슨(Harold Morrison)과 결혼

1961년 첫째 아들 해롤드 포드(Harold Ford) 태어남

1964년 가족과 유럽 여행 직후 이혼. 둘째 아들 슬레이드 케빈(Slade Kevin) 태어남

1964년 랜덤하우스(Random House)의 편집인으로 일하기 위해 뉴욕 주의 시라큐스(Syracuse)로 감.

1965년 뉴욕 랜덤하우스의 편집장으로 전보발령.

1970년 첫번째 소설 『제일 파란 눈(*The Bluest Eye*)』 출판.

1971-72년 퍼처스(Purchase) 소재 뉴욕 주립 대학(State University of New York)에서 부교수.

1973년 두 번째 소설 『술라(*Sula*)』 출판. 미들턴 해리스(Middleton Harris)의 『블랙 북(*The Black Book*)』 (選集) 편집 및 출판.

1975년 『술라』로 전국저술상 지명후보 및 오호아나(Ohoana) 저술상 수상.

1976년-77년 예일 대학(Yale University) 강사.

1977년 세 번째 소설 『솔로몬의 노래(*Song of Solomon*)』 출판. (이달의 저서 선정). 전국 비평가 협회상(National Book Critics Circle Award) 및 아메리칸 아카데미 문학예술상(American Academy and Institute of Arts and Letters Award) 수상.

1980 카터 대통령 당시 전국예술위원회(National Council on the Arts)에 위원으로 지명됨.

1981년 네 번째 소설 『타르 베이비(*Tar Baby*)』가 출판. 미국예술원(American Academy and Institute of Arts and Letters)에 선출됨. 『뉴스위크(Newsweek)』지 표지에 나옴.

1984-89년 올버니(Albany) 소재 뉴욕 주립 대학(State of University of New York)에서 알버트 슈바이처 인문학 석좌교수(Albert Schweitzer Professorship).

1986년 1월 4일 희곡 『꿈꾸는 에멧(*Dreaming Emmet*)』이 뉴욕주 올버니에서 공연됨. 뉴욕 주지사 예술상(New York State Governor's Art Award) 수상.

1986-88년 바드 대학(Bard College)에서 객원교수.

1987년 다섯 번째 소설 『빌러비드 (*Beloved*)』 출판됨. 버클리 캘리포니아 주립대 이사회 초청 연사.

1988년 『빌러비드』로 퓰리처 소설작품상(Pulitzer Prize)과 로버트 케네디 상(Robert F. Kenney Award) 등을 수상. 멜처상(Melcher Award), 콜럼버스 이전 재단상(Before Columbus Foundation Award) 수상. 전국여성연합회(National Organization for Women) 의 엘리자베스 캐디 스탠튼상(Elizabeth Cady Stanton Award) 수상.

1989년 프린스턴 대학교 로버트 F. 고힌 인문학 석좌교수 (Robert F. Goheen Professorship of Humanities). 미연방 MLA (Modern Language Association of America's Commonwealth Award) 문학상 수상.

1990년 키안티 루피노 안티코 파토레 국제 문학상(Chianti Ruffino

Antico Fattore International Literary Prize) 수상.

1992년 여섯 번째 소설 『재즈(*Jazz*)』 출간됨. 평론집 『어둠 속의 연주(*Playing in the Dark: Whiteness and the Literary Imagination*)』 출간. Race-ing Justice, En-Gendering Power: Essays on Anita Hill, Clarence Thomas, and the Construction of Social Reality 편집.

1993년 노벨 문학상 수상

1997년 일곱 번째 소설 『파라다이스(*Paradise*)』 출간

2003년 여덟 번째 소설 『사랑(*Love*)

Further Reading:

《Articles》

Alexander. Allen. "The Fourth Face: The Image of God in Toni Morrison's *The Bluest Eye.*" *African American Review.* 32:2 (June 1998).

Awkward, Michael. "Roadblocks and Relatives: Critical Revision in Toni Morrison's *The Bluest Eye.*" Ed. Nellie Y. McKay. *Critical Essays on Toni Morrison.* Boston: G.K.Hall, 1988.

Bishop, John. "Morrison's *The Bluest Eye.*" *Explicator.* 51:4 (Summer 1993). 252-55.

Brown, Joseph A. "To Cheer the Weary Traveler: Toni Morrison, William Faulkner, and History." *Mississippi Quarterly* 49:4 (Fall 1996). 709-26.

Byerman, Keith E. "Beyond Realism: The Fictions of Toni Morrison." *Modern Critical Views: Toni Morrison.* Ed. Harold Bloom. NY: Chelsea, 1990.

Caputi, Jane. "Specifying" Fannie Hurst: Langston Hughes's "*Limitations of Life*," Zora Neale Hurston's *Their Eyes were Watching God*, and Toni Morrison's *The Bluest Eye* as "Answers" to Hurst's *Imitation of Life.*" *Black American Literature Forum: Women Writers Issue.* 24:4 (Winter 1990). 697-716

Dahill-Baue, William. "Insignificant Monkeys: Preaching Black English in Faulkner's *The Sound and the Fury* and Morrison's *The Bluest Eye* and *Beloved.*" *Mississippi Quarterly: The Journal of Southern Culture.* 49:3 (Summer 1996). 457-73.

Dittmar. Linda "Will the Circle be Unbroken? The Politics of Form in *The Bluest Eye.*" *Novel: A Forum on Fiction.* 23:2 (Dec 1990).

Gillan. Jennifer "Focusing on the Wrong Front: Historical Displacement, The Maginot Line, and *The Bluest Eye.*" *African American Review.* 36:2 (Summer 2002).

Klotman, Phyllis R. "Dick-and-Jane and the Shirley Temple Sensibility in *The Bluest Eye*." *Black American Literature Forum*. 13:4 (Winter 1979). 123-25.

Kuenz, Jane. "*The Bluest Eye*: Notes on History, Community, and Black Female Subjectivity." *African American Review: Women's Culture Issue*. 27:3 (Autumn 1993). 421-31

Lee, Young-Oak. "Teaching Multiethnic Literatures of the United States to Korean Students: Language, Gender, and History." *English Language and Literature* 48:4 (2002), 1005-1026.

_________ . "African American Literature: T. Morrison's *The Bluest Eye*." *Gender and History: Understanding U. S. Multiethnic Literatures*. Seoul: Thaehak, 2005.

Malmgren, Carl D. "Texts, Primers, and Voices in Toni Morrison's *The Bluest Eye*." *Studies in Contemporary Fiction*. 41:3 (March 2000).

Mayo, James. "Morrison's *The Bluest Eye*." *Explicator*. 60:4 (Summer 2002). 231-34.

McKay, Nellie Y., Earle, Kathryn. "Approaches to Teaching the Novels of Toni Morrison." *Approaches to Teaching World Literature*. No. 59. New York, 1997

Mermann-Jozwiak, Elisabeth. "Re-Membering the Body: Body Politics in Toni Morrison's *The Bluest Eye*." *Literature Interpretation Theory*. 12:2 (June 2001). 189-203.

Miner, Madonne M. "Rape, Madness, and Silence in *The Bluest Eye*." *Modern Critical Views: Toni Morrison*. Ed. Harold Bloom. NY: Chelsea, 1990.

Moses, Cat "The Blues Aesthetic in Toni Morrison's *The Bluest Eye*." *African American Review*. 33:4 (1999). 623-37.

Napieralski, Edmund A. "Morrison's *The Bluest Eye*." *Explicator*. 53:1 (Fall 1994). 59-62.

Ogunyemi, Chikwenye Okonjo. "Order and Disorder in Toni Morrison's

The Bluest Eye." Critique: *Studies in Modern Fiction* (Atlanta, GA). 19:1 (1977). 112-20.

Powell, Timothy B. "Toni Morrison: The Struggle to Depict the Black Figure on the White Page." *Black American Literature Forum: Women Writers Issue.* 24:4 (Winter 1990). 747-60

Rosenberg, Ruth. "Seeds in Hard Ground: Black Girlhood in *The Bluest Eye.*" *Black American Literature Forum.* 21:4 (Winter 1987). 435-45.

Wong, Shelly. "Transgression as Poesis in *The Bluest Eyes.*" *Callaloo* 13, 1990, 471-481.

Wren, James A."Morrison's *The Bluest Eye.*" *Explicator* 55:3 (Spring 1997). 172-75.

Yancy, George. "The Black Self Within a Semiotic Space of Whiteness: Reflections on the Racial Deformation of Pecola Breedlove in Toni Morrison's *The Bluest Eye.*" *CLA Journal* 43:3. 2000. 299-319.

《Books》

Beaulieu, Elizabeth Ann. Ed. *The Toni Morrison Encyclopedia.* Westpoint: Greenwood Pub Group Press, 2003.

Bjork, Patrick Bryce. *The Novels of Toni Morrison: The Search for Self and Place within the Community.* NY: Peter Lang, 1992.

Bloom, Harold. Ed. *Toni Morrison.* NY: Chelsea, 1990.

Carmean, Karen *Toni Morrison's World of Fiction.* Troy, NY: Whitston, 1993.

Duvall, John N. *The Identifying Fictions of Toni Morrison: Modernist Authenticity and Postmodern Blackness* NY, Hampshire: Palgrave, 2000.

Furman, Jan. *Toni Morrison's Fiction.* Columbia: U of South Carolina Press, 1996.

Gates, Jr., Henry Louis, K.A. Appiah. Ed. T*oni Morrison: Critical Perspectives Past and Present.* NY: Amistad, 1993.

Harris, Trudier. *Fiction and Folklore: The Novels of Toni Morrison.* Knoxville: U of Tennessee Press, 1991.

Higgins, Therese E. *Religiosity, Cosmology and Folklore: The African Influence in the Novels of Toni Morrison.* London: Rouuledge, 2001.

Otten, T. *The Crime of Innocence in the Fiction of Toni Morrison.* Columbia & London: U of Missouri Press, 1989.

Peach, Linden. *Toni Morrison.* NY: St. Martin's, 2000. Second Edition.

Peterson, N.J. Ed. *Toni Morrison.* Baltimore, NY: The Johns Hopkins UP, 1997.

Ryan, Michael. *Literary Theory: A Practical Introduction.* Malden: Blackwell, 1999.

Samuels, Wilfred D., & Clenora Hudson-Weems. *Toni Morrison.* Boston: Twayne, 1990.

Winfrey, Oprah. *Journey to Beloved.* Hyperion, 1998.

Text

Toni Morrison

The Bluest Eye

To the two who gave me life

and the one who made me free

The Bluest Eye

Here is the house. It is green and white. It has a red door. It is very pretty. Here is the family. Mother, Father, Dick, and Jane live in the green-and-white house. They are very happy. See Jane. She has a red dress. She wants to play. Who will play with Jane? See the cat. It goes meow-meow. Come and play. Come play with Jane. The kitten will not play. See Mother. Mother is very nice. Mother, will you play with Jane? Mother laughs. Laugh, Mother, laugh. See Father. He is big and strong. Father, will you play with Jane? Father is smiling. Smile, Father, smile. See the dog. Bowwow goes the dog. Do you want to play with Jane? See the dog run. Run, dog, run. Look, look. Here comes a friend. The friend will play with Jane. They will play a good game. Play, Jane, play.[1]

---

1 미국 초등학교에서 사용하는 교과서(primer) "The Story of Dick and Jane" 내용. 흑인과 백인 모두에게 익숙한 내용으로 인간이 행복하기 위해 추구하는 풍요롭고 평화로운 이상적인 가족의 모습. 그러나 행복한 백인 가정에 초점을 맞추고 있어 자칫 어린 학생들에게 아름답고 좋은 것은 백인들만 꿈 꿀 수 있는 것으로 잘못 인식시킬 수 있다.

Here is the house it is green and white it has a red door it is very pretty here is the family mother father dick and jane live in the green-and-white house they are very happy see jane she has a red dress she wants to play who will play with jane see the cat it goes meow-meow come and play come play with jane the kitten will not play see mother mother is very nice mother will you play with jane mother laughs laugh mother laugh see father he is big and strong father will you play with jane father is smiling smile father smile see the dog bowwow goes the dog do you want to play do you want to play with jane see the dog run run dog run look look here comes a friend the friend will play with jane they will play a good game play jane play[2]

Hereisthehouseitisgreenandwhiteithasareddooritisveryprettyhereist hefamilymotherfatherdickandjaneliveinthegreenandwhitehousethe yareveryhappyseejaneshehasareddressshewantstoplaywhowillplayw ithjaneseethecatitgoesmeowmeowcomeandplaycomeplaywithjaneth ekittenwillnotplayseemothermotherisverynicemotherwillyouplayw ithjanemotherlaughslaughmotherlaughseefatherheisbigandstrongfat herwillyouplaywithjanefatherissmilingsmilefathersmileseethedogbo wwowgoesthedogdoyouwanttoplaydoyouwanttoplaywithjaneseethe dogrunrundogrunlooklookherecomesafriendthefriendwillplaywithj anetheywillplayagoodgameplayjaneplay[3]

---

2 바로 앞에 인용된 부분의 반복으로 구두점이 사라지고 대문자와 소문자 구분이 무시됨으로써 급박한 느낌을 준다.

3 전체 인용문이 구두점이나 간격이 생략된 채 다닥다닥 붙어있어 속도감이 숨가쁘고 내적인 혼란이 있음을 보여준다.

Quiet as it's kept, there were no marigolds[4] in the fall of 1941. We thought, at the time, that it was because Pecola was having her father's baby that the marigolds did not grow. A little examination and much less melancholy would have proved to us that our seeds were not the only ones that did not sprout; nobody's did. Not even the gardens fronting the lake showed marigolds that year. But so deeply concerned were we with the health and safe delivery of Pecola's baby we could think of nothing but our own magic: if we planted the seeds, and said the right words over them, they would blossom, and everything would be all right.

It was a long time before my sister and I admitted to ourselves that no green was going to spring from our seeds. Once we knew, our guilt was relieved only by fights and mutual accusations about who was to blame. For years I thought my sister was right: it was my fault. I had

---

4 A plant of the daisy family, typically with yellow, orange, or copper-brown flowers, which is widely cultivated as an ornamental.

planted them too far down in the earth. It never occurred to either of us that the earth itself might have been unyielding. We had dropped our seeds in our own little plot of black dirt just as Pecola's father had dropped his seeds in his own plot of black dirt. Our innocence and faith were no more productive than his lust or despair. What is clear now is that of all of that hope, fear, lust, love, and grief, nothing remains but Pecola and the unyielding earth. Cholly Breedlove is dead; our innocence too. The seeds shriveled and died; her baby too.

There is really nothing more to say—except why. But since why is difficult to handle, one must take refuge in how.

Autumn

Nuns go by as quiet as lust, and drunken men and sober eyes sing in the lobby of the Greek hotel. Rosemary Villanucci, our next-door friend who lives above her father's cafe, sits in a 1939 Buick[5] eating bread and butter.[6] She rolls down the window to tell my sister Frieda and me that we can't come in. We stare at her, wanting her bread, but more than that wanting to poke the arrogance out of her eyes and smash the pride of ownership that curls her chewing mouth. When she comes out of the car we will beat her up, make red marks on her white skin, and she will cry and ask us do we want her to pull her pants down. We will say no. We don't know what we should feel or do if she does, but whenever she asks us, we know she is offering us something precious and that our own pride must be asserted by refusing to accept.

---

5 General Motors가 생산하는 보수적 이미지의 고급 승용차.

6 버터 바른 빵을 먹으며(Butter was a treat not often enjoyed by the poor)

School has started, and Frieda and I get new brown stockings and cod-liver oil. Grown-ups talk in tired, edgy voices about Zick's Coal Company and take us along in the evening to the railroad tracks where we fill burlap sacks with the tiny pieces of coal lying about. Later we walk home, glancing back to see the great carloads of slag being dumped, red hot and smoking, into the ravine that skirts the steel mill. The dying fire lights the sky with a dull orange glow. Frieda and I lag behind, staring at the patch of color surrounded by black. It is impossible not to feel a shiver when our feet leave the gravel path and sink into the dead grass in the field.

Our house is old, cold, and green. At night a kerosene lamp lights one large room. The others are braced in darkness, peopled by roaches and mice. Adults do not talk to us—they give us directions. They issue orders without providing information. When we trip and fall down they glance at us; if we cut or bruise ourselves, they ask us are we crazy. When we catch colds, they shake their heads in disgust at our lack of consideration. How, they ask us, do you expect anybody to get anything done if you all are sick? We cannot answer them. Our illness is treated with contempt, foul Black Draught,[7] and castor oil that blunts our minds.

When, on a day after a trip to collect coal, I cough once, loudly, through bronchial tubes already packed tight with phlegm, my mother frowns. "Great Jesus. Get on in that bed. How many times do I have to tell you to wear something on your head? You must be

7 의사 처방 없이 직접 매매되는 액체 하제(下劑), 때로는 감기약으로도 사용.

the biggest fool in this town. Frieda? Get some rags and stuff that window."

Frieda restuffs the window. I trudge off to bed, full of guilt and self-pity. I lie down in my underwear, the metal in my black garters hurts my legs, but I do not take them off, for it is too cold to lie stockingless. It takes a long time for my body to heat its place in the bed. Once I have generated a silhouette of warmth, I dare not move, for there is a cold place one-half inch in any direction. No one speaks to me or asks how I feel. In an hour or two my mother comes. Her hands are large and rough, and when she rubs the Vicks salve on my chest, I am rigid with pain. She takes two fingers' full of it at a time, and massages my chest until I am faint. Just when I think I will tip over into a scream, she scoops out a little of the salve on her forefinger and puts it in my mouth, telling me to swallow. A hot flannel is wrapped about my neck and chest. I am covered up with heavy quilts and ordered to sweat, which I do—promptly.

Later I throw up, and my mother says, "What did you puke on the bed clothes for? Don't you have sense enough to hold your head out the bed? Now, look what you did. You think I got time for nothing but washing up your puke?"

The puke swaddles down the pillow onto the sheet—green-gray, with flecks of orange. It moves like the insides of an uncooked egg. Stubbornly clinging to its own mass, refusing to break up and be removed. How, I wonder, can it be so neat and nasty at the same time?

My mother's voice drones on. She is not talking to me. She is talking to the puke, but she is calling it my name: Claudia. She wipes it up as best she can and puts a scratchy towel over the large wet place. I lie down again. The rags have fallen from the window crack, and the air is cold. I dare not call her back and am reluctant to leave my warmth. My mother's anger humiliates me; her words chafe my cheeks, and I am crying. I do not know that she is not angry at me, but at my sickness. I believe she despises my weakness for letting the sickness "take holt."[8] By and by I will not get sick; I will refuse to. But for now I am crying. I know I am making more snot, but I can't stop.

My sister comes in. Her eyes are full of sorrow. She sings to me: "When the deep purple falls over sleepy garden walls, someone thinks of me...." I doze, thinking of plums, walls, and "someone."

But was it really like that? As painful as I remember? Only mildly. Or rather, it was a productive and fructifying pain. Love, thick and dark as Alaga syrup,[9] eased up into that cracked window. I could smell it—taste it—sweet, musty, with an edge of wintergreen[10] in its base—everywhere in that house. It[11] stuck, along with my tongue, to the frosted windowpanes. It coated my chest, along with the salve, and when the flannel came undone in my sleep, the clear, sharp curves of air outlined its presence on my throat. And in the night, when my coughing was dry and tough, feet padded into the room, hands repinned the flannel, readjusted the quilt, and rested a moment on my forehead. So when I think of autumn, I think of somebody with hands who does not want me to die.

It was autumn too when Mr. Henry came. Our roomer. Our roomer.[12] The words ballooned from the lips and hovered about our heads[13]—silent, separate, and pleasantly mysterious. My mother was all ease and satisfaction in discussing his coming.

"You know him," she said to her friends. "Henry Washington.

---

8 병에 쉽게 걸리게 되는 나의 나약함(take holt는 take hold of의 사투리임.)
9 흑인들, 특히 미국 남부 흑인들 사이에서 잘 쓰이는 알라가 감기 시럽
10 노루발풀. 일명 "evergreen."이 식물로부터 껌이나 사탕을 만드는데 넣는 강한 약 냄새가 나는 기름을 추출함.
11 10행의 Love를 가리킴. 질병의 고통 중에도 돌보는 손길에서 사랑을 느낌.
12 세입자. Our roomer의 반복. 세입자는 곧 수입을 의미함.
13 세입자에 대한 이야기가 퍼져나감을 표현.

He's been living over there with Miss Della Jones on Thirteenth Street. But she's too addled now to keep up. So he's looking for another place."

"Oh, yes." Her friends do not hide their curiosity. "I been wondering how long he was going to stay up there with her. They say she's real bad off. Don't know who he is half the time, and nobody else."

"Well, that old crazy nigger she married up with didn't help her head none."[14]

"Did you hear what he told folks when he left her?"

"Uh-uh. What?"

"Well, he run off with that trifling Peggy—from Elyria. You know."

"One of Old Slack Bessie's girls?"

"That's the one. Well, somebody asked him why he left a nice good church woman like Della for that heifer.[15] You know Della always did keep a good house. And he said the honest-to-God real reason was he couldn't take no more of that violet water[16] Della Jones used. Said he wanted a woman to smell like a woman. Said Della was just too clean for him."

"Old dog. Ain't that nasty!"

"You telling me. What kind of reasoning is that?"

"No kind. Some men just dogs."

"Is that what give her them strokes?"

"Must have helped. But you know, none of them[17] girls wasn't too bright. Remember that grinning Hattie? She wasn't never right. And their Auntie Julia is still trotting up and down Sixteenth Street talking to herself."

---

14 아무 도움도 되지 못했다.

15 A woman, generally a girl.

16 ultra violet water purifier

17 strokes

"Didn't she get put away?"

"Naw. County wouldn't take her. Said she wasn't harming anybody."

"Well, she's harming me. You want something to scare the living shit out of you,[18] you get up at five-thirty in the morning like I do and see that old hag floating by in that bonnet. Have mercy!"

They laugh.

Frieda and I are washing Mason jars.[19] We do not hear their words, but with grown-ups we listen to and watch out for their voices.

"Well, I hope don't nobody let me roam around like that when I get senile. It's a shame."

"What they going to do about Della? Don't she have no people?"

"A sister's coming up from North Carolina to look after her. I expect she wants to get aholt of Della's house."[20]

"Oh, come on. That's a evil thought, if ever I heard one."

"What you want to bet? Henry Washington said that sister ain't seen Della in fifteen years."

"I kind of thought Henry would marry her one of these days."

"That old woman?"

"Well, Henry ain't no chicken."[21]

"No, but he ain't no buzzard, either."[22]

"He ever been married to anybody?"

"No."

---

18 놀라 자빠지고 싶은 생각이 든다면(scare the living shit out of는 누구를 심하게 놀라게 한다는 뜻으로 이를 완곡하게 표현하자면 "scare the living daylight out of," 혹은 "scare the pants off"라고 말할 수 있다)

19 꽉 맞는 나사 마개가 달린, 식품(집에서 재배한 과일과 채소) 저장용 유리병.

20 내가 보기에는 Della의 집을 차지하려는 것 같은데. get aholt of는 get ahold of (=occupy, take possession of, secure)를 달리 쓴 표현이다.

21 그렇다고 Henry도 영계는 아니지. ("no chicken"은 일반적으로 나이든 사람 ("elderly")이라는 의미로 쓰인다.

22 물론이지, 하지만 그렇게 늙지도 않았어.

"How come? Somebody cut it off?"

"He's just picky."

"He ain't picky. You see anything around here you'd marry?"

"Well ... no."

"He's just sensible. A steady worker with quiet ways. I hope it works out all right."

"It will. How much you charging?"

"Five dollars every two weeks."

"That'll be a big help to you."

"I'll say."

Their conversation is like a gently wicked dance: sound meets sound, curtsies, shimmies, and retires.[23] Another sound enters but is upstaged by still another: the two circle each other and stop. Sometimes their words move in lofty spirals; other times they take strident leaps, and all of it is punctuated with warm-pulsed laughter—like the throb of a heart made of jelly. The edge, the curl, the thrust of their emotions is always clear to Frieda and me. We do not, cannot, know the meanings of all their words, for we are nine and ten years old. So we watch their faces, their hands, their feet, and listen for truth in timbre.

So when Mr. Henry arrived on a Saturday night, we smelled him. He smelled wonderful. Like trees and lemon vanishing cream, and Nu Nile Hair Oil[24] and flecks of Sen-Sen.[25]

He smiled a lot, showing small even teeth with a friendly gap in the middle. Frieda and I were not introduced to him—merely pointed out. Like, here is the bathroom; the clothes closet is here;

---

23 소리와 소리가 만나 서로에게 절을 하고, 시미 춤도 추고 그리고는 물러난다. (*curtsy: a woman's or girl's formal greeting made by bending the knees with one foot in front of the other. * shimmy: a kind of ragtime dance in which the whole body shakes or sways)

24 뉴 나일 머리 기름(흑인 남성들이 애용하는 모발용품)

25 입 냄새를 없애는 센-센 사탕

and these are my kids, Frieda and Claudia; watch out for this window; it don't open all the way.

We looked sideways at him, saying nothing and expecting him to say nothing. Just to nod, as he had done at the clothes closet, acknowledging our existence. To our surprise, he spoke to us.

"Hello there. You must be Greta Garbo,[26] and you must be Ginger Rogers."[27] We giggled. Even my father was startled into a smile.

"Want a penny?" He held out a shiny coin to us. Frieda lowered her head, too pleased to answer. I reached for it. He snapped his thumb and forefinger, and the penny disappeared. Our shock was laced with delight. We searched all over him, poking our fingers into his socks, looking up the inside back of his coat. If happiness is anticipation with certainty, we were happy. And while we waited for the coin to reappear, we knew we were amusing Mama and Daddy. Daddy was smiling, and Mama's eyes went soft as they followed our hands wandering over Mr. Henry's body.

We loved him. Even after what came later, there was no bitterness in our memory of him.

She[28] slept in the bed with us. Frieda on the outside because she is brave—it never occurs to her that if in her sleep her hand hangs over the edge of the bed "something" will crawl out from under it and bite her fingers off. I sleep near the wall because that thought has occurred to me. Pecola, therefore, had to sleep in the middle.

Mama had told us two days earlier that a "case" was coming—a girl who had no place to go. The county had placed her in our

26 Greta Garbo: This Swedish-American actress(1905-1990) began her career in silent films and successfully switched to "talkies" in the 1930s. Her most famous films include 《Anna Christie》 (1930), 《Mata Hari》 (1931), and 《Anna Karenina》 (1935).

27 Ginger Rogers: Best known for the movie musicals she made as Fred Astaire's dance partner, Rogers received a 1940 Academy Award for best actress for her role in Kitty Foyle.

28 Pecola Breedlove를 가리킴.

house for a few days until they could decide what to do, or, more precisely, until the family was reunited. We were to be nice to her and not fight. Mama didn't know "what got into people," but that old Dog Breedlove[29] had burned up his house, gone upside his wife's head, and everybody, as a result, was outdoors.

Outdoors, we knew, was the real terror of life.[30] The threat of being outdoors surfaced frequently in those days. Every possibility of excess was curtailed with it.[31] If somebody ate too much, he could end up outdoors. If somebody used too much coal, he could end up outdoors. People could gamble themselves outdoors, drink themselves outdoors. Sometimes mothers put their sons outdoors, and when that happened, regardless of what the son had done, all sympathy was with him. He was outdoors, and his own flesh had done it. To be put outdoors by a landlord was one thing—unfortunate, but an aspect of life over which you had no control, since you could not control your income. But to be slack enough to put oneself outdoors, or heartless enough to put one's own kin outdoors—that was criminal.

There is a difference between being put *out* and being put out*doors*. If you are put out, you go somewhere else; if you are outdoors, there is no place to go. The distinction was subtle but final. Outdoors was the end of something, an irrevocable, physical fact, defining and complementing our metaphysical condition. Being a minority in both caste and class, we moved about anyway on the hem of life, struggling to consolidate our weaknesses and hang on, or to creep singly up into the major folds of the garment.[32]

---

29 Dog: (Informal) a person regarded as unpleasant, contemptible, or wicked (used as a term of abuse)

30 길거리로 나앉는 건, 정말이지, 살면서 가장 무서운 일이었다.

31 누구나 지나치게 욕심을 부리면 거리로 나앉을 수도 있었다.

32 to creep singly up into the major folds of the garment: 삶의 중심부에 혼자의 힘으로 기어들어가기 위해. (여기서 'folds'는 바로 윗 줄의 'the hem'(가장자리)과 대비를 이루고 있다.)

Our peripheral existence, however, was something we had learned to deal with—probably because it was abstract. But the concreteness of being outdoors was another matter—like the difference between the concept of death and being, in fact, dead. Dead doesn't change, and outdoors is here to stay.

Knowing that there was such a thing as outdoors bred in us a hunger for property, for ownership. The firm possession of a yard, a porch, a grape arbor. Propertied black people spent all their energies, all their love, on their nests. Like frenzied, desperate birds, they overdecorated everything; fussed and fidgeted over their hard-won homes; canned, jellied, and preserved all summer to fill the cupboards and shelves; they painted, picked, and poked at every corner of their houses. And these houses loomed like hothouse sunflowers among the rows of weeds that were the rented houses. Renting blacks cast furtive glances at these owned yards and porches, and made firmer commitments to buy themselves "some nice little old place." In the meantime, they saved, and scratched, and piled away what they could in the rented hovels, looking forward to the day of property.

Cholly Breedlove, then, a renting black, having put his family outdoors, had catapulted himself beyond the reaches of human consideration.[33] He had joined the animals; was, indeed, an old dog, a snake, a ratty nigger. Mrs. Breedlove was staying with the woman she worked for; the boy, Sammy, was with some other family; and Pecola was to stay with us. Cholly was in jail.

She came with nothing. No little paper bag with the other dress, or a nightgown, or two pair of whitish cotton bloomers.[34] She just appeared with a white woman and sat down.

We had fun in those few days Pecola was with us. Frieda and I

---

33 had catapulted himself beyond the reaches of human consideration: 사람이 생각이 미치는 한도를 넘어서까지 자신을 타락 속에 내던지고 있었다.

34 bloomers: 블루머. 무릎 길이의 헐렁한 여성용 속바지

stopped fighting each other and concentrated on our guest, trying hard to keep her from feeling outdoors.

When we discovered that she clearly did not want to dominate us,[35] we liked her. She laughed when I clowned for her, and smiled and accepted gracefully the food gifts my sister gave her.

"Would you like some graham crackers?"[36]

"I don't care."

Frieda brought her four graham crackers on a saucer and some milk in a blue-and-white Shirley Temple[37] cup. She was a long time with the milk,[38] and gazed fondly at the silhouette of Shirley Temple's dimpled face. Frieda and she had a loving conversation about how cu-ute Shirley Temple was. I couldn't join them in their adoration because I hated Shirley. Not because she was cute, but because she danced with Bojangles,[39] who was *my* friend, *my* uncle, *my* daddy, and who ought to have been soft-shoeing[40] it and chuckling with me. Instead he was enjoying, sharing, giving a lovely dance thing with one of those little white girls whose socks never slid down under their heels. So I said, "I like Jane Withers."[41]

They gave me a puzzled look, decided I was incomprehensible, and continued their reminiscing about old squint-eyed Shirley.[42]

---

35 that she clearly did not want to dominate us: Pecola가 우리들을 휘두르고 싶어하지 않는다는 사실

36 graham crackers: 19세기 중반에 나온 그레이엄 밀가루(=unbolted whole-wheat flour)로 만든 크래커. Graham은 미국의 식이 요법 개량가인 S. Graham(1794-1851)에서 따온 이름.

37 Shirley Temple(1928~): With her hallmark dimples, corkscrew golden curls, and twinkling eyes, she became a unique symbol of American movies.

38 She was a long time with the milk: Pecola는 오랫동안 우유를 마시고 있었다

39 Bill "Bojangles" Robinson(1878-1949): US dancer of Broadway and Hollywood, best known for his dancing roles with Shirley Temple in films of the 1930s.

40 who ought to have been soft-shoeing: 나와 탭 댄스를 춰야 했을

41 Jane Withers(1928-): A 1930s-40s tomboy actress with dark eyes and dark hair, she was the antithesis of the Shirley Temple icon. She appeared with Shirley Temple in 《Bright Eyes》 (1934).

42 old squint-eyed Shirley: 교활하고 사시 눈을 한 셜리 템플. Claudia는 셜리 템

Younger than both Frieda and Pecola, I had not yet arrived at the turning point in the development of my psyche which would allow me to love her. What I felt at that time was unsullied hatred. But before that I had felt a stranger, more frightening thing than hatred for all the Shirley Temples of the world.

It had begun with Christmas and the gift of dolls. The big, the special, the loving gift was always a big, blue-eyed Baby Doll. From the clucking sounds of adults I knew that the doll represented what they thought was my fondest wish. I was bemused with the thing itself, and the way it looked. What was I supposed to do with it? Pretend I was its mother? I had no interest in babies or the concept of motherhood. I was interested only in humans my own age and size, and could not generate any enthusiasm at the prospect of being a mother. Motherhood was old age, and other remote possibilities. I learned quickly, however, what I was expected to do with the doll: rock it, fabricate storied situations around it, even sleep with it. Picture books were full of little girls sleeping with their dolls. Raggedy Ann[43] dolls usually, but they were out of the question. I was physically revolted by and secretly frightened of those round moronic eyes, the pancake face, and orangeworms hair.

The other dolls, which were supposed to bring me great pleasure, succeeded in doing quite the opposite. When I took it to bed, its hard unyielding limbs resisted my flesh—the tapered fingertips on those dimpled hands scratched. If, in sleep, I turned, the bone-cold head collided with my own. It was a most uncomfortable, patently aggressive sleeping companion. To hold it was no more rewarding. The starched gauze or lace on the cotton dress irritated any embrace. I had only one desire: to dismember it. To see of what it was made, to discover the dearness, to find the beauty, the

---

플을 깎아 내리고 있다.

43 Raggedy Anne: a blue-eyed, yellow-haired, pink-skinned doll.

desirability that had escaped me, but apparently only me.[44] Adults, older girls, shops, magazines, newspapers, window signs—all the world had agreed that a blue-eyed, yellow-haired, pink-skinned doll was what every girl child treasured. "Here," they said, "this is beautiful, and if you are on this day 'worthy' you may have it." I fingered the face, wondering at the single-stroke eyebrows; picked at the pearly teeth stuck like two piano keys between red bowline lips. Traced the turned-up nose, poked the glassy blue eyeballs, twisted the yellow hair. I could not love it. But I could examine it to see what it was that all the world said was lovable. Break off the tiny fingers, bend the flat feet, loosen the hair, twist the head around, and the thing made one sound—a sound they said was the sweet and plaintive cry "Mama," but which sounded to me like the bleat of a dying lamb, or, more precisely, our icebox door opening on rusty hinges in July. Remove the cold and stupid eyeball, it would bleat still, "Ahhhhhh," take off the head, shake out the sawdust, crack the back against the brass bed rail, it would bleat still. The gauze back would split, and I could see the disk with six holes, the secret of the sound. A mere metal roundness.

Grown people frowned and fussed: "You-don't-know-how-to-take-care-of-nothing. I-never-had-a-baby-doll-in-my-whole-life-and-used-to-cry-my-eyes-out-for-them. Now-you-got-one-a-beautiful-one-and-you-tear-it-up-what's-the-matter-with-you?"

How strong was their outrage. Tears threatened to erase the aloofness of their authority. The emotion of years of unfulfilled longing preened in their voices. I did not know why I destroyed those dolls. But I did know that nobody ever asked me what I wanted for Christmas. Had any adult with the power to fulfill my desires taken me seriously and asked me what I wanted, they would have known that I did not want to have anything to own, or to

---

44 the desirability that had escaped me, but apparently only me: (그 인형을) 갖고 싶다는 욕망이 나를 피해갔던 것이다. 분명히 내게만 그런 욕심이 안 생겼다.

possess any object. I wanted rather to feel something on Christmas day. The real question would have been, "Dear Claudia, what experience would you like on Christmas?" I could have spoken up, "I want to sit on the low stool in Big Mama's kitchen with my lap full of lilacs and listen to Big Papa play his violin for me alone." The lowness of the stool made for my body, the security and warmth of Big Mama's kitchen, the smell of the lilacs, the sound of the music, and, since it would be good to have all of my senses engaged, the taste of a peach, perhaps, afterward.

Instead I tasted and smelled the acridness of tin plates and cups designed for tea parties that bored me. Instead I looked with loathing on new dresses that required a hateful bath in a galvanized zinc tub before wearing. Slipping around on the zinc, no time to play or soak, for the water chilled too fast, no time to enjoy one's nakedness, only time to make curtains of soapy water careen down between the legs. Then the scratchy towels and the dreadful and humiliating absence of dirt. The irritable, unimaginative cleanliness. Gone the ink marks from legs and face, all my creations and accumulations of the day gone, and replaced by goose pimples.

I destroyed white baby dolls.

But the dismembering of dolls was not the true horror. The truly horrifying thing was the transference of the same impulses to little white girls. The indifference with which I could have axed them was shaken only by my desire to do so. To discover what eluded me: the secret of the magic they weaved on others. What made people look at them and say, "Awwwww," but not for me? The eye slide of black women as they approached them on the street, and the possessive gentleness of their touch as they handled them.

If I pinched them, their eyes—unlike the crazed glint of the baby doll's eyes—would fold in pain, and their cry would not be the sound of an icebox door, but a fascinating cry of pain. When I learned how repulsive this disinterested violence was, that it was repulsive because it was disinterested, my shame floundered about for refuge. The best hiding place was love. Thus the conversion from pristine sadism to fabricated hatred, to fraudulent love. It was a small step to Shirley Temple. I learned much later to worship her, just as I learned to delight in cleanliness, knowing, even as I learned, that the change was adjustment without improvement.

"Three quarts of milk. That's what was *in* that icebox yesterday. Three whole quarts. Now they ain't none. Not a drop. I don't mind folks coming in and getting what they want, but three quarts of milk! What the devil does *any*body need with *three* quarts of milk?"

The "folks" my mother was referring to was Pecola. The three of us, Pecola, Frieda, and I, listened to her downstairs in the kitchen fussing about the amount of milk Pecola had drunk. We knew she was fond of the Shirley Temple cup and took every opportunity to drink milk out of it just to handle and see sweet Shirley's face. My mother knew that Frieda and I hated milk and assumed Pecola drank it out of greediness. It was certainly not for us to "dispute" her. We didn't initiate talk with grown-ups; we answered their questions.

Ashamed of the insults that were being heaped on our friend, we just sat there: I picked toe jam,[45] Frieda cleaned her fingernails with her teeth, and Pecola finger-traced some scars on her knee—her head cocked to one side. My mother's fussing soliloquies always irritated and depressed us. They were interminable, insulting, and although indirect (Mama never named anybody—just talked about folks and *some* people), extremely painful in their thrust. She would go on like that for hours, connecting one offense to another until all of the things that chagrined her were spewed out. Then, having told everybody and everything off, she would burst into

45 toe jam: the grey-brown shit that accumulates between your toes.

song and sing the rest of the day. But it was such a long time before the singing part came. In the meantime, our stomachs jellying and our necks burning, we listened, avoided each other's eyes, and picked toe jam or whatever.

"... I don't know what I'm suppose to be running here, a charity ward, I guess. Time for me to get out of the *giving* line and get in the *getting* line. I guess I ain't sup*posed* to have nothing. I'm sup*posed* to end up in the poorhouse.[46] Look like nothing I do is going to keep me out of there.[47] Folks just spend all their time trying to figure out ways to send *me* to the poorhouse. I got about as much business with another mouth to feed as a cat has with side pockets.[48] As if I don't have trouble enough trying to feed my own and keep out the poorhouse, now I got something else in here that's just going to *drink* me on in there.[49] Well, naw, she ain't. Not long as I got strength in my body and a tongue in my head. There's a limit to everything. I ain't got nothing to just throw *away*. Don't nobody need *three* quarts of milk. Henry *Ford*[50] don't need three quarts of milk. That's just downright *sin*ful. I'm willing to do what I can for folks. Can't nobody say I ain't. But this has got to stop, and I'm just the one to stop it. Bible say watch as *well* as pray. Folks just dump they children off on you and go on 'bout they business. Ain't nobody even *peeped* in here to see whether that child has a loaf of bread. Look like they would just *peep* in to see whether I had a loaf of bread to give her. But naw. That thought don't cross they[51] mind.

---

46 poorhouse: 구빈원(救貧院), 양육원

47 Look like nothing I do is going to keep me out of there: 내가 아무리 한 들 구빈원을 벗어날 도리가 없겠네.

48 as a cat has with side pockets: (은유적 표현) 돌봐주어야 하는 새끼고양이들이 더 있는 것처럼

49 now I got something else in here that's just going to *drink* me on in there: 이제는 우유를 마셔대어(하루에 3리터나 마셔버리니) 나를 구빈원에 가게 만들 존재가 여기 있구나.

50 Henry *Ford*: A car manufacturer; one of America's richest men during the 1940s.

51 they=their

That old trifling Cholly been out of jail *two* whole days and ain't been here *yet* to see if his own child was 'live[52] or dead. She could be *dead* for all he know. And that *mama* [53] neither.What kind of something is that?"[54]

When Mama got around to Henry Ford and all those people who didn't care whether she had a loaf of bread, it was time to go. We wanted to miss the part about Roosevelt and the CCC [55] camps.

Frieda got up and started down the stairs. Pecola and I followed, making a wide arc to avoid the kitchen doorway. We sat on the steps of the porch, where my mother's words could reach us only in spurts.

It was a lonesome Saturday. The house smelled of Fels Naphtha[56] and the sharp odor of mustard greens cooking. Saturdays were lonesome, fussy, soapy days. Second in misery only to those tight, starchy, cough-drop Sundays, so full of "don'ts" and "set'cha self downs."[57]

If my mother was in a singing mood, it wasn't so bad. She would sing about hard times, bad times, and somebody-done-gone-and-left-me times. But her voice was so sweet and her singing-eyes so melty I found myself longing for those hard times, yearning to be grown without "a thin di-i-ime to my name."[58] I looked forward to

---

52 'live=alive

53 mama: 엄마라는 작자도

54 What kind of something is that?: 어떻게 되어먹은 작자들이야?

55 CCC(Civilian Conservatory Corps): 미국 민간자원 보존단. 미국이 경제대공황 이후 300만 명 이상의 청장년에게 일자리를 제공할 목적으로 1933년에 시작한 연방 취업 프로그램

56 Fels Naphtha: 펠스 나프타 비누. A brand of heavy duty laundry soap. It is used everyday for poison ivy treatment, laundry, to rid plants of pests and remedy black spot fungus in roses.

57 Set'cha self downs: 가만히 앉아 있어.

58 yearning to be grown without "a thin di-i-ime to my name": 성인이 되어서 내 돈이라곤 얄팍한 십전짜리 한 개도 없이 되기를 바랬다. (여기서 di-i-ime은 dime 다임, 10센트 백동화로 단돈 한 푼의 적은 돈을 말함.)

the delicious time when "my man" would leave me, when I would "hate to see that evening sun go down ..." 'cause then I would know "my man has left this town." Misery colored by the greens and blues in my mother's voice took all of the grief out of the words and left me with a conviction that pain was not only endurable, it was sweet.

But without song, those Saturdays sat on my head like a coal scuttle, and if Mama was fussing, as she was now, it was like somebody throwing stones at it.

"...and here I am poor as a bowl of yak-me. What do they think I am? Some kind of Sandy Claus?[59] Well, they can just take they stocking down 'cause it *ain't* Christmas...."

We fidgeted.

"Let's do something," Frieda said.

"What do you want to do?" I asked.

"I don't know. Nothing." Frieda stared at the tops of the trees. Pecola looked at her feet.

"You want to go up to Mr. Henry's room and look at his girlie magazines?"[60]

Frieda made an ugly face. She didn't like to look at dirty pictures. "Well," I continued, "we could look at his Bible. *That's* pretty." Frieda sucked her teeth and made a *phttt* sound with her lips. "O.K., then. We could go thread needles for the half-blind lady. She'll give us a penny."

Frieda snorted. "Her eyes look like snot. I don't feel like looking at them. What *you* want to do, Pecola?"

"I don't care," she said. "Anything you want."

I had another idea. "We could go up the alley and see what's in the trash cans."

---

59 Sandy Claus =Santa Claus

60 girlie magazines: 누드 잡지(Here, "girlie" depicts or features nude or partially nude young women in erotic poses)

"Too cold," said Frieda. She was bored and irritable.

"I know. We could make some fudge."[61]

"You kidding? With Mama in there fussing? When she starts fussing at the walls, you know she's gonna be at it all day. She wouldn't even let us."

"Well, let's go over to the Greek hotel and listen to them cuss."

"Oh, who wants to do *that*? Besides, they say the same old words all the time."

My supply of ideas exhausted, I began to concentrate on the white spots on my fingernails. The total signified the number of boyfriends I would have. Seven.

Mama's soliloquy slid into the silence "... Bible say feed the hungry. That's fine. That's all right. But I ain't feeding no elephants.... Anybody need three quarts of milk to *live* need to get out of here. They in the wrong place. What is this? Some kind of *dairy* farm?"

Suddenly Pecola bolted straight up, her eyes wide with terror. A whinnying sound came from her mouth.

"What's the matter with *you*?" Frieda stood up too. Then we both looked where Pecola was staring. Blood was running down her legs. Some drops were on the steps. I leaped up. "Hey. You cut yourself? Look. It's all over your dress."

A brownish-red stain discolored the back of her dress. She kept whinnying, standing with her legs far apart.

Frieda said, "Oh. Lordy![62] I know. I know what that is!"

"What?" Pecola's fingers went to her mouth.

"That's ministratin'."[63]

"What's that?"

"You know."

---

61 fudge: 퍼지(설탕, 버터, 우유, 초콜릿으로 만드는 과자)

62 Lordy!: 이런! 어마!(놀람 당황 등을 나타냄) (used to express surprise or dismay)

63 ministratin': Frieda가 아직 어려서 menstruation(월경)을 잘못 말한 것.

"Am I going to die?" she asked.

"Noooo. You won't die. It just means you can have a baby!"

"What?"

"How do *you* know?" I was sick and tired of Frieda knowing everything.

"Mildred told me, and Mama too."

"I don't believe it."

"You don't have to, dummy. Look. Wait here. Sit down, Pecola. Right here." Frieda was all authority and zest. "And you," she said to me, "you go get some water."

"Water?"

"Yes, stupid. Water. And be quiet, or Mama will hear you."

Pecola sat down again, a little less fear in her eyes. I went into the kitchen.

"What you want, girl?" Mama was rinsing curtains in the sink.

"Some water, ma'am."

"Right where I'm working, naturally. Well, get a glass. Not no clean one neither. Use that jar."

I got a Mason jar and filled it with water from the faucet. It seemed a long time filling.

"Don't nobody never want nothing till they see me at the sink. Then everybody got to drink water...."

When the jar was full, I moved to leave the room.

"Where you going?"

"Outside."

"Drink that water right here!"

"I ain't gonna break nothing."

"You don't know what you gonna do."

"Yes, ma'am. I do. Lemme take it out. I won't spill none."

"You bed' not."[64]

I got to the porch and stood there with the Mason jar of water.

---

64 You bed'not.=You better not.

Pecola was crying.

"What you crying for? Does it hurt?"

She shook her head.

"Then stop slinging snot."

Frieda opened the back door. She had something tucked in her blouse. She looked at me in amazement and pointed to the jar. "What's that supposed to do?"

"You told me. You *said* get some water."

"Not a little old jar full. Lots of water. To scrub the steps with, dumbbell!"[65]

"How was I supposed to know?"

"Yeah. How was you. Come on." She pulled Pecola up by the arm. "Let's go back here." They headed for the side of the house where the bushes were thick.

"Hey. What about me? I want to go."

"Shut uuuup," Frieda stage-whispered.[66] "Mama will hear you. You wash the steps."

They disappeared around the corner of the house.

I was going to miss something. Again. Here was something important, and I had to stay behind and not see any of it. I poured the water on the steps, sloshed it with my shoe, and ran to join them.

Frieda was on her knees; a white rectangle of cotton was near her on the ground. She was pulling Pecola's pants off. "Come on. Step out of them." She managed to get the soiled pants down and flung them at me. "Here."

"What am I supposed to do with these?"

"Bury them, moron."[67]

Frieda told Pecola to hold the cotton thing between her legs.

---

65 dumbbell: 《미 구어》 얼간이(a stupid person)

66 stage-whisper: (들으라고 하는) 혼잣말.

67 moron: 《구어》 (경멸적) 저능아, 바보(a stupid person)

"How she gonna walk like that?" I asked.

Frieda didn't answer. Instead she took two safety pins from the hem of her skirt and began to pin the ends of the napkin to Pecola's dress.

I picked up the pants with two fingers and looked about for something to dig a hole with. A rustling noise in the bushes startled me, and turning toward it, I saw a pair of fascinated eyes in a dough-white face. Rosemary was watching us. I grabbed for her face and succeeded in scratching her nose. She screamed and jumped back.

"Mrs. MacTeer! Mrs. MacTeer!" Rosemary hollered. "Frieda and Claudia are out here playing nasty! Mrs. MacTeer!"

Mama opened the window and looked down at us.

"What?"

"They're playing nasty, Mrs. MacTeer. Look. And Claudia hit me 'cause I seen them!"

Mama slammed the window shut and came running out the back door.

"What you all doing? Oh. Uh-huh. Uh-huh. Playing nasty, huh?" She reached into the bushes and pulled off a switch. "I'd rather raise pigs than some nasty girls. Least I can slaughter *them*!"[68]

We began to shriek. "No, Mama. No, ma'am. We wasn't! She's a liar! No, ma'am, Mama! No, ma'am, Mama!"

Mama grabbed Frieda by the shoulder, turned her around, and gave her three or four stinging cuts on her legs. "Gonna be nasty, huh? Naw you ain't!"

Frieda was destroyed. Whippings wounded and insulted her.

Mama looked at Pecola. "You too!" she said. "Child of mine or not!" She grabbed Pecola and spun her around. The safety pin snapped open on one end of the napkin, and Mama saw it fall from under her dress. The switch hovered in the air while Mama blinked.

---

68 Least I can slaughter *them*!": 돼지라면 차라리 잡아 먹을 수나 있지!

"What the devil is going on here?"

Frieda was sobbing. I, next in line, began to explain. "She was bleeding. We was just trying to stop the blood!"

Mama looked at Frieda for verification. Frieda nodded. "She's ministratin'. We was just helping."

Mama released Pecola and stood looking at her. Then she pulled both of them toward her, their heads against her stomach. Her eyes were sorry. "All right, all right. Now, stop crying. I didn't know. Come on, now. Get on in the house. Go on home, Rosemary. The show is over."

We trooped in, Frieda sobbing quietly, Pecola carrying a white tail, me carrying the little-girl-gone-to-woman pants.[69]

Mama led us to the bathroom. She prodded Pecola inside, and taking the underwear from me, told us to stay out.

We could hear water running into the bathtub.

"You think she's going to drown her?"

"Oh, Claudia. You so dumb. She's just going to wash her clothes and all."

"Should we beat up Rosemary?"

"No. Leave her alone."

The water gushed, and over its gushing we could hear the music of my mother's laughter.

That night, in bed, the three of us lay still. We were full of awe and respect for Pecola. Lying next to a real person who was really ministratin' was somehow sacred. She was different from us now—grown-up-like. She, herself, felt the distance, but refused to lord it over us.

After a long while she spoke very softly. "Is it true that I can have

69 me carrying the little-girl-gone-to-woman-pants: 나는 이제 어른이 된 소녀의 팬티를 손에 들고 있었다.

a baby now?"

"Sure," said Frieda drowsily. "Sure you can."

"But ... how?" Her voice was hollow with wonder.

"Oh," said Frieda, "somebody has to love you."

"Oh."

There was a long pause in which Pecola and I thought this over. It would involve, I supposed, "my man," who, before leaving me, would love me. But there weren't any babies in the songs my mother sang. Maybe that's why the women were sad: the men left before they could make a baby.

Then Pecola asked a question that had never entered my mind. "How do you do that? I mean, how do you get somebody to love you?" But Frieda was asleep. And I didn't know.

HEREISTHEHOUSEITISGREENANDWH ITEITHASAREDDOORITISVERYPRETT YITISVERYPRETTYPRETTYPRETTYP

There is an abandoned store on the southeast corner of Broadway and Thirty-fifth Street in Lorain, Ohio. It does not recede into its background of leaden sky, nor harmonize with the gray frame houses and black telephone poles around it. Rather, it foists itself on the eye of the passerby in a manner that is both irritating and melancholy. Visitors who drive to this tiny town wonder why it has not been torn down, while pedestrians, who are residents of the neighborhood, simply look away when they pass it.

At one time, when the building housed a pizza parlor, people saw only slow-footed teen-aged boys huddled about the corner. These young boys met there to feel their groins, smoke cigarettes, and plan mild outrages. The smoke from their cigarettes they inhaled deeply, forcing it to fill their lungs, their hearts, their thighs, and keep at bay the shiveriness, the energy of their youth. They moved slowly, laughed slowly, but flicked the ashes from their cigarettes too quickly, too often, and exposed themselves, to those who were interested, as novices to the habit. But long before the sound of their lowing and the sight of their preening, the building was leased to a Hungarian baker, modestly famous for his brioche[70] and poppy-seed[71] rolls. Earlier than that, there was a real-estate office there, and even before that, some gypsies used it as a base of operations. The gypsy family gave the large plate-glass window as much distinction and character as it ever had. The girls of the family took turns sitting between yards of velvet draperies and Oriental rugs hanging at the windows. They looked out and occasionally smiled, or winked, or beckoned—only occasionally. Mostly they looked, their elaborate dresses, long-sleeved and long-skirted, hiding the nakedness that stood in their eyes.

So fluid has the population in that area been, that probably no one remembers longer, longer ago, before the time of the gypsies and the time of the teen-agers when the Breedloves lived there, nestled together in the storefront. Festering together in the debris of a realtor's whim. They slipped in and out of the box of peeling gray, making no stir in the neighborhood, no sound in the labor force, and no wave in the mayor's office. Each member of the family in his own cell of consciousness, each making his own patchwork quilt of reality—collecting fragments of experience here, pieces of information there. From the tiny impressions gleaned from one another, they created a sense of belonging and tried to make do with the way they found each other.

The plan of the living quarters was as unimaginative as a first-generation Greek landlord could contrive it to be. The large "store" area was partitioned into two rooms by beaverboard planks that did not reach to the ceiling. There was a living room, which the family

---

70 brioche: A soft roll made of butter, eggs, flour, and yeast

71 poppy-seed: 양귀비의 씨(빵이나 과자 등의 위에 붙이는 장식)

called the front room, and the bedroom, where all the living was done. In the front room were two sofas, an upright piano, and a tiny artificial Christmas tree which had been there, decorated and dust-laden, for two years. The bedroom had three beds: a narrow iron bed for Sammy, fourteen years old, another for Pecola, eleven years old, and a double bed for Cholly and Mrs. Breedlove. In the center of the bedroom, for the even distribution of heat, stood a coal stove. Trunks, chairs, a small end table, and a cardboard "wardrobe" closet were placed around the walls. The kitchen was in the back of this apartment, a separate room. There were no bath facilities. Only a toilet bowl, inaccessible to the eye, if not the ear, of the tenants.

There is nothing more to say about the furnishings. They were anything but describable, having been conceived, manufactured, shipped, and sold in various states of thoughtlessness, greed, and indifference. The furniture had aged without ever having become familiar. People had owned it, but never known it. No one had lost a penny or a brooch under the cushions of either sofa and remembered the place and time of the loss or the finding. No one had clucked and said, "But I *had* it just a minute ago. I was sitting right there talking to..." or "Here it is. It must have slipped down while I was feeding the baby!" No one had given birth in one of the beds—or remembered with fondness the peeled paint places, because that's what the baby, when he learned to pull himself up, used to pick loose. No thrifty child had tucked a wad of gum under the table. No happy drunk—a friend of the family, with a fat neck, unmarried, you know, but God how he eats!—had sat at the piano and played "You Are My Sunshine."[72] No young girl had stared at the tiny Christmas tree and remembered when she had decorated it,

72 "You Are My Sunshine": A song written by former Louisiana State Governor Jimmie Davis and Charles Mitchell (1940). This song is one of two official songs for the State of Louisiana.

or wondered if that blue ball was going to hold, or if HE would ever come back to see it.

There were no memories among those pieces. Certainly no memories to be cherished. Occasionally an item provoked a physical reaction: an increase of acid irritation in the upper intestinal tract, a light flush of perspiration at the back of the neck as circumstances surrounding the piece of furniture were recalled. The sofa, for example. It had been purchased new, but the fabric had split straight across the back by the time it was delivered. The store would not take the responsibility....

"Looka here, buddy. It was O.K. when I put it on the truck. The store can't do anything about it once it's on the truck...." Listerine[73] and Lucky Strike[74] breath.

"But I don't want no tore couch if'n it's bought new." Pleading eyes and tightened testicles.

"Tough shit, buddy. *Your* tough shit...."

You could hate a sofa, of course—that is, if you could hate a sofa. But it didn't matter. You still had to get together $4.80 a month. If you had to pay $4.80 a month for a sofa that started off split, no good, and humiliating—you couldn't take any joy in owning it. And the joylessness stank, pervading everything. The stink of it kept you from painting the beaverboard walls; from getting a matching piece of material for the chair; even from sewing up the split, which became a gash, which became a gaping chasm that exposed the cheap frame and cheaper upholstery. It withheld the refreshment in a sleep slept on it. It imposed a furtiveness on the loving done on it.[75] Like a sore tooth that is not content to throb in isolation, but must diffuse its own pain to other parts of the body—making breathing difficult, vision limited, nerves unsettled, so a hated piece

73 Listerine: 구강 청결제, 구취 제거제 브랜드

74 Lucky Strike: 미국의 유명 담배 브랜드

75 It imposed a furtiveness on the loving done on it: 그 소파의 찢어진 부분 때문에 그 위에서 성행위 하는 것조차 불편하게 느껴졌다.

of furniture produces a fretful malaise that asserts itself throughout the house and limits the delight of things not related to it.

The only living thing in the Breedloves' house was the coal stove, which lived independently of everything and everyone, its fire being "out," "banked," or "up" at its own discretion, in spite of the fact that the family fed it and knew all the details of its regimen: sprinkle, do not dump, not too much.... The fire seemed to live, go down, or die according to its own schemata. In the morning, however, it always saw fit to die.

HEREISTHEFAMILYMOTHERFATHER DICKANDJANETHEYLIVEINTHEGREE NANDWHITEHOUSETHEYAREVERYH

The Breedloves did not live in a storefront because they were having temporary difficulty adjusting to the cutbacks at the plant. They lived there because they were poor and black, and they stayed there because they believed they were ugly. Although their poverty was traditional and stultifying, it was not unique. But their ugliness was unique. No one could have convinced them that they were not relentlessly and aggressively ugly. Except for the father, Cholly, whose ugliness (the result of despair, dissipation, and violence directed toward petty things and weak people) was behavior, the rest of the family—Mrs. Breedlove, Sammy Breedlove, and Pecola Breedlove—wore their ugliness, put it on, so to speak, although it did not belong to them. The eyes, the small eyes set closely together under narrow foreheads. The low, irregular hairlines, which seemed even more irregular in contrast to the straight, heavy eyebrows which nearly met. Keen but crooked noses, with insolent nostrils. They had high cheekbones, and their ears turned forward. Shapely lips which called attention not to themselves but to the rest of the face. You looked at them and wondered why they were so ugly; you looked closely and could not find the source. Then you realized that it came from conviction, their conviction. It was as though some mysterious all-knowing master had given each one a cloak of ugliness to wear, and they had each accepted it without question. The master had said, "You are ugly people." They had looked about themselves and saw nothing to contradict the statement; saw, in fact, support for it leaning at them from every billboard, every movie, every glance. "Yes," they had said. "You are right." And they took the ugliness in their hands, threw it as a mantle over them, and went about the world with it. Dealing with it each according to his way. Mrs. Breedlove handled hers as an actor does a prop: for the articulation of character, for support of a role she frequently imagined was hers—martyrdom. Sammy used his as a weapon to cause others pain. He adjusted his behavior to it, chose his companions on the basis of it: people who could be fascinated, even intimidated by it. And Pecola. She hid behind hers. Concealed, veiled, eclipsed—peeping out from behind the shroud very seldom, and then only to yearn for the return of her mask.

This family, on a Saturday morning in October, began, one by one, to stir out of their dreams of affluence and vengeance into the anonymous misery of their storefront.

Mrs. Breedlove slipped noiselessly out of bed, put a sweater on over her nightgown (which was an old day dress), and walked toward the kitchen. Her one good foot made hard, bony sounds; the twisted one whispered on the linoleum. In the kitchen she made noises with doors, faucets, and pans. The noises were hollow, but the threats they implied were not. Pecola opened her eyes and lay staring at the dead coal stove. Cholly mumbled, thrashed about in the bed for a minute, and then was quiet.

Even from where Pecola lay, she could smell Cholly's whiskey. The noises in the kitchen became louder and less hollow. There was direction and purpose in Mrs. Breedlove's movements that had nothing to do with the preparation of breakfast. This awareness, supported by ample evidence from the past, made Pecola tighten her stomach muscles and ration her breath.

Cholly had come home drunk. Unfortunately he had been too drunk to quarrel, so the whole business would have to erupt this morning. Because it had not taken place immediately, the oncoming fight would lack spontaneity; it would be calculated, uninspired, and deadly.

Mrs. Breedlove came swiftly into the room and stood at the foot of the bed where Cholly lay.

"I need some coal in this house."

Cholly did not move.

"Hear me?" Mrs. Breedlove jabbed Cholly's foot.

Cholly opened his eyes slowly. They were red and menacing. With no exception, Cholly had the meanest eyes in town.

"Awwwwww, woman!"

"I said I need some coal. It's as cold as a witch's tit in this house. Your whiskey ass wouldn't feel hellfire, but I'm cold.[76] I got to do a lot of things, but I ain't got to freeze."

"Leave me 'lone."

"Not until you get me some coal. If working like a mule don't give me the right to be warm, what am I doing it for? You sure ain't bringing in nothing. If it was left up to you, we'd all be dead...." Her voice was like an earache in the brain. "... If you think I'm going to wade out in the cold and get it myself, you'd better think

---

76 Your whisky ass wouldn't feel hellfire, but I'm cold: 당신의 그 술에 절어버린 몸뚱이는 지옥 불이 뜨거운지도 못 느낄지 모르지만, 나는 추워 죽겠다구요.

again."

"I don't give a shit how you get it." A bubble of violence burst in his throat.

"You going to get your drunk self out of that bed and get me some coal or not?"

Silence.

"Cholly!"

Silence.

"Don't try me this morning, man. You say one more word, and I'll split you open!"

Silence.

"All right. All right. But if I sneeze once, just once, God help your butt!"[77]

Sammy was awake now too, but pretending to be asleep. Pecola still held her stomach muscles taut and conserved her breath. They all knew that Mrs. Breedlove could have, would have, and had, gotten coal from the shed, or that Sammy or Pecola could be directed to get it. But the unquarreled evening hung like the first note of a dirge in sullenly expectant air. An escapade of drunkenness, no matter how routine, had its own ceremonial close. The tiny, undistinguished days that Mrs. Breedlove lived were identified, grouped, and classed by these quarrels. They gave substance to the minutes and hours otherwise dim and unrecalled. They relieved the tiresomeness of poverty, gave grandeur to the dead rooms. In these violent breaks in routine that were themselves routine, she could display the style and imagination of what she believed to be her own true self. To deprive her of these fights was to deprive her of all the zest and reasonableness of life. Cholly, by his habitual drunkenness and orneriness, provided them both with the material they needed to make their lives tolerable. Mrs. Breedlove considered herself an upright

---

77 God help your butt!: 그땐 각오해요.

and Christian woman, burdened with a no-count man,[78] whom God wanted her to punish. (Cholly was beyond redemption, of course, and redemption was hardly the point—Mrs. Breedlove was not interested in Christ the Redeemer, but rather Christ the Judge.) Often she could be heard discoursing with Jesus about Cholly, pleading with Him to help her "strike the bastard down from his pea-knuckle of pride." And once when a drunken gesture catapulted Cholly into the red-hot stove, she screamed, "Get him, Jesus! Get him!" If Cholly had stopped drinking, she would never have forgiven Jesus. She needed Cholly's sins desperately. The lower he sank, the wilder and more irresponsible he became, the more splendid she and her task became. In the name of Jesus.

No less did Cholly need her. She was one of the few things abhorrent to him that he could touch and therefore hurt. He poured out on her the sum of all his inarticulate fury and aborted desires. Hating her, he could leave himself intact. When he was still very young, Cholly had been surprised in some bushes by two white men while he was newly but earnestly engaged in eliciting sexual pleasure from a little country girl. The men had shone a flashlight right on his behind. He had stopped, terrified. They chuckled. The beam of the flashlight did not move. "Go on," they said. "Go on and finish. And, nigger, make it good." The flashlight did not move. For some reason Cholly had not hated the white men; he hated, despised, the girl.[79] Even a half-remembrance of this episode, along with myriad other humiliations, defeats, and emasculations, could stir him

---

78 a no-count man: 무능한 사람, 무책임한 사람(= a no-account man) (No account = worthless, of little or no importance or value)

79 For some reason Cholly had not hated the white men; he hated, despised, the girl: 왠지 모르지만 Cholly는 그 백인 남자들을 증오하지 않았다. 그는 상대방 여자를 미워하고 멸시했다. (그는 백인들이 못되게 굴었지만, 그들 앞에서 꼼짝도 못 한 자신의 무능한 모습을 모두 목격한 데이트 상대가 더 미웠던 것이다. 스스로 약자이면서, 자신보다 더 약자인 자에게 보복하는 심리가 작용한 것.)

into flights of depravity that surprised himself–but only himself. Somehow he could not astound. He could only be astounded. So he gave that up, too.

Cholly and Mrs. Breedlove fought each other with a darkly brutal formalism that was paralleled only by their lovemaking. Tacitly they had agreed not to kill each other. He fought her the way a coward fights a man—with feet, the palms of his hands, and teeth. She, in turn, fought back in a purely feminine way—with frying pans and pokers, and occasionally a flatiron would sail toward his head. They did not talk, groan, or curse during these beatings. There was only the muted sound of falling things, and flesh on unsurprised flesh.

There was a difference in the reaction of the children to these battles. Sammy cursed for a while, or left the house, or threw himself into the fray. He was known, by the time he was fourteen, to have run away from home no less than twenty-seven times. Once he got to Buffalo and stayed three months. His returns, whether by force or circumstance, were sullen. Pecola, on the other hand, restricted by youth and sex, experimented with methods of endurance. Though the methods varied, the pain was as consistent as it was deep. She struggled between an overwhelming desire that one would kill the other, and a profound wish that she herself could die. Now she was whispering, "Don't, Mrs. Breedlove. Don't." Pecola, like Sammy and Cholly, always called her mother Mrs. Breedlove.[80]

"Don't, Mrs. Breedlove. Don't."

But Mrs. Breedlove did.

By the grace, no doubt, of God, Mrs. Breedlove sneezed. Just once.

She ran into the bedroom with a dishpan full of cold water and threw it in Cholly's face. He sat up, choking and spitting. Naked and

---

80 Pecola, like Sammy and Cholly, called her mother Mrs. Breedlove: Pecola는 Sammy와 Cholly와 마찬가지로 엄마를 Breedlove 여사라고 불렀다. (이는 Pecola가 다른 가족구성원들과 마찬가지로 어머니와 심리적 거리를 두고 있음을 암시한다.)

ashen, he leaped from the bed, and with a flying tackle, grabbed his wife around the waist, and they hit the floor. Cholly picked her up and knocked her down with the back of his hand. She fell in a sitting position, her back supported by Sammy's bed frame. She had not let go of the dishpan, and began to hit at Cholly's thighs and groin with it. He put his foot in her chest, and she dropped the pan. Dropping to his knee, he struck her several times in the face, and she might have succumbed early had he not hit his hand against the metal bed frame when his wife ducked. Mrs. Breedlove took advantage of this momentary suspension of blows and slipped out of his reach. Sammy, who had watched in silence their struggling at his bedside, suddenly began to hit his father about the head with both fists, shouting "You naked fuck!" over and over and over. Mrs. Breedlove, having snatched up the round, flat stove lid, ran tippy-toe to Cholly as he was pulling himself up from his knees, and struck him two blows, knocking him right back into the senselessness out of which she had provoked him. Panting, she threw a quilt over him and let him lie.

Sammy screamed, "Kill him! Kill him!"

Mrs. Breedlove looked at Sammy with surprise. "Cut out that noise, boy." She put the stove lid back in place, and walked toward the kitchen. At the doorway she paused long enough to say to her son, "Get up from there anyhow. I need some coal."

Letting herself breathe easy now, Pecola covered her head with the quilt. The sick feeling, which she had tried to prevent by holding in her stomach, came quickly in spite of her precaution. There surged in her the desire to heave, but as always, she knew she would not.

"Please, God," she whispered into the palm of her hand. "Please make me disappear." She squeezed her eyes shut. Little parts of her body faded away. Now slowly, now with a rush. Slowly again. Her fingers went, one by one; then her arms disappeared all the way to the elbow. Her feet now. Yes, that was good. The legs all at once. It was hardest above the thighs. She had to be real still and pull. Her stomach would not go. But finally it, too, went away. Then her chest, her neck. The face was hard, too. Almost done, almost. Only her tight, tight eyes were left. They were always left.

Try as she might, she could never get her eyes to disappear. So what was the point? They were everything. Everything was there, in them. All of those pictures, all of those faces. She had long ago given up the idea of running away to see new pictures, new faces, as Sammy had so often done. He never took her, and he never thought about his going ahead of time, so it was never planned. It wouldn't have worked anyway. As long as she looked the way she did, as long as she was ugly, she would have to stay with these people. Somehow she belonged to them. Long hours she sat looking in the mirror, trying to discover the secret of the ugliness, the ugliness that made her ignored or despised at school, by teachers and classmates alike. She was the only member of her class who sat alone at a double desk. The first letter of her last name forced her to sit in the front of the room always. But what about Marie Appolonaire? Marie was in front of her, but she shared a desk with Luke Angelino. Her teachers had always treated her this way. They tried never to glance at her, and called on her only when everyone was required to respond. She also knew that when one of the girls at school wanted to be particularly insulting to a boy, or wanted to get an immediate response from him, she could say, "Bobby loves Pecola Breedlove! Bobby loves Pecola Breedlove!" and never fail to get peals of laughter from those in earshot, and mock anger from the accused.

It had occurred to Pecola some time ago that if her eyes, those eyes that held the pictures, and knew the sights—if those eyes of hers were different, that is to say, beautiful, she herself would be different. Her teeth were good, and at least her nose was not big and flat like some of those who were thought so cute. If she looked different, beautiful, maybe Cholly would be different, and Mrs. Breedlove too.[81] Maybe they'd say, "Why, look at pretty-eyed Pecola. We mustn't do bad things in front of those pretty eyes."

Pretty eyes. Pretty blue eyes. Big blue pretty eyes.
Run, Jip, run. Jip runs, Alice runs. Alice has blue eyes.
Jerry has blue eyes. Jerry runs. Alice runs. They run
with their blue eyes. Four blue eyes. Four pretty
blue eyes. Blue-sky eyes. Blue-like Mrs. Forrest's
blue blouse eyes. Morning-glory-blue-eyes.
Alice-and-Jerry-blue-storybook-eyes.

Each night, without fail, she prayed for blue eyes. Fervently, for a year she had prayed. Although somewhat discouraged, she was not without hope. To have something as wonderful as that happen would take a long, long time.

Thrown, in this way, into the binding conviction that only a miracle could relieve her, she would never know her beauty. She would see only what there was to see: the eyes of other people.

She walks down Garden Avenue to a small grocery store which sells penny candy. Three pennies are in her shoe—slipping back and forth between the sock and the inner sole. With each step she feels the painful press of the coins against her foot. A sweet, endurable, even cherished irritation, full of promise and delicate security. There is plenty of time to consider what to buy. Now, however, she moves down an avenue gently buffeted by the familiar and therefore loved images. The dandelions at the base of the

---

81 It had occurred to Pecola some time ago . . . maybe Cholly would be different, and Mrs. Breedlove too. (☞ Pecola는 여기서 자신과 가족의 모든 불행을 눈의 탓으로 돌리고 있다.)

telephone pole. Why, she wonders, do people call them weeds? She thought they were pretty. But grown-ups say, "Miss Dunion keeps her yard so nice. Not a dandelion anywhere." Hunkie women in black babushkas[82] go into the fields with baskets to pull them up. But they do not want the yellow heads—only the jagged leaves. They make dandelion soup. Dandelion wine. Nobody loves the head of a dandelion. Maybe because they are so many, strong, and soon.

There was the sidewalk crack shaped like a Y, and the other one that lifted the concrete up from the dirt floor. Frequently her sloughing step had made her trip over that one. Skates would go well over this sidewalk–old it was, and smooth; it made the wheels glide evenly, with a mild whirr. The newly paved walks were bumpy and uncomfortable, and the sound of skate wheels on new walks was grating.

These and other inanimate things she saw and experienced. They were real to her. She knew them. They were the codes and touchstones of the world, capable of translation and possession. She owned the crack that made her stumble; she owned the clumps of dandelions whose white heads, last fall, she had blown away; whose yellow heads, this fall, she peered into. And owning them made her part of the world, and the world a part of her.

She climbs four wooden steps to the door of Yacobowski's Fresh Veg. Meat and Sundries Store. A bell tinkles as she opens it. Standing before the counter, she looks at the array of candies. All Mary Janes, she decides.[83] Three for a penny. The resistant sweetness that breaks open at last to deliver peanut butter–the oil and salt which complement the sweet pull of caramel. A peal of anticipation unsettles her stomach.

She pulls off her shoe and takes out the three pennies. The gray head of Mr. Yacobowski looms up over the counter. He urges his

---

82 babushkas: 바부시카(폴란드나 러시아 여성들이 머리에 쓰는 삼각형 스카프)
83 All Mary Janes, she decides: Pecola는 '메리 제인스' 사탕만 사겠다고 결심했다.

eyes out of his thoughts to encounter her. Blue eyes. Blear-dropped. Slowly, like Indian summer[84] moving imperceptibly toward fall, he looks toward her. Somewhere between retina and object, between vision and view, his eyes draw back, hesitate, and hover. At some fixed point in time and space he senses that he need not waste the effort of a glance. He does not see her, because for him there is nothing to see. How can a fifty-two-year-old white immigrant storekeeper with the taste of potatoes and beer in his mouth, his mind honed on the doe-eyed Virgin Mary, his sensibilities blunted by a permanent awareness of loss, *see* a little black girl? Nothing in his life even suggested that the feat was possible, not to say desirable or necessary.

"Yeah?"

She looks up at him and sees the vacuum where curiosity ought to lodge. And something more. The total absence of human recognition—the glazed separateness. She does not know what keeps his glance suspended. Perhaps because he is grown, or a man, and she a little girl. But she has seen interest, disgust, even anger in grown male eyes. Yet this vacuum is not new to her. It has an edge; somewhere in the bottom lid is the distaste. She has seen it lurking in the eyes of all white people. So. The distaste must be for her, her blackness. All things in her are flux and anticipation. But her blackness is static and dread. And it is the blackness that accounts for, that creates, the vacuum edged with distaste in white eyes.

She points her finger at the Mary Janes—a little black shaft of finger, its tip pressed on the display window. The quietly inoffensive assertion of a black child's attempt to communicate with a white adult.

"Them." The word is more sigh than sense.

"What? These? These?" Phlegm and impatience mingle in his voice.

---

84 Indian summer: a period of warm or mild weather in late autumn or early winter

She shakes her head, her fingertip fixed on the spot which, in her view, at any rate, identifies the Mary Janes. He cannot see her view—the angle of his vision, the slant of her finger, makes it incomprehensible to him. His lumpy red hand plops around in the glass casing like the agitated head of a chicken outraged by the loss of its body.

"Christ. Kantcha talk?"[85]

His fingers brush the Mary Janes.

She nods.

"Well, why'nt you say so? One? How many?"

Pecola unfolds her fist, showing the three pennies. He scoots three Mary Janes toward her—three yellow rectangles in each packet. She holds the money toward him. He hesitates, not wanting to touch her hand. She does not know how to move the finger of her right hand from the display counter or how to get the coins out of her left hand. Finally he reaches over and takes the pennies from her hand. His nails graze her damp palm.

Outside, Pecola feels the inexplicable shame ebb.

Dandelions. A dart of affection leaps out from her to them. But they do not look at her and do not send love back. She thinks, "They *are* ugly. They *are* weeds." Preoccupied with that revelation, she trips on the sidewalk crack. Anger stirs and wakes in her; it opens its mouth, and like a hot-mouthed puppy, laps up the dredges of her shame.

Anger is better. There is a sense of being in anger. A reality and presence. An awareness of worth. It is a lovely surging. Her thoughts fall back to Mr. Yacobowski's eyes, his phlegmy voice. The anger will not hold; the puppy is too easily surfeited. Its thirst too quickly quenched, it sleeps. The shame wells up again, its muddy rivulets seeping into her eyes. What to do before the tears come. She

---

85 "Christ. Kantcha talk?"(= Jesus Christ, Can't you talk?"): "세상에, 말도 못하니?"

remembers the Mary Janes.

Each pale yellow wrapper has a picture on it. A picture of little Mary Jane, for whom the candy is named. Smiling white face. Blond hair in gentle disarray, blue eyes looking at her out of a world of clean comfort. The eyes are petulant, mischievous. To Pecola they are simply pretty. She eats the candy, and its sweetness is good. To eat the candy is somehow to eat the eyes, eat Mary Jane. Love Mary Jane. Be Mary Jane.

Three pennies had bought her nine lovely orgasms with Mary Jane. Lovely Mary Jane, for whom a candy is named.

Three whores lived in the apartment above the Breedloves' storefront. China, Poland, and Miss Marie. Pecola loved them, visited them, and ran their errands. They, in turn, did not despise her.

On an October morning, the morning of the stove-lid triumph,[86] Pecola climbed the stairs to their apartment.

Even before the door was opened to her tapping, she could hear Poland singing—her voice sweet and hard, like new strawberries:

I got blues in my mealbarrel
Blues up on the shelf
I got blues in my mealbarrel
Blues up on the shelf
Blues in my bedroom
'Cause I'm sleepin' by myself

"Hi, dumplin'.[87] Where your socks?" Marie seldom called Pecola the same thing twice, but invariably her epithets were fond ones

---

86 the morning of the stove-lid triumph: (Breedlove 부인이) 난로 뚜껑으로 승리를 거둔 날 아침

87 dumplin': dumpling. 만두, 혹은 땅딸보라는 뜻. Maginot Line이 Pecola를 음식 이름으로 부르는 별명의 첫번째.

chosen from menus and dishes that were forever uppermost in her mind.

"Hello, Miss Marie. Hello, Miss China. Hello, Miss Poland."

"You heard me. Where your socks? You as bare-legged as a yard dog."

"I couldn't find any."

"Couldn't find any? Must be somethin' in your house that loves socks."[88]

China chuckled. Whenever something was missing, Marie attributed its disappearance to "something in the house that loved it." "There is somethin' in this house that loves brassieres," she would say with alarm.

Poland and China were getting ready for the evening. Poland, forever ironing, forever singing. China, sitting on a pale-green kitchen chair, forever and forever curling her hair. Marie never got ready.

The women were friendly, but slow to begin talk. Pecola always took the initiative with Marie, who, once inspired, was difficult to stop.

"How come you got so many boyfriends, Miss Marie?"

"*Boy*friends? *Boy*friends? Chittlin',[89] I ain't seen a *boy* since nineteen and twenty-seven."

"You didn't see none then." China stuck the hot curlers into a tin of Nu Nile hair dressing. The oil hissed at the touch of the hot metal.

"How come, Miss Marie?" Pecola insisted.

"How come what? How come I ain't seen a boy since nineteen and twenty-seven? Because they ain't *been* no boys since then. That's

---

88 Must be somethin' in your house that loves socks: 너희 집에 양말 좋아하는 괴물이 살고 있는 게 틀림없어.

89 Cittlin': chitterings (요리용 돼지, 송아지 따위의) 소장(곱창). 역시 Maginot Line이 Pecola를 음식이름으로 부른 것.

when they stopped. Folks started gettin' born old."

"You mean that's when *you* got old," China said.

"I ain't never got old. Just fat."

"Same thing."

"You think 'cause you skinny, folks think you young? You'd mak a haint buy a girdle."

"And you look like the north side of a southbound mule."

"All I know is, them bandy little legs of yours is every bit as old as mine."

"Don't worry 'bout my bandy legs. That's the first thing they push aside."

All three of the women laughed. Marie threw back her head. From deep inside, her laughter came like the sound of many rivers, freely, deeply, muddily, heading for the room of an open sea. China giggled spastically. Each gasp seemed to be yanked out of her by an unseen hand jerking an unseen string. Poland, who seldom spoke unless she was drunk, laughed without sound. When she was sober she hummed mostly or chanted blues songs, of which she knew many.

Pecola fingered the fringe of a scarf that lay on the back of a sofa. "I never seen nobody with as many boyfriends as you got, Miss Marie. How come they all love you?"

Marie opened a bottle of root beer[90]. "What else they gone do? They know I'm rich and good-lookin'. They wants to put their toes in my curly hair, and get at my money."

"You rich, Miss Marie?"

"Puddin', I got money's mammy."

"Where you get it from? You don't do no work."

"Yeah," said China, "where you get it from?"

---

90 root beer: 《미국, 캐나다》 루트 비어(나무 뿌리, 껍질, 약초에서 짜낸 즙에 시럽을 타서 만드는 탄산 음료)

"Hoover[91] give it me. I did him a favor once, for the F. B. and I."[92]

"What'd you do?"

"I did him a favor. They wanted to catch this crook, you see. Name of Johnny. He was as low-down as they come...."

"We *know* that." China arranged a curl.

"... the F. B. and I. wanted him bad. He killed more people than TB. And if you *crossed* him? Whoa, Jesus! He'd run you as long as there was ground.[93] Well, I was little and cute then. No more than ninety pounds, soaking wet."[94]

"You ain't never been soaking wet," China said.

"Well, you ain't never been dry.[95] Shut up. Let me tell you, sweetnin'. To tell it true, I was the only one could handle him. He'd go out and rob a bank or kill some people, and I'd say to him, soft-like, 'Johnny, you shouldn't do that.' And he'd say he just had to bring me pretty things. Lacy drawers and all. And every Saturday we'd get a case of beer and fry up some fish. We'd fry it in meal and egg batter, you know, and when it was all brown and crisp—not hard, though—we'd break open that cold beer...." Marie's eyes went soft as the memory of just such a meal sometime, somewhere transfixed her. All her stories were subject to breaking down at descriptions of food. Pecola saw Marie's teeth settling down into the back of crisp sea bass; saw the fat fingers putting back into her mouth tiny flakes of white, hot meat that had escaped from her lips; she heard the "pop" of the beer-bottle cap; smelled the acridness of the first stream of vapor; felt

---

91 Edgar Hoover (1885–1972): US government official; director of the FBI (1924–72). He organized the FBI into an efficient, scientific law-enforcement agency, but came under criticism for the organization's role during the McCarthy era and for its reactionary political stance in the 1960s.

92 the F.B. and I: FBI (Federal Bureau of Investigation); 미연방수사국

93 And if you crossed him? Whoa, Jesus! He'd run you as long as there was ground: 누구라도 그를 배반하기만 한다면, 아 세상에, 땅 끝까지 쫓아올 걸.

94 soaking wet (=extremely small and thin)

95 You ain't never been dry. (=You are not particularly thin yourself, i.e. fat.)

the cold beeriness hit the tongue. She ended the daydream long before Marie.

"But what about the money?" she asked.

China hooted. "She's makin' like she's the Lady in Red that told on Dillinger.[96] Dillinger wouldn't have come near you lessen[97] he was going hunting in Africa and shoot you for a hippo."

"Well, this hippo had a ball back in Chicago. Whoa Jesus, ninety-nine!"

"How come you always say 'Whoa Jesus' and a number?" Pecola had long wanted to know.

"Because my mama taught me never to cuss."

"Did she teach you not to drop your drawers?" China asked.

"Didn't have none," said Marie. "Never saw a pair of drawers till I was fifteen, when I left Jackson and was doing day work in Cincinnati. My white lady gave me some old ones of hers. I thought they was some kind of stocking cap. I put it on my head when I dusted. When she saw me, she liked to fell out."

"You must have been one dumb somebody." China lit a cigarette and cooled her irons.

"How'd I know?" Marie paused. "And what's the use of putting on something you got to keep taking off all the time? Dewey never let me keep them on long enough to get used to them."

"Dewey who?" This was a somebody new to Pecola.

"Dewey who? Chicken![98] You never heard me tell of *Dewey*?" Marie was shocked by her negligence.

"No, ma'am."

---

96 She's makin' like(=pretending) she's the Lady in Red that told on Dillinger: 자기가 무슨 딜린저를 팔아 넘긴 붉은 의상의 여인이라도 된 줄 아나. (*John Dillinger (1903-1934): 살인범, 은행강도. 감옥소를 탈출한 이후 FBI가 지목한 "공공의 적 1호"가 됐으나, 후에 FBI에 의해 매수된 붉은 의상의 여인(the Lady wearing a red gown)의 밀고로 체포됨.)

97 lessen= unless

98 Chicken! (=shit! 여성은 이런 말을 입에 담을 수 없었다.)

"Oh, honey, you've missed half your life. Whoa Jesus, one-nine-five! You talkin' 'bout smooth![99] I met him when I was fourteen. We ran away and lived together like married for three years. You know all those klinker-tops[100] you see runnin' up here? Fifty of 'em in a bowl wouldn't make a Dewey Prince ankle bone.[101] Oh, Lord. How that man loved me!"

China arranged a fingerful of hair into a bang[102] effect. "Then why left you to sell tail?"[103]

"Girl, when I found out I could sell it—that somebody would pay cold cash for it, you could have knocked me over with a feather."[104]

Poland began to laugh. Soundlessly. "Me too. My auntie[105] whipped me good that first time when I told her I didn't get no money. I said 'Money? For what? He didn't owe me nothin'.' She said, 'The hell he didn't!'"

They all dissolved in laughter.

Three merry gargoyles. Three merry harridans. Amused by a long-ago time of ignorance. They did not belong to those generations of prostitutes created in novels, with great and generous hearts, dedicated, because of the horror of circumstance, to ameliorating the luckless, barren life of men, taking money incidentally and humbly for their "understanding." Nor were they from that sensitive breed of young girl, gone wrong at the hands of fate, forced to cultivate an outward brittleness in order to protect her springtime

---

99 You talkin'about smooth! 사람들을, 특히 여자들을 잘 다루는 사람. 여기서는 Dewey를 가리킴.

100 klinker-tops: 놈팡이들

101 Fifty of 'em in a bowl wouldn't make a Dewey Prince ankle bone: 그런 놈들 한 사발을 합쳐도 듀이 프린스 발뒤꿈치도 못 따라갈걸.

102 "Bangs": a fringe of hair cut straight across the forehead.

103 "Then why he left you to sell tail?": "그런데 왜 그가 네가 몸을 파는 걸 그냥 놔두었지?"

104 you could have knocked me over with a feather: 당시는 하도 어려워 누가 깃털 하나만 건드려도 내가 쓸어질 지경이었지.

105 auntie: 일반적으로 아줌마(aunt), 유모의 뜻이지만 여기서는 포주를 말함

from further shock, but knowing full well she was cut out for better things, and could make the right man happy. Neither were they the sloppy, inadequate whores who, unable to make a living at it alone, turn to drug consumption and traffic or pimps to help complete their scheme of self-destruction, avoiding suicide only to punish the memory of some absent father or to sustain the misery of some silent mother. Except for Marie's fabled love for Dewey Prince, these women hated men, all men, without shame, apology, or discrimination. They abused their visitors with a scorn grown mechanical from use. Black men, white men, Puerto Ricans, Mexicans, Jews, Poles, whatever—all were inadequate and weak, all came under their jaundiced eyes and were the recipients of their disinterested wrath. They took delight in cheating them. On one occasion the town well knew, they lured a Jew up the stairs, pounced on him, all three, held him up by the heels, shook everything out of his pants pockets, and threw him out of the window.

Neither did they have respect for women, who, although not their colleagues, so to speak, nevertheless deceived their husbands —regularly or irregularly, it made no difference. "Sugar-coated whores," they called them, and did not yearn to be in their shoes. Their only respect was for what they would have described as "good Christian colored women." The woman whose reputation was spotless, and who tended to her family, who didn't drink or smoke or run around. These women had their undying, if covert, affection. They would sleep with their husbands, and take their money, but always with a vengeance.

Nor were they protective and solicitous of youthful innocence. They looked back on their own youth as a period of ignorance, and regretted that they had not made more of it. They were not young girls in whores' clothing, or whores regretting their loss of innocence. They were whores in whores' clothing, whores who had never been young and had no word for innocence. With Pecola they were as free as they were with each other. Marie concocted stories for her because she was a child, but the stories were breezy and rough. If Pecola had announced her intention to live the life they did, they would not have tried to dissuade her or voiced any alarm.

"You and Dewey Prince have any children, Miss Marie?"

"Yeah. Yeah. We had some." Marie fidgeted. She pulled a bobby pin from her hair and began to pick her teeth. That meant she didn't want to talk anymore.

Pecola went to the window and looked down at the empty street. A tuft of grass had forced its way up through a crack in the sidewalk, only to meet a raw October wind. She thought of Dewey Prince and how he loved Miss Marie. What did love feel like? she wondered. How do grown-ups act when they love each other? Eat fish together? Into her eyes came the picture of Cholly and Mrs. Breedlove in bed. He making sounds as though he were in pain, as though something had him by the throat and wouldn't let go. Terrible as his noises were, they were not nearly as bad as the no noise at all from her mother. It was as though she was not even there. Maybe that was love. Choking sounds and silence.

Turning her eyes from the window, Pecola looked at the women.

China had changed her mind about the bangs and was arranging a small but sturdy pompadour.[106] She was adept in creating any number of hair styles, but each one left her with a pinched and harassed look. Then she applied makeup heavily. Now she gave herself surprised eyebrows and a cupid-bow mouth. Later she would make Oriental eyebrows and an evilly slashed mouth.

Poland, in her sweet strawberry voice, began another song:

I know a boy who is sky-soft brown
I know a boy who is sky-soft brown

---

106 pompadour: 퐁파두르. 치켜올린 여성의 트레머리

The dirt leaps for joy when his feet touch the ground.
His strut is a peacock
His eye is burning brass
His smile is sorghum syrup drippin' slow-sweet to the last
I know a boy who is sky-soft brown[107]

Marie sat shelling peanuts and popping them into her mouth. Pecola looked and looked at the women. Were they real? Marie belched, softly, purringly, lovingly.

107 sky-soft brown: African American "light-skinned, soft-brown complexion." "high yellow."

Winter

My daddy's face is a study. Winter moves into it and presides there. His eyes become a cliff of snow threatening to avalanche; his eyebrows bend like black limbs of leafless trees. His skin takes on the pale, cheerless yellow of winter sun; for a jaw he has the edges of a snowbound field dotted with stubble; his high forehead is the frozen sweep of the Erie,[108] hiding currents of gelid thoughts that eddy in darkness. Wolf killer turned hawk fighter,[109] he worked night and day to keep one from the door and the other from under the windowsills. A Vulcan[110] guarding the flames, he gives us instructions about which doors to keep closed or opened for proper distribution of heat, lays kindling by, discusses qualities of coal, and teaches us how to rake, feed, and bank the fire. And he will not unrazor his lips until spring.

---

108 Erie: Lake Erie. 이리 호(湖)(미국 동북부와 캐나다 동남부에 위치)

109 Wolf killer turned hawk fighter: earning enough money to survive

110 Vulcan: 《로마 신화》 불의 신(Jupiter와 Juno 사이에 태어난 불과 대장장이의 신)

Winter tightened our heads with a band of cold and melted our eyes. We put pepper in the feet of our stockings, Vaseline on our faces, and stared through dark icebox mornings at four stewed prunes, slippery lumps of oatmeal, and cocoa with a roof of skin.

But mostly we waited for spring, when there could be gardens.

By the time this winter had stiffened itself into a hateful knot that nothing could loosen, something did loosen it, or rather someone. A someone who splintered the knot into silver threads that tangled us, netted us, made us long for the dull chafe of the previous boredom.

This disrupter of seasons was a new girl in school named Maureen Peal. A high-yellow dream child[111] with long brown hair braided into two lynch ropes that hung down her back. She was rich, at least by our standards, as rich as the richest of the white girls, swaddled in comfort and care. The quality of her clothes threatened to derange Frieda and me. Patent-leather shoes with buckles, a cheaper version of which we got only at Easter and which had disintegrated by the end of May. Fluffy sweaters the color of lemon drops tucked into skirts with pleats so orderly they astounded us. Brightly colored knee socks with white borders, a brown velvet coat trimmed in white rabbit fur, and a matching muff.[112] There was a hint of spring in her sloe green eyes, something summery in her complexion, and a rich autumn ripeness in her walk.

She enchanted the entire school. When teachers called on her, they smiled encouragingly. Black boys didn't trip her in the halls; white boys didn't stone her, white girls didn't suck their teeth when she was assigned to be their work partners; black girls stepped aside when she wanted to use the sink in the girls' toilet,

---

111 A high-yellow dream child: Maureen Peal(Maureen Peal)이 흑백혼혈아임을 의미한다.

112 muff: 머프(양손을 따뜻하게 하는 원통 모양의 모피 토시 방한구)

and their eyes genuflected under sliding lids. She never had to search for anybody to eat with in the cafeteria—they flocked to the table of her choice, where she opened fastidious lunches, shaming our jelly-stained bread with egg-salad sandwiches cut into four dainty squares, pink-frosted cupcakes, stocks of celery and carrots, proud, dark apples. She even bought and liked white milk.

Frieda and I were bemused, irritated, and fascinated by her. We looked hard for flaws to restore our equilibrium, but had to be content at first with uglying up her name, changing Maureen Peal to Meringue[113] Pie. Later a minor epiphany was ours when we discovered that she had a dog tooth[114]—a charming one to be sure—but a dog tooth nonetheless. And when we found out that she had been born with six fingers on each hand and that there was a little bump where each extra one had been removed, we smiled. They were small triumphs, but we took what we could get—snickering behind her back and calling her Six-finger-dog-tooth-meringue-pie. But we had to do it alone, for none of the other girls would cooperate with our hostility. They adored her.

When she was assigned a locker next to mine, I could indulge my jealousy four times a day. My sister and I both suspected that we were secretly prepared to be her friend, if she would let us, but I knew it would be a dangerous friendship, for when my eye traced the white border patterns of those Kelly-green[115] knee socks, and felt the pull and slack of my brown stockings, I wanted to kick her. And when I thought of the unearned haughtiness in

---

113 Meringue: 머렝(달걀의 흰자위를 거품을 일게 만들어 설탕을 섞은 것. 파이 등에 얹음)

114 A minor epiphany was ours when we discovered that she had a dog tooth: 그 애에게 송곳니가 있었다는 사실을 알았을 때 우리는 적잖이 즐거웠다. (Epiphany originally means the manifestation of Christ to the Gentiles as represented by the Magi (Matthew 2:1-12). But here, a new discovery.)

115 Kelly-green knee socks: Royal blue and black striped overknee socks.

her eyes, I plotted accidental slammings of locker doors on her hand.

As locker friends, however, we got to know each other a little, and I was even able to hold a sensible conversation with her without visualizing her fall off a cliff, or giggling my way into what I thought was a clever insult.

One day, while I waited at the locker for Frieda, she joined me.

"Hi."

"Hi."

"Waiting for your sister?"

"Uh-huh."

"Which way do you go home?"

"Down Twenty-first Street to Broadway."

"Why don't you go down Twenty-second Street?"

" 'Cause I live on Twenty-first Street."

"Oh. I can walk that way, I guess. Partly, anyway."

"Free country."

Frieda came toward us, her brown stockings straining at the knees because she had tucked the toe under to hide a hole in the foot.

"Maureen's gonna walk part way with us."

Frieda and I exchanged glances, her eyes begging my restraint, mine promising nothing.

It was a false spring day, which, like Maureen, had pierced the shell of a deadening winter. There were puddles, mud, and an inviting warmth that deluded us. The kind of day on which we draped our coats over our heads, left our galoshes in school, and came down with croup[116] the following day. We always responded to the slightest change in weather, the most minute shifts in time of day. Long before seeds were stirring, Frieda and I were

---

116 Croup is characterized by a loud cough that resembles the barking of a seal, difficulty breathing, and a grunting noise or wheezing during breathing.

scruffing and poking at the earth, swallowing air, drinking rain....

As we emerged from the school with Maureen, we began to moult immediately. We put our head scarves in our coat pockets, and our coats on our heads. I was wondering how to maneuver Maureen's fur muff into a gutter when a commotion in the playground distracted us. A group of boys was circling and holding at bay a victim, Pecola Breedlove.

Bay Boy, Woodrow Cain, Buddy Wilson, Junie Bug—like a necklace of semiprecious stones they surrounded her. Heady with the smell of their own musk, thrilled by the easy power of a majority, they gaily harassed her.

"Black e mo.[117] Black e mo. Yadaddsleepsnekked.[118] Black e mo black e mo ya dadd sleeps nekked. Black e mo ..."

They had extemporized a verse made up of two insults about matters over which the victim had no control; the color of her skin and speculations on the sleeping habits of an adult, wildly fitting in its incoherence. That they themselves were black, or that their own father had similarly relaxed habits was irrelevant. It was their contempt for their own blackness that gave the first insult its teeth. They seemed to have taken all of their smoothly cultivated ignorance, their exquisitely learned self-hatred, their elaborately designed hopelessness and sucked it all up into a fiery cone of scorn that had burned for ages in the hollows of their minds—cooled—and spilled over lips of outrage, consuming whatever was in its path. They danced a macabre ballet around the victim, whom, for their own sake, they were prepared to sacrifice to the flaming pit.

Black e mo Black e mo Ya daddy sleeps nekked

---

117 Emo: someone who is very emotional and is not afraid to cry. Example: Cheer up emo kid and wipe those tears from your eyes!!

118 Yadaddsleepsnekked.=Your daddy sleeps naked.

Stch ta ta stch ta ta
stach ta ta ta ta ta

Pecola edged around the circle crying. She had dropped her notebook, and covered her eyes with her hands.

We watched, afraid they might notice us and turn their energies our way. Then Frieda, with set lips and Mama's eyes, snatched her coat from her head and threw it on the ground. She ran toward them and brought her books down on Woodrow Cain's head. The circle broke.

Woodrow Cain grabbed his head.

"Hey, girl!"

"You cut that out, you hear?" I had never heard Frieda's voice so loud and clear.

Maybe because Frieda was taller than he was, maybe because he saw her eyes, maybe because he had lost interest in the game, or maybe because he had a crush on Frieda, in any case Woodrow looked frightened just long enough to give her more courage.

"Leave her 'lone, or I'm gone tell everybody what you did!"

Woodrow did not answer; he just walled his eyes.

Bay Boy piped up, "Go on, gal! Ain't nobody bothering you."

"You shut up, Bullet Head."[119] I had found my tongue.

"Who you calling Bullet Head?"

"I'm calling you Bullet Head, Bullet Head."

Frieda took Pecola's hand. "Come on."

"You want a fat lip?"[120] Bay Boy drew back his fist at me.

"Yeah. Gimme one of yours."

"You gone[121] get one."

---

119 Bullet Head: ⟨derogatory⟩ A person's head that is small and round. A stupid, self-important, or obstinate person.

120 You want a fat lip? = (You want to) get hit in the face?

121 You gone(=gonna) get one.

Maureen appeared at my elbow, and the boys seemed reluctant to continue under her springtime eyes so wide with interest. They buckled in confusion, not willing to beat up three girls under her watchful gaze. So they listened to a budding male instinct that told them to pretend we were unworthy of their attention.

"Come on, man."

"Yeah. Come on. We ain't got time to fool with them."

Grumbling a few disinterested epithets, they moved away.

I picked up Pecola's notebook and Frieda's coat, and the four of us left the playground.

"Old Bullet Head, he's always picking on girls."

Frieda agreed with me. "Miss Forrester said he was incorrigival."[122]

"Really?" I didn't know what that meant, but it had enough of a doom sound in it to be true of Bay Boy.

While Frieda and I clucked on about the near fight, Maureen, suddenly animated, put her velvet-sleeved arm through Pecola's and began to behave as though they were the closest of friends.

"I just moved here. My name is Maureen Peal. What's yours?"

"Pecola."

"Pecola? Wasn't that the name of the girl in *Imitation of Life?"*[123]

"I don't know. What is that?"

"The picture show, you know. Where this mulatto girl hates her mother cause she is black and ugly but then cries at the funeral. It

---

122 Miss Forrester said he was incorrigival: Forrester 선생님도 재는 구제불능이라고 하셨어. (*incorrigible: a youthful mispronunciation of "incorrigible," unable to be corrected, improved, or reformed.)

123 《Imitation of Life》 : A black-and-white film released in 1934, in which a white woman becomes rich through the pancake recipe of her black servant; meantime, the black servant is deeply saddened when her light-skinned daughter chooses to pass for white. This version of the Fannie Hurst novel starred Claudette Colbert.

was real sad. Everybody cries in it. Claudette Colbert[124] too."

"Oh." Pecola's voice was no more than a sigh.

"Anyway, her name was Pecola too. She was so pretty. When it comes back, I'm going to see it again. My mother has seen it four times."

Frieda and I walked behind them, surprised at Maureen's friendliness to Pecola, but pleased. Maybe she wasn't so bad, after all. Frieda had put her coat back on her head, and the two of us, so draped, trotted along enjoying the warm breeze and Frieda's heroics.

"You're in my gym class, aren't you?" Maureen asked Pecola.

"Yes."

"Miss Erkmeister's legs sure are bow. I bet she thinks they're cute.

How come she gets to wear real shorts, and we have to wear those old bloomers? I want to die every time I put them on."

Pecola smiled but did not look at Maureen.

"Hey." Maureen stopped short. "There's an Isaley's. Want some ice cream? I have money."

She unzipped a hidden pocket in her muff and pulled out a multifolded dollar bill. I forgave her those knee socks.[125]

"My uncle sued Isaley's." Maureen said to the three of us. "He sued the Isaley's in Akron. They said he was disorderly and that that was why they wouldn't serve him, but a friend of his, a policemen, came in and beared the witness, so the suit went

---

124 Claudette Colbert: 클로데트 콜베르(1903–1996). 프랑스 출신 미국의 여배우. 프랭크 카프라(Frank Capra) 감독 《하루 밤에 생긴 일(It Happened One Night)》(1934)로 여우주연상 수상. 같은 해 《슬픔은 그대 가슴에(The Imitation of Life)》 도 출연했다.

125 I forgave her those knee socks: 이제 Maureen이 신은 양말에 더 이상 앙심을 품지 않기로 했다. (☞ 여기서 양말은 앞서 100쪽에서 Maureen Peal이 신고 있었던 "brightly colored knee socks with white borders"를 말한다. 화자 Claudia는 애초에 이를 질투하고 경멸했다.)

through."

"What's a suit?"

"It's when you can beat them up if you want to and won't anybody do nothing. Our family does it all the time. We believe in suits."

At the entrance to Isaley's Maureen turned to Frieda and me, asking, "You all going to buy some ice cream?"

We looked at each other. "No," Frieda said.

Maureen disappeared into the store with Pecola.

Frieda looked placidly down the street; I opened my mouth, but quickly closed it. It was extremely important that the world not know that I fully expected Maureen to buy us some ice cream, that for the past 120 seconds I had been selecting the flavor, that I had begun to like Maureen, and that neither of us had a penny.

We supposed Maureen was being nice to Pecola because of the boys, and were embarrassed to be caught—even by each other—thinking that she would treat us, or that we deserved it as much as Pecola did.

The girls came out. Pecola with two dips of orange-pineapple, Maureen with black raspberry.

"You should have got some," she said. "They had all kinds. Don't eat down to the tip of the cone," she advised Pecola.

"Why?"

"Because there's a fly in there."

"How you know?"

"Oh, not really. A girl told me she found one in the bottom of hers once, and ever since then she throws that part away."

"Oh."

We passed the Dreamland Theater, and Betty Grable[126] smiled

126 Betty Grable(1916-1973): 《Pin Up Girl》 (1944)로 잘 알려져 있고, 마릴린 몬로와 함께 《백만장자와 결혼하는 법(How to Marry a Millionaire)》 (1953)에 출현했던 미국의 육체파 배우.

down at us.

"Don't you just love her?" Maureen asked.

"Uh-huh," said Pecola.

I differed. "Hedy Lamarr[127] is better."

Maureen agreed. "Ooooo yes. My mother told me that a girl named Audrey, she went to the beauty parlor where we lived before, and asked the lady to fix her hair like Hedy Lamarr's,[128] and the lady said, 'Yeah, when you grow some hair like Hedy Lamarr's.'" She laughed long and sweet.

"Sounds crazy," said Frieda.

"She sure is. Do you know she doesn't even menstrate yet, and she's sixteen. Do you, yet?"

"Yes." Pecola glanced at us.

"So do I." Maureen made no attempt to disguise her pride. "Two months ago I started. My girl friend in Toledo, where we lived before, said when she started she was scared to death. Thought she had killed herself."

"Do you know what it's for?" Pecola asked the question as though hoping to provide the answer herself.

"For babies." Maureen raised two pencil-stroke eyebrows at the obviousness of the question. "Babies need blood when they are inside you, and if you are having a baby, then you don't menstrate. But when you're not having a baby, then you don't have to save the blood, so it comes out."

"How do babies get the blood?" asked Pecola.

"Through the like-line.[129] You know. Where your belly button is. That is where the like-line grows from and pumps the blood to the baby."

---

127 Hedy Lamarr (1913–2000): 오스트리아 출신 배우. 영화 《삼손과 데릴라(Samson and Delilah)》 (1949)에 출연하여 명성을 얻었다.

128 hair like Hedy Lamarr's: the long dark hair, arranged perfectly but not too "done"

129 like-line = life-line. 귀동냥한 내용을 잘 모르는 채 발음을 흉내 내고 있다.

"Well, if the belly buttons are to grow like-lines to give the baby blood, and only girls have babies, how come boys have belly buttons?"

Maureen hesitated. "I don't know," she admitted. "But boys have all sorts of things they don't need." Her tinkling laughter was somehow stronger than our nervous ones. She curled her tongue around the edge of the cone, scooping up a dollop[130] of purple that made my eyes water. We were waiting for a stop light to change. Maureen kept scooping the ice cream from around the cone's edge with her tongue; she didn't bite the edge as I would have done. Her tongue circled the cone. Pecola had finished hers; Maureen evidently liked her things to last. While I was thinking about her ice cream, she must have been thinking about her last remark, for she said to Pecola, "Did you ever see a naked man?"

Pecola blinked, then looked away. "No. Where would I see a naked man?"

"I don't know. I just asked."

"I wouldn't even look at him, even if I did see him. That's dirty. Who wants to see a naked man?" Pecola was agitated. "Nobody's father would be naked in front of his own daughter. Not unless he was dirty too."

"I didn't say 'father.' I just said 'a naked man.'"

"Well..."

"How come you said 'father'?" Maureen wanted to know.

"Who else would she see, dog tooth?" I was glad to have a chance to show anger. Not only because of the ice cream, but because we had seen our own father naked and didn't care to be reminded of it and feel the shame brought on by the absence of shame. He had been walking down the hall from the bathroom into his bedroom and passed the open door of our room. We had lain there wide-eyed. He stopped and looked in, trying to see in

---

130 a dollop of (ice cream): a large lump or portion of a solid matter

the dark room whether we were really asleep—or was it his imagination that opened eyes were looking at him? Apparently he convinced himself that we were sleeping. He moved away, confident that his little girls would not lie open-eyed like that, staring, staring. When he had moved on, the dark took only him away, not his nakedness. That stayed in the room with us. Friendly-like.

"I'm not talking to you," said Maureen. "Besides, I don't care if she sees her father naked. She can look at him all day if she wants to. Who cares?"

"You do," said Frieda. "That's all you talk about."

"It is not."

"It is so. Boys, babies, and somebody's naked daddy. You must be boy-crazy."

"You better be quiet."

"Who's gonna make me?" Frieda put her hand on her hip and jutted her face toward Maureen.

"You all ready made. Mammy made."

"You stop talking about my mama."

"Well, you stop talking about my daddy."

"Who said anything about your old daddy?"

"You did."

"Well, you started it."

"I wasn't even talking to you. I was talking to Pecola."

"Yeah. About seeing her naked daddy."

"So what if she did see him?"

Pecola shouted, "I never saw my daddy naked. Never."

"You did too," Maureen snapped. "Bay Boy said so."

"I did not."

"You did."

"I did not."

"Did Your own daddy, too!"

Pecola tucked her head in—a funny, sad, helpless movement. A kind of hunching of the shoulders, pulling in of the neck, as though she wanted to cover her ears.

"You stop talking about her daddy," I said.

"What do I care about her old black daddy?" asked Maureen.

"Black? Who you calling black?"

"You!"

"You think you so cute!" I swung at her and missed, hitting Pecola in the face. Furious at my clumsiness, I threw my notebook at her, but it caught her in the small of her velvet back, for she had turned and was flying across the street against traffic.

Safe on the other side, she screamed at us, "I *am* cute! And you ugly! Black and ugly black e mos. I *am* cute!"

She ran down the street, the green knee socks making her legs look like wild dandelion stems that had somehow lost their heads. The weight of her remark stunned us, and it was a second or two before Frieda and I collected ourselves enough to shout, "Six-finger-dog-tooth-meringue-pie!" We chanted this most powerful of our arsenal of insults as long as we could see the green stems and rabbit fur.

Grown people frowned at the three girls on the curbside, two with their coats draped over their heads, the collars framing the eyebrows like nuns' habits, black garters showing where they bit the tops of brown stockings that barely covered the knees, angry faces knotted like dark cauliflowers.

Pecola stood a little apart from us, her eyes hinged in the direction in which Maureen had fled. She seemed to fold into herself, like a pleated wing. Her pain antagonized me. I wanted to open her up, crisp her edges, ram a stick down that hunched and curving spine, force her to stand erect and spit the misery out on the streets. But she held it in where it could lap up into her eyes.

Frieda snatched her coat from her head. "Come on, Claudia. 'Bye,

Pecola."

We walked quickly at first, and then slower, pausing every now and then to fasten garters, tie shoelaces, scratch, or examine old scars. We were sinking under the wisdom, accuracy, and relevance of Maureen's last words. If she was cute—and if anything could be believed, she *was*—then we were not. And what did that mean? We were lesser. Nicer, brighter, but still lesser. Dolls we could destroy, but we could not destroy the honey voices of parents and aunts, the obedience in the eyes of our peers, the slippery light in the eyes of our teachers when they encountered the Maureen Peals of the world. What was the secret? What did we lack? Why was it important? And so what? Guileless and without vanity, we were still in love with ourselves then. We felt comfortable in our skins, enjoyed the news that our senses released to us, admired our dirt, cultivated our scars, and could not comprehend this unworthiness. Jealousy we understood and thought natural—a desire to have what somebody else had; but envy was a strange, new feeling for us. And all the time we knew that Maureen Peal was not the Enemy and not worthy of such intense hatred. The *Thing* to fear was the *Thing* that made *her* beautiful, and not us.

The house was quiet when we opened the door. The acrid smell of simmering turnips filled our cheeks with sour saliva.

"Mama!"

There was no answer, but a sound of feet. Mr. Henry shuffled part of the way down the stairs. One thick, hairless leg leaned out of his bathrobe.

"Hello there, Greta Garbo; hello, Ginger Rogers."

We gave him the giggle he was accustomed to. "Hello, Mr. Henry. Where's Mama?"

"She went to your grandmaw's. Left word for you to cut off the turnips and eat some graham crackers till she got back. They in the kitchen."

We sat in silence at the kitchen table, crumbling the crackers into anthills. In a little while Mr. Henry came back down the stairs. Now he had his trousers on under his robe.

"Say. Wouldn't you all like some cream?"

"Oh, yes, sir."

"Here. Here's a quarter. Gone over to Isaley's and get yourself some cream. You been good girls, ain't you?"

His light-green words restored color to the day. "Yes, sir. Thank you, Mr. Henry. Will you tell Mama for us if she comes?"

"Sure. But she ain't due back for a spell."

Coatless, we left the house and had gotten all the way to the corner when Frieda said, "I don't want to go to Isaley's."

"What?"

"I don't want ice cream. I want potato chips."

"They got potato chips at Isaley's."

"I know, but why go all that long way? Miss Bertha got potato chips."

"But I want ice cream."

"No you don't, Claudia."

"I do too."

"Well, you go on to Isaley's. I'm going to Miss Bertha's."

"But you got the quarter, and I don't want to go all the way up there by myself."

"Then let's go to Miss Bertha's. You like her candy, don't you?"

"It's always stale, and she always runs out of stuff."

"Today is Friday. She orders fresh on Friday."

"And then that crazy old Soaphead Church lives there."

"So what? We're together. We'll run if he does anything at us."

"He scares me."

"Well, I don't want to go up by Isaley's. Suppose Meringue Pie is hanging around. You want to run into her, Claudia?"

"Come on, Frieda. I'll get candy."

Miss Bertha had a small candy, snuff, and tobacco store. One brick room sitting in her front yard. You had to peep in the door, and if she wasn't there, you knocked on the door of her house in back. This day she was sitting behind the counter reading a Bible in a tube of sunlight.

Frieda bought potato chips, and we got three Powerhouse bars for ten cents, and had a dime left. We hurried back home to sit under the lilac bushes on the side of the house. We always did our Candy Dance there so Rosemary could see us and get jealous. The Candy Dance was a humming, skipping, foot-tapping, eating, smacking combination that overtook us when we had sweets. Creeping between the bushes and the side of the house, we heard voices and laughter. We looked into the living-room window, expecting to see Mama. Instead we saw Mr. Henry and two women. In a playful manner, the way grandmothers do with babies, he was sucking the fingers of one of the women, whose laughter filled a tiny place over his head. The other woman was buttoning her coat. We knew immediately who they were, and our flesh crawled. One was China, and the other was called the Maginot Line.[131] The back of my neck itched. These were the fancy women of the maroon nail polish that Mama and Big Mama hated. And in our house.

China was not too terrible, at least not in our imaginations. She was thin, aging, absentminded, and unaggressive. But the Maginot Line. That was the one my mother said she "wouldn't let eat out of one of her plates."[132] That was the one church women never

---

131 Maginot Line: Maginot Line의 이름은 마지노 선에서 나왔다. 마지노 선은 프랑스가 1925년-35년에 독일과 프랑스 국경에 구축했던 요새선으로 비유적으로 난공불락으로 여기는 방어선을 의미한다. 그러나 결국 나치의 침공을 막지는 못했다.

132 she "wouldn't let eat out of one of her plates": 그녀는 "사람들에게 음식도 나누지 않을 사람," 즉 인정머리도 없는 사람.

allowed their eyes to rest on. That was the one who had killed people, set them on fire, poisoned them, cooked them in lye. Although I thought the Maginot Line's face, hidden under all that fat, was really sweet, I had heard too many black and red words about her, seen too many mouths go triangle at the mention of her name, to dwell on any redeeming features she might have.

Showing brown teeth, China seemed to be genuinely enjoying Mr. Henry. The sight of him licking her fingers brought to mind the girlie magazines in his room. A cold wind blew somewhere in me, lifting little leaves of terror and obscure longing. I thought I saw a mild lonesomeness cross the face of the Maginot Line. But it may have been my own image that I saw in the slow flaring of her nostrils, in her eyes that reminded me of waterfalls in movies about Hawaii.

The Maginot Line yawned and said, "Come on, China. We can't hang in here all day. Them people be home soon." She moved toward the door.

Frieda and I dropped down to the ground, looking wildly into each other's eyes. When the women were some distance away, we went inside. Mr. Henry was in the kitchen opening a bottle of pop.

"Back already?"

"Yes, sir."

"Cream all gone?" His little teeth looked so kindly and helpless. Was that really our Mr. Henry with China's fingers?

"We got candy instead."

"You did huh? Ole sugar-tooth Greta Garbo."

He wiped the bottle sweat and turned it up to his lips—a gesture that made me uncomfortable.

"Who were those women, Mr. Henry?"

He choked on the pop and looked at Frieda. "What you say?"

"Those women," she repeated, "who just left. Who were they?"

"Oh." He laughed the grown-up getting-ready-to-lie laugh. A

heh-heh we knew well.

"Those were some members of my Bible class. We read the scriptures together, and so they came today to read with me."

"Oh," said Frieda. I was looking at his house slippers to keep from seeing those kindly teeth frame a lie. He walked toward the stairs and then turned back to us.

"Bed'[133] not mention it to your mother. She don't take to so much Bible study and don't like me having visitors, even if they good Christians."

"No, sir, Mr. Henry. We won't."

He rapidly mounted the stairs.

"Should we?" I asked. "Tell Mama?"

Frieda sighed. She had not even opened her Powerhouse bar or her potato chips, and now she traced the letters on the candy wrappers with her fingers. Suddenly she lifted her head and began to look all around the kitchen.

"No. I guess not. No plates are out."

"Plates? What you talking about now?"

"No plates are out. The Maginot Line didn't eat out of one of Mama's plates. Besides, Mama would just fuss all day if we told her,"

We sat down and looked at the graham-cracker anthills we had made. "We better cut off the turnips. They'll burn, and Mama will whip us," she said.

"I know."

"But if we let them burn, we won't have to eat them."

"Heyyy, what a lovely idea," I thought.

"Which you want? A whipping and no turnips, or turnips and no whippings?"

"I don't know. Maybe we could burn them just a little so Mama and Daddy can eat them, but we can say we can't."

---

133 Bed'=Better

"O.K."

I made a volcano out of my anthill.

"Frieda?"

"What?"

"What did Woodrow that you was gonna tell?"

"Wet the bed. Mrs. Cain told Mama he won't quit."

"Old nasty."

The sky was getting dark; I looked out of the window and saw snow falling. I poked my finger down into the mouth of my volcano, and it toppled, dispersing the golden grains into little swirls. The turnip pot crackled.

SEETHECATITGOESMEOWMEOWCOM EANDPLAYCOMEPLAYWITHJANETHE KITTENWILLNOTPLAYPLAYPLAYPLA

They come from Mobile. Aiken. From Newport News. From Marietta. From Meridian.[134] And the sounds of these places in their mouths make you think of love. When you ask them where they are from, they tilt their heads and say "Mobile" and you think you've been kissed. They say "Aiken" and you see a white butterfly glance off a fence with a torn wing. They say "Nagadoches"[135] and you want to say "Yes, I will." You don't know what these towns are like, but you love what happens to the air when they open their lips and let the names ease out.

---

134 Mobile, an industrial city and port on the coast of southern Alabama; Aiken, a resort city in west central South Carolina; Newport News, a city in southeastern Virginia, at the mouth of the James River on the Hampton Roads estuary; Marietta, a city in northwestern Georgia, a northwestern suburb of Atlanta; Meridian, a city in southwestern Idaho.

135 Nagadoches. Indian name: a place in Texas.

Meridian. The sound of it opens the windows of a room like the first four notes of a hymn. Few people can say the names of their home towns with such sly affection. Perhaps because they don't have home towns, just places where they were born. But these girls soak up the juice of their home towns, and it never leaves them. They are thin brown girls who have looked long at hollyhocks[136] in the backyards of Meridian, Mobile, Aiken, and Baton Rouge. And like hollyhocks they are narrow, tall, and still. Their roots are deep, their stalks are firm, and only the top blossom nods in the wind. They have the eyes of people who can tell what time it is by the color of the sky. Such girls live in quiet black neighborhoods where everybody is gainfully employed. Where there are porch swings hanging from chains. Where the grass is cut with a scythe, where rooster combs and sunflowers grow in the yards, and pots of bleeding heart,[137] ivy, and mother-in-law tongue[138] line the steps and windowsills. Such girls have bought watermelon and snapbeans from the fruit man's wagon. They have put in the window the cardboard sign that has a pound measure printed on each of three edges—10 lbs., 25 lbs., 50 lbs.—and NO ICE on the fourth. These particular brown girls from Mobile and Aiken are not like some of their sisters. They are not fretful, nervous, or shrill; they do not have lovely black necks that stretch as though against an invisible collar; their eyes do not bite.[139] These sugar-brown Mobile girls move through the streets without a stir. They are as sweet and plain as buttercake. Slim ankles; long, narrow feet. They wash themselves

---

136 hollyhocks: 접시꽃(A hollyhock is a tall Eurasian plant of the mallow family, widely cultivated for its large showy flowers)

137 bleeding heart: 금낭화(Any of a number of plants that have heart-shaped flowers, typically pink or red, in particular)

138 mother-in-law tongue: 산세베리아(Or, mother-in-law's tongue; a West African plant of the agave family, having long slender leaves with yellow marginal stripes, often grown as a houseplant)

139 Their eyes do not bite: 그들의 눈은 사납지 않다.

with orange-colored Lifebuoy soap,[140] dust themselves with Cashmere Bouquet talc,[141] clean their teeth with salt on a piece of rag, soften their skin with Jergens Lotion. They smell like wood, newspapers, and vanilla. They straighten their hair with Dixie Peach, and part it on the side. At night they curl it in paper from brown bags, tie a print scarf around their heads, and sleep with hands folded across their stomachs. They do not drink, smoke, or swear, and they still call sex "nookey."[142] They sing second soprano[143] in the choir, and although their voices are clear and steady, they are never picked to solo. They are in the second row, white blouses starched, blue skirts almost purple from ironing.

They go to land-grant colleges, normal schools, and learn how to do the white man's work with refinement: home economics to prepare his food; teacher education to instruct black children in obedience; music to soothe the weary master and entertain his blunted soul. Here they learn the rest of the lesson begun in those soft houses with porch swings and pots of bleeding heart: how to behave. The careful development of thrift, patience, high morals, and good manners. In short, how to get rid of the funkiness. The dreadful funkiness of passion, the funkiness of nature, the funkiness of the wide range of human emotions.

Wherever it erupts, this Funk, they wipe it away; where it crusts, they dissolve it; wherever it drips, flowers, or clings, they find it and fight it until it dies. They fight this battle all the way to the grave. The laugh that is a little too loud; the enunciation a little too round; the gesture a little too generous. They hold their behind in

---

140 Lifebuoy Royal Disinfectant Soap was launched in 1894 as an affordable new product in the UK, to support people. ... Soon after launch, Lifebuoy soap travelled across the world, reaching countries such as India.

141 Cashmere Bouquet Powder is made of fine Italian talc, world renowned for its soft, smooth feel. It helps absorb perspiration and prevent chafing.

142 "nookie": 《비어》 성교(性交) (vulgar slang) sexual activity or intercourse

143 second soprano: 메조 소프라노(mezzo soprano)

for fear of a sway too free;[144] when they wear lipstick, they never cover the entire mouth for fear of lips too thick, and they worry, worry, worry about the edges of their hair.

They never seem to have boyfriends, but they always marry. Certain men watch them, without seeming to, and know that if such a girl is in his house, he will sleep on sheets boiled white, hung out to dry on juniper bushes, and pressed flat with a heavy iron. There will be pretty paper flowers decorating the picture of his mother, a large Bible in the front room. They feel secure. They know their work clothes will be mended, washed, and ironed on Monday, that their Sunday shirts will billow on hangers from the door jamb, stiffly starched and white. They look at her hands and know what she will do with biscuit dough; they smell the coffee and the fried ham; see the white, smoky grits with a dollop of butter on top. Her hips assure them that she will bear children easily and painlessly. And they are right.

What they do not know is that this plain brown girl[145] will build her nest stick by stick, make it her own inviolable world, and stand guard over its every plant, weed, and doily, even against him. In silence will she return the lamp to where she put it in the first place; remove the dishes from the table as soon as the last bite is taken; wipe the doorknob after a greasy hand has touched it. A sidelong look will be enough to tell him to smoke on the back porch. Children will sense instantly that they cannot come into her yard to retrieve a ball. But the men do not know these things. Nor do they know that she will give him her body sparingly and partially. He must enter her surreptitiously, lifting the hem of her nightgown only to her navel. He must rest his weight on his elbows when they make love, ostensibly to avoid hurting her breasts but

144 They hold their behind in for fear of a sway too free: 그들은 엉덩이가 너무 흔들릴까 봐 엉덩이를 바짝 조이며 걷는다.

145 this plain brown girl: Geraldine을 지칭

actually to keep her from having to touch or feel too much of him.

While he moves inside her, she will wonder why they didn't put the necessary but private parts of the body in some more convenient place—like the armpit, for example, or the palm of the hand. Someplace one could get to easily, and quickly, without undressing. She stiffens when she feels one of her paper curlers coming undone from the activity of love; imprints in her mind which one it is that is coming loose so she can quickly secure it once he is through. She hopes he will not sweat—the damp may get into her hair; and that she will remain dry between her legs—she hates the glucking sound they make when she is moist. When she senses some spasm about to grip him, she will make rapid movements with her hips, press her fingernails into his back, suck in her breath, and pretend she is having an orgasm. She might wonder again, for the six hundredth time, what it would be like to have *that* feeling while her husband's penis is inside her. The closest thing to it was the time she was walking down the street and her napkin slipped free of her sanitary belt. It moved gently between her legs as she walked. Gently, ever so gently. And then a slight and distinctly delicious sensation collected in her crotch. As the delight grew, she had to stop in the street, hold her thighs together to contain it. That must be what it is like, she thinks, but it never happens while he is inside her. When he withdraws, she pulls her nightgown down, slips out of the bed and into the bathroom with relief.

Occasionally some living thing will engage her affections. A cat, perhaps, who will love her order, precision, and constancy; who will be as clean and quiet as she is. The cat will settle quietly on the windowsill and caress her with his eyes. She can hold him in her arms, letting his back paws struggle for footing on her breast and his forepaws cling to her shoulder. She can rub the smooth fur and feel the unresisting flesh underneath. At her gentlest touch he will preen, stretch, and open his mouth. And she will accept the strangely pleasant sensation that comes when he writhes beneath her hand and flattens his eyes with a surfeit of sensual delight. When she stands cooking at the table, he will circle about her shanks, and the trill of his fur spirals up her legs to her thighs, to make her fingers tremble a little in the pie dough.

Or, as she sits reading the "Uplifting Thoughts" in *The Liberty Magazine,*[146] the cat will jump into her lap. She will fondle that soft hill of hair and let the warmth of the animal's body seep over and into the deeply private areas of her lap. Sometimes the magazine drops, and she opens her legs just a little, and the two of them will be still together, perhaps shifting a little together, sleeping a little together, until four o'clock, when the intruder comes home from work vaguely anxious about what's for dinner.

The cat will always know that he is first in her affections. Even after she bears a child. For she does bear a child—easily, and painlessly. But only one. A son. Named Junior.

One such girl from Mobile, or Meridian, or Aiken who did not sweat in her armpits nor between her thighs, who smelled of wood and vanilla, who had made soufflés[147] in the Home Economics Department, moved with her husband, Louis, to Lorain, Ohio. Her name was Geraldine. There she built her nest, ironed shirts, potted bleeding hearts, played with her cat, and birthed Louis Junior.

Geraldine did not allow her baby, Junior, to cry. As long as his needs were physical, she could meet them—comfort and satiety. He was always brushed, bathed, oiled, and shod. Geraldine did not talk to him, coo to him, or indulge him in kissing bouts, but she saw that every other desire was fulfilled. It was not long before the child discovered the difference in his mother's behavior to himself and the cat. As he grew older, he learned how to direct his hatred

---

146 The Liberty Magazine: A magazine on religious freedom

147 soufflés: 수플레 요리(달걀 노른자, 화이트 소스, 생선살, 치즈 따위를 넣고 달걀 흰자를 거품 내어 구운 요리)

of his mother to the cat, and spent some happy moments watching it suffer. The cat survived, because Geraldine was seldom away from home, and could effectively soothe the animal when Junior abused him.

Geraldine, Louis, Junior, and the cat lived next to the playground of Washington Irving School. Junior considered the playground his own, and the schoolchildren coveted his freedom to sleep late, go home for lunch, and dominate the playground after school. He hated to see the swings, slides, monkey bars, and seesaws empty and tried to get kids to stick around as long as possible. White kids; his mother did not like him to play with niggers. She had explained to him the difference between colored people and niggers.[148] They were easily identifiable. Colored people were neat and quiet; niggers were dirty and loud. He belonged to the former group: he wore white shirts and blue trousers; his hair was cut as close to his scalp as possible to avoid any suggestion of wool, the part was etched into his hair by the barber. In winter his mother put Jergens Lotion[149] on his face to keep the skin from becoming ashen. Even though he was light-skinned, it was possible to ash. The line between colored and nigger was not always clear; subtle and telltale signs threatened to erode it, and the watch had to be constant.

Junior used to long to play with the black boys. More than anything in the world he wanted to play King of the Mountain and have them push him down the mound of dirt and roll over him. He wanted to feel their hardness pressing on him, smell their wild blackness, and say "Fuck you" with that lovely casualness. He wanted to sit with them on curbstones[150] and compare the sharpness of jackknives, the distance and arcs of spitting. In the

148 She had explained to him the difference between colored people and niggers: 그녀는 아들에게 흑인과 깜둥이의 차이점을 설명해 주었다.

149 Jergens Lotion=hand lotion의 일종

150 curbstone: 연석(緣石, 차도와 인도 사이의 경계가 되는 돌)

toilet he wanted to share with them the laurels of being able to pee far and long. Bay Boy and P. L. had at one time been his idols. Gradually he came to agree with his mother that neither Bay Boy nor P. L. was good enough for him. He played only with Ralph Nisensky, who was two years younger, wore glasses, and didn't want to *do* anything. More and more Junior enjoyed bullying girls. It was easy making them scream and run. How he laughed when they fell down and their bloomers showed. When they got up, their faces red and crinkled, it made him feel good. The nigger girls he did not pick on very much. They usually traveled in packs, and once when he threw a stone at some of them, they chased, caught, and beat him witless. He lied to his mother, saying Bay Boy did it. His mother was very upset. His father just kept on reading the Lorain *Journal.*

When the mood struck him, he would call a child passing by to come play on the swings or the seesaw. If the child wouldn't, or did and left too soon, Junior threw gravel at him. He became a very good shot.

Alternately bored and frightened at home, the playground was his joy. On a day when he had been especially idle, he saw a very black girl taking a shortcut through the playground. She kept her head down as she walked. He had seen her many times before, standing alone, always alone, at recess. Nobody ever played with her. Probably, he thought, because she was ugly.

Now Junior called to her. "Hey! What are you doing walking through my yard?"

The girl stopped.

"Nobody can come through this yard 'less I say so."

"This ain't your yard. It's the school's."

"But I'm in charge of it."

The girl started to walk away.

"Wait." Junior walked toward her. "You can play in it if you want to. What's your name?"

"Pecola. I don't want to play."

"Come on. I'm not going to bother you."

"I got to go home."

"Say, you want to see something? I got something to show you."

"No. What is it?"

"Come on in my house. See, I live right there. Come on. I'll show you."

"Show me what?"

"Some kittens. We got some kittens. You can have one if you want."

"Real kittens?"

"Yeah. Come on."

He pulled gently at her dress. Pecola began to move toward his house. When he knew she had agreed, Junior ran ahead excitedly, stopping only to yell back at her to come on. He held the door open for her, smiling his encouragement. Pecola climbed the porch stairs and hesitated there, afraid to follow him. The house looked dark. Junior said, "There's nobody here. My ma's gone out, and my father's at work. Don't you want to see the kittens?"

Junior turned on the lights. Pecola stepped inside the door.

How beautiful, she thought. What a beautiful house. There was a big red-and-gold Bible on the dining-room table. Little lace doilies[151] were everywhere—on arms and backs of chairs, in the center of a large dining table, on little tables. Potted plants were on all the windowsills. A color picture of Jesus Christ hung on a wall with the prettiest paper flowers fastened on the frame. She wanted to see everything slowly, slowly. But Junior kept saying, "Hey, you. Come on. Come on." He pulled her into another room, even more beautiful than the first. More doilies, a big lamp with green-and-gold base and white shade. There was even a rug on the floor, with

---

151 doilies: 도일리(doily). 식탁의 꽃병 따위 아래 까는 레이스 장식 있는 깔개.

enormous dark-red flowers. She was deep in admiration of the flowers when Junior said, "Here!" Pecola turned. "Here is your kitten!" he screeched. And he threw a big black cat right in her face. She sucked in her breath in fear and surprise and felt fur in her mouth. The cat clawed her face and chest in an effort to right itself, then leaped nimbly to the floor.

Junior was laughing and running around the room clutching his stomach delightedly. Pecola touched the scratched place on her face and felt tears coming. When she started toward the doorway, Junior leaped in front of her.

"You can't get out. You're my prisoner," he said. His eyes were merry but hard.

"You let me go."

"No!" He pushed her down, ran out the door that separated the rooms, and held it shut with his hands. Pecola's banging on the door increased his gasping, high-pitched laughter.

The tears came fast, and she held her face in her hands. When something soft and furry moved around her ankles, she jumped, and saw it was the cat. He wound himself in and about her legs. Momentarily distracted from her fear, she squatted down to touch him, her hands wet from the tears. The cat rubbed up against her knee. He was black all over, deep silky black, and his eyes, pointing down toward his nose, were bluish green. The light made them shine like blue ice. Pecola rubbed the cat's head; he whined, his tongue flicking with pleasure. The blue eyes in the black face held her.

Junior, curious at not hearing her sobs, opened the door, and saw her squatting down rubbing the cat's back. He saw the cat stretching its head and flattening its eyes. He had seen that expression many times as the animal responded to his mother's touch.

"Gimme my cat!" His voice broke. With a movement both awkward and sure he snatched the cat by one of its hind legs and began to swing it around his head in a circle.

"Stop that!" Pecola was screaming. The cat's free paws were stiffened, ready to grab anything to restore balance, its mouth wide, its eyes blue streaks of horror.

Still screaming, Pecola reached for Junior's hand. She heard her dress rip under her arm. Junior tried to push her away, but she grabbed the arm which was swinging the cat. They both fell, and in falling, Junior let go the cat, which, having been released in mid-motion, was thrown full force against the window. It slithered down and fell on the radiator behind the sofa. Except for a few shudders, it was still. There was only the slightest smell of singed fur.

Geraldine opened the door.

"What is this?" Her voice was mild, as though asking a perfectly reasonable question. "Who is this girl?"

"She killed our cat," said Junior. "Look." He pointed to the radiator, where the cat lay, its blue eyes closed, leaving only an empty, black, and helpless face.

Geraldine went to the radiator and picked up the cat. He was limp in her arms, but she rubbed her face in his fur. She looked at Pecola. Saw the dirty torn dress, the plaits sticking out on her head, hair matted where the plaits had come undone, the muddy shoes with the wad of gum peeping out from between the cheap soles, the soiled socks, one of which had been walked down into the heel of the shoe. She saw the safety pin holding the hem of the dress up. Up over the hump of the cat's back she looked at her. She had seen this little girl all of her life. Hanging out of windows over saloons in Mobile, crawling over the porches of shotgun houses on the edge of town, sitting in bus stations holding paper bags and crying to mothers who kept saying "Shet up![152]" Hair uncombed, dresses falling apart, shoes untied and caked with dirt. They had stared at

152 Shet up! (= "Shut up!")

her with great uncomprehending eyes. Eyes that questioned nothing and asked everything. Unblinking and unabashed, they stared up at her. The end of the world lay in their eyes, and the beginning, and all the waste in between.

They were everywhere. They slept six in a bed, all their pee mixing together in the night as they wet their beds each in his own candy-and-potato-chip dream. In the long, hot days, they idled away, picking plaster from the walls and digging into the earth with sticks. They sat in little rows on street curbs, crowded into pews at church, taking space from the nice, neat, colored children; they clowned on the playgrounds, broke things in dime stores, ran in front of you on the street, made ice slides on the sloped sidewalks in winter. The girls grew up knowing nothing of girdles, and the boys announced their manhood by turning the bills of their caps backward. Grass wouldn't grow where they lived.[153] Flowers died. Shades fell down. Tin cans and tires blossomed where they lived. They lived on cold black-eyed peas and orange pop. Like flies they hovered; like flies they settled. And this one had settled in her house. Up over the hump of the cat's back she looked.

"Get out," she said, her voice quiet. "You nasty little black bitch. Get out of my house."

The cat shuddered and flicked his tail.

Pecola backed out of the room, staring at the pretty milk-brown lady in the pretty gold-and-green house who was talking to her through the cat's fur. The pretty lady's words made the cat fur move; the breath of each word parted the fur. Pecola turned to find the front door and saw Jesus looking down at her with sad and unsurprised eyes, his long brown hair parted in the middle, the gay paper flowers twisted around his face.

---

153 Grass wouldn't grow where they lived: 그들이 사는 곳에는 풀이 자라지 않았다. (☞ 이는 이 소설의 처음 부분에 금잔화가 피지 않아 Pecola와 불모(不毛)만 남았음을 슬퍼하는 클로디아의 독백을 연상시킨다.)

Outside, the March wind blew into the rip in her dress. She held her head down against the cold. But she could not hold it low enough to avoid seeing the snowflakes falling and dying on the pavement

Spring

The first twigs are thin, green, and supple. They bend into a complete circle, but will not break. Their delicate, showy hopefulness shooting from forsythia and lilac bushes meant only a change in whipping style. They beat us differently in the spring. Instead of the dull pain of a winter strap, there were these new green switches that lost their sting long after the whipping was over. There was a nervous meanness in these long twigs that made us long for the steady stroke of a strap or the firm but honest slap of a hairbrush. Even now spring for me is shot through with the remembered ache of switchings, and forsythia holds no cheer.

Sunk in the grass of an empty lot on a spring Saturday, I split the stems of milkweed and thought about ants and peach pits and death and where the world went when I closed my eyes. I must have lain long in the grass, for the shadow that was in front of me when I left the house had disappeared when I went back. I entered the house, as the house was bursting with an uneasy quiet. Then I heard my mother singing something about trains and Arkansas. She came in the back door with some folded yellow curtains which she piled on the kitchen table. I sat down on the floor to listen to the song's story, and noticed how strangely she was behaving. She still had her hat on, and her shoes were dusty, as though she had been walking in deep dirt. She put on some water to boil and then swept the porch; then she hauled out the curtain stretcher, but instead of putting the damp curtains on it, she swept the porch again. All the time singing about trains and Arkansas.

When she finished, I went to look for Frieda. I found her upstairs lying on our bed, crying the tired, whimpering cry that follows the first wailings—mostly gasps and shudderings. I lay on the bed and looked at the tiny bunches of wild roses sprinkled over her dress. Many washings had faded their color and dimmed their outlines.

"What happened, Frieda?"

She lifted a swollen face from the crook of her arm. Shuddering still, she sat up, letting her thin legs dangle over the bedside. I knelt on the bed and picked up the hem of my dress to wipe her running nose. She never liked wiping noses on clothes, but this time she let me. It was the way Mama did with her apron.

"Did you get a whipping?"

She shook her head no.

"Then why you crying?"

"Because."

"Because what?"

"Mr. Henry."

"What'd he do?"

"Daddy beat him up."

"What for? The Maginot Line? Did he find out about the Maginot Line?"

"No."

"Well, what, then? Come on, Frieda. How come I can't know?"

"He ... *picked* at me."[154]

"Picked at you? You mean like Soaphead Church?"

"Sort of."

"He showed his privates at you?"

"Noooo. He touched me."

"Where?"

"Here and here." She pointed to the tiny breasts that, like two fallen acorns, scattered a few faded rose leaves on her dress.

"Really? How did it feel?"

"Oh, Claudia." She sounded put-out.[155] I wasn't asking the right questions.

"It didn't feel like anything."

"But wasn't it supposed to? Feel good, I mean?" Frieda sucked her teeth.

"What'd he do? Just walk up and pinch them?"

She sighed. "First he said how pretty I was. Then he grabbed my arm and touched me."

"Where was Mama and Daddy?"

"Over at the garden weeding."

"What'd you say when he did it?"

"Nothing. I just ran out the kitchen and went to the garden."

"Mama said we was never to cross the tracks by ourselves."

"Well, what would you do? Set there and let him pinch you?"

I looked at my chest. "I don't have nothing to pinch. I'm never going to have nothing."

"Oh, Claudia, you're jealous of everything. You *want* him to?"

"No, I just get tired of having everything last."[156]

"You do not. What about scarlet fever?[157] You had that first."

---

154 "He…picked at me.": "그가…나를 집적댔어."

155 She sounded put-out. (=deeply annoyed, insulted): 그녀는 화가 난 것처럼 보였다.

156 "No, I just get tired of having everything last.": 그게 아니라 내가 항상 무엇이든 마지막으로 알게 되는 게 지긋지긋할 따름이야.

"Yes, but it didn't last. Anyway, what happened at the garden?"

"I told Mama, and she told Daddy, and we all come home, and he was gone, so we waited for him, and when Daddy saw him come up on the porch, he threw our old tricycle at his head and knocked him off the porch."

"Did he die?"

"Naw. He got up and started singing 'Nearer My God to Thee.' Then Mama hit him with a broom and told him to keep the Lord's name out of his mouth, but he wouldn't stop, and Daddy was cussing, and everybody was screaming."

"Oh, shoot, I always miss stuff."

"And Mr. Buford came running out with his gun, and Mama told him to go somewhere and sit down, and Daddy said no, give him the gun, and Mr. Buford did, and Mama screamed, and Mr. Henry shut up and started running, and Daddy shot at him and Mr. Henry jumped out of his shoes and kept on running in his socks. Then Rosemary Came out and said that Daddy was going to jail, and I hit her."

"Real hard?"

"Real hard."

"Is that when Mama whipped you?"

"She didn't whip me, I told you."

"Then why you crying?"

"Miss Dunion came in after everybody was quiet, and Mama and Daddy was fussing about who let Mr. Henry in anyway, and she said that Mama should take me to the doctor, because I might be ruined, and Mama started screaming all over again."

"At you?"

"No. At Miss Dunion."

"But why were you crying?"

"I don't want to be *ruined*!"

"What's ruined?"

---

157 scarlet fever: 성홍열(scarlatina)

"You know. Like the Maginot Line. She's ruined. Mama said so." The tears came back.

An image of Frieda, big and fat, came to mind. Her thin legs swollen, her face surrounded by layers of rouged skin.[158] I too begin to feel tears.

"But, Frieda, you could exercise and not eat."

She shrugged.

"Besides, what about China and Poland? They're ruined too, aren't they? And they ain't fat."

"That's because they drink whiskey. Mama says whiskey ate them up."

"You could drink whiskey."

"Where would I get whiskey?"

We thought about this. Nobody would sell it to us; we had no money, anyway. There was never any in our house. Who would have some?

"Pecola," I said. "Her father's always drunk. She can get us some."

"You think so?"

"Sure. Cholly's always drunk. Let's go ask her. We don't have to tell her what for."

"Now?"

"Sure, now."

"What'll we tell Mama?"

"Nothing. Let's just go out the back. One at a time. So she won't notice."

"O.K. You go first, Claudia."

We opened the fence gate at the bottom of the backyard and ran down the alley.

Pecola lived on the other side of Broadway. We had never been in her house, but we knew where it was. A two-story gray building

---

158 her face surrounded by layers of rouged skin: 그녀는 얼굴에 겹겹이 화장으로 떡칠을 하고 있었다.

that had been a store downstairs and had an apartment upstairs.

Nobody answered our knock on the front door, so we walked around to the side door. As we approached, we heard radio music and looked to see where it came from. Above us was the second-story porch, lined with slanting, rotting rails, and sitting on the porch was the Maginot Line herself. We stared up and automatically reached for the other's hand. A mountain of flesh, she lay rather than sat in a rocking chair. She had no shoes on, and each foot was poked between a railing: tiny baby toes at the tip of puffy feet; swollen ankles smoothed and tightened the skin; massive legs like tree stumps parted wide at the knees, over which spread two roads of soft flabby inner thigh that kissed each other deep in the shade of her dress and closed. A dark-brown root-beer bottle, like a burned limb, grew out of her dimpled hand. She looked at us down through the porch railings and emitted a low, long belch. Her eyes were as clean as rain, and again I remembered the waterfall. Neither of us could speak. Both of us imagined we were seeing what was to become of Frieda. The Maginot Line smiled at us.

"You all looking for somebody?"

I had to pull my tongue from the roof of my mouth to say, "Pecola—she live here?"

"Uh-huh, but she ain't here now. She gone to her mama's work place to git the wash."[159]

"Yes, ma'am. She coming back?"

"Uh-huh. She got to hang up the clothes before the sun goes down."

"Oh."

"You can wait for her. Wanna come up here and wait?"

We exchanged glances. I looked back up at the broad cinnamon roads[160] that met in the shadow of her dress.

---

159 to git the wash (=to get the wash). 세탁물을 가지러

160 the broad cinnamon roads: Maginot Line의 계피빛(검붉은) 허벅지를 말한다.

Frieda said, "No, ma'am."

"Well," the Maginot Line seemed interested in our problem. "Yo can go to her mama's work place, but it's way over by the lake."

"Where by the lake?"

"That big white house with the wheelbarrow full of flowers."

It was a house that we knew, having admired the large white wheelbarrow tilted down on spoked wheels and planted with seasonal flowers.

"Ain't that too far for you all to go walking?"

Frieda scratched her knee.

"Why don't you wait for her? You can come up here. Want some pop?" Those rain-soaked eyes lit up, and her smile was full, not like the pinched and holding-back smile of other grown-ups.

I moved to go up the stairs, but Frieda said, "No, ma'am, we ain't allowed."

I was amazed at her courage, and frightened of her sassiness. The smile of the Maginot Line slipped. "Ain't 'llowed?"

"No'm."

"Ain't 'llowed to what?"

"Go in your house."

"Is that right?" The waterfalls were still. "How come?"

"My mama said so. My mama said you ruined."

The waterfalls began to run again. She put the root-beer bottle to her lips and drank it empty. With a graceful movement of the wrist, a gesture so quick and small we never really saw it, only remembered it afterward, she tossed the bottle over the rail at us. It split at our feet, and shards of brown glass dappled our legs before we could jump back. The Maginot Line put a fat hand on one of the folds of her stomach and laughed. At first just a deep humming with her mouth closed, then a larger, warmer sound. Laughter at once beautiful and frightening. She let her head tilt sideways, closed her eyes, and shook her massive trunk, letting the laughter fall like a wash of red leaves all around us. Scraps and curls of the laughter followed us as we ran. Our breath gave out at the same time our legs did. After we rested against a tree, our heads on crossed forearms, I said, "Let's go home."

Frieda was still angry—fighting, she believed, for her life. "No, we got to get it now."

"We can't go all the way to the lake."

"Yes we can. Come on."

"Mama gone get us."

"No she ain't. Besides, she can't do nothing but whip us."

That was true. She wouldn't kill us, or laugh a terrible laugh at us, or throw a bottle at us.

We walked down tree-lined streets of soft gray houses leaning like tired ladies.... The streets changed; houses looked more sturdy, their paint was newer, porch posts straighter, yards deeper. Then came brick houses set well back from the street, fronted by yards edged in shrubbery clipped into smooth cones and balls of velvet green.

The lakefront houses were the loveliest. Garden furniture, ornaments, windows like shiny eyeglasses, and no sign of life. The backyards of these houses fell away in green slopes down to a strip of sand, and then the blue Lake Erie, lapping all the way to Canada. The orange-patched sky of the steel-mill section never reached this part of town. This sky was always blue.

We reached Lake Shore Park, a city park laid out with rosebuds, fountains, bowling greens, picnic tables. It was empty now, but sweetly expectant of clean, white, well-behaved children and parents who would play there above the lake in summer before half-running, half-stumbling down the slope to the welcoming water. Black people were not allowed in the park, and so it filled our dreams.

Right before the entrance to the park was the large white house with the wheelbarrow full of flowers. Short crocus blades sheathed the purple-and-white hearts that so wished to be first they endured the chill and rain of early spring. The walkway was flagged in calculated disorder, hiding the cunning symmetry. Only fear of discovery and the knowledge that we did not belong kept us from loitering. We circled the proud house and went to the back.

There on the tiny railed stoop sat Pecola in a light red sweater and blue cotton dress. A little wagon was parked near her. She seemed glad to see us.

"Hi."

"Hi."

"What you all doing here?" She was smiling, and since it was a rare thing to see on her, I was surprised at the pleasure it gave me.

"We're looking for you."

"Who told you I was here?"

"The Maginot Line."

"Who is that?"

"That big fat lady. She lives over you."

"Oh, you mean Miss Marie. Her name is Miss Marie."

"Well, everybody calls her Miss Maginot Line. Ain't you scared?"

"Scared of what?"

"The Maginot Line."

Pecola looked genuinely puzzled. "What for?"

"Your mama let you go in her house? And eat out of her plates?"

"She don't know I go. Miss Marie is nice. They all nice."

"Oh, yeah," I said, "she tried to kill us."

"Who? Miss Marie? She don't bother nobody."

"Then how come your mama don't let you go in her house if she so nice?"

"I don't know. She say she's bad, but they ain't bad. They give me stuff all the time."

"What stuff?"

"Oh, lots of stuff, pretty dresses, and shoes. I got more shoes than I ever wear. And jewelry and candy and money. They take me to the movies, and once we went to the carnival. China gone take me to Cleveland to see the square, and Poland gone take me to Chicago to see the Loop.[161] We going everywhere together."

"You lying. You don't have no pretty dresses."

"I do, too."

"Oh, come on, Pecola, what you telling us all that junk for?" Frieda asked.

"It ain't junk." Pecola stood up ready to defend her words, when the door opened.

Mrs. Breedlove stuck her head out the door and said, "What's going on out here? Pecola, who are these children?"

"That's Frieda and Claudia, Mrs. Breedlove."

"Whose girls are you?" She came all the way out on the stoop. She looked nicer than I had ever seen her, in her white uniform and her hair in a small pompadour.

"Mrs. MacTeer's girls, ma'am."

"Oh, yes. Live over on Twenty-first Street?"

"Yes, ma'am."

"What are you doing 'way over here?"

"Just walking. We came to see Pecola."

"Well, you better get on back. You can walk with Pecola. Come on in while I get the wash."

We stepped into the kitchen, a large spacious room. Mrs. Breedlove's skin glowed like taffeta[162] in the reflection of white porcelain, white woodwork, polished cabinets, and brilliant copperware. Odors of meat, vegetables, and something freshly

---

161 the Loop: 미국 시카고 내의 상업중심지구(Informal name for the commercial district in downtown Chicago, so named for the railway tracks that circle around part of it.)

162 taffeta: 호박단(琥珀緞), 태피터(비단의 평직) (A fine lustrous silk or similar synthetic fabric with a crisp texture.)

baked mixed with a scent of Fels Naphtha.

"I'm gone get the wash. You all stand stock still right there and don't mess up nothing." She disappeared behind a white swinging door, and we could hear the uneven flap of her footsteps as she descended into the basement.

Another door opened, and in walked a little girl, smaller and younger than all of us. She wore a pink sunback dress and pink fluffy bedroom slippers with two bunny ears pointed up from the tips. Her hair was corn yellow and bound in a thick ribbon. When she saw us, fear danced across her face for a second. She looked anxiously around the kitchen.

"Where's Polly?" she asked.

The familiar violence rose in me. Her calling Mrs. Breedlove Polly, when even Pecola called her mother Mrs. Breedlove, seemed reason enough to scratch her.

"She's downstairs," I said.

"Polly!" she called.

"Look," Frieda whispered, "look at that." On the counter near the stove in a silvery pan was a deep-dish berry cobbler.[163] The purple juice bursting here and there through crust. We moved closer.

"It's still hot," Frieda said.

Pecola stretched her hand to touch the pan, lightly, to see if it was hot.

"Polly, come here," the little girl called again.

It may have been nervousness, awkwardness, but the pan tilted under Pecola's fingers and fell to the floor, splattering blackish blueberries everywhere. Most of the juice splashed on Pecola's legs, and the burn must have been painful, for she cried out and began hopping about just as Mrs. Breedlove entered with a tightly packed laundry bag. In one gallop she was on Pecola, and with the back of

---

163 cobbler: 프루트 파이(fruit pie)의 일종 (A fruit pie with a rich, thick, cake-like crust.)

her hand knocked her to the floor. Pecola slid in the pie juice, one leg folding under her. Mrs. Breedlove yanked her up by the arm, slapped her again, and in a voice thin with anger, abused Pecola directly and Frieda and me by implication.

"Crazy fool ... my floor, mess ... look what you ... work ... get on out ... now that... crazy ... my floor, my floor ... my floor." Her words were hotter and darker than the smoking berries, and we backed away in dread.

The little girl in pink started to cry. Mrs. Breedlove turned to her. "Hush, baby, hush. Come here. Oh, Lord, look at your dress. Don't cry no more. Polly will change it." She went to the sink and turned tap water on a fresh towel. Over her shoulder she spit out words to us like rotten pieces of apple. "Pick up that wash and get on out of here, so I can get this mess cleaned up."

Pecola picked up the laundry bag, heavy with wet clothes, and we stepped hurriedly out the door. As Pecola put the laundry bag in the wagon, we could hear Mrs. Breedlove hushing and soothing the tears of the little pink-and-yellow girl.

"Who were they, Polly?"

"Don't worry none, baby."

"You gonna make another pie?"

"'Course I will."

"Who were they, Polly?"

"Hush. Don't worry none," she whispered, and the honey in her words complemented the sundown spilling on the lake.

SEEMOTHERMOTHERISVERYNICEMO THERWILLYOUPLAYWITHJANEMOTH ERLAUGHSLAUGHMOTHERLAUGHLA

The easiest thing to do would be to build a case out of her foot. That is what she herself did. But to find out the truth about how dreams die, one should never take the word of the dreamer. The end of her lovely beginning was probably the cavity in one of her front teeth. She preferred, however, to think always of her foot. Although she was the ninth of eleven children and lived on a ridge of red Alabama clay seven miles from the nearest road, the complete indifference with which a rusty nail[164] was met when it punched clear through her foot during her second year of life saved Pauline Williams from total anonymity. The wound left her with a crooked, archless foot that flopped when she walked—not a limp that would have eventually twisted her spine, but a way of lifting

---

164 a rusty nail: (☞ Pauline에게는 두 살 때 녹슨 못을 밟았던 사건이 충치와 함께 커다란 정신적 상처로 남는다.)

the bad foot as though she were extracting it from little whirlpools that threatened to pull it under. Slight as it was, this deformity explained for her many things that would have been otherwise incomprehensible: why she alone of all the children had no nickname; why there were no funny jokes and anecdotes about funny things she had done; why no one ever remarked on her food preferences—no saving of the wing or neck for her—no cooking of the peas in a separate pot without rice because she did not like rice; why nobody teased her; why she never felt at home anywhere, or that she belonged anyplace. Her general feeling of separateness and unworthiness she blamed on her foot. Restricted, as a child, to this cocoon of her family's spinning, she cultivated quiet and private pleasures. She liked, most of all, to arrange things.[165] To line things up in rows—jars on shelves at canning, peach pits on the step, sticks, stones, leaves—and the members of her family let these arrangements be. When by some accident somebody scattered her rows, they always stopped to retrieve them for her, and she was never angry, for it gave her a chance to rearrange them again. Whatever portable plurality she found, she organized into neat lines, according to their size, shape, or gradations of color. Just as she would never align a pine needle with the leaf of a cottonwood tree, she would never put the jars of tomatoes next to the green beans. During all of her four years of going to school, she was enchanted by numbers and depressed by words. She missed—without knowing what she missed—paints and crayons.

Near the beginning of World War I, the Williamses discovered, from returning neighbors and kin, the possibility of living better in another place. In shifts, lots, batches, mixed in with other families, they migrated, in six months and four journeys, to Kentucky, where

---

165 She liked, most of all, to arrange things: 물건들을 정리하는 일에 즐거움을 느낀다는 것은 그녀의 강박관념을 나타낸다.

there were mines and millwork.

"When all us left from dawn home and was waiting down by the depot for the truck, it was nighttime. June bugs[166] was shooting everywhere. They lighted up a tree leaf, and I seen a streak of green every now and again. That was the last time I seen real june bugs. These things up here ain't june bugs. They's something else. Folks here call them fireflies. Down home they was different. But I recollect that streak of green. I recollect it well."

In Kentucky they lived in a real town, ten to fifteen houses on a single street, with water piped right into the kitchen. Ada and Fowler Williams found a five-room frame house for their family. The yard was bounded by a once-white fence against which Pauline's mother planted flowers and within which they kept a few chickens. Some of her brothers joined the Army, one sister died, and two got married, increasing the living space and giving the entire Kentucky venture a feel of luxury. The relocation was especially comfortable to Pauline, who was old enough to leave school. Mrs. Williams got a job cleaning and cooking for a white minister on the other side of town, and Pauline, now the oldest girl at home, took over the care of the house. She kept the fence in repair, pulling the pointed stakes erect, securing them with bits of wire, collected eggs, swept, cooked, washed, and minded the two younger children—a pair of twins called Chicken and Pie, who were still in school. She was not only good at housekeeping, she enjoyed it. After her parents left for work and the other children were at school or in mines, the house was quiet. The stillness and isolation both calmed and energized her. She could arrange and clean without interruption until two o'clock, when Chicken and Pie came home.

---

166 june bug: 미국산 풍뎅이

When the war ended and the twins were ten years old, they too left school to work. Pauline was fifteen, still keeping house, but with less enthusiasm. Fantasies about men and love and touching were drawing her mind and hands away from her work. Changes in weather began to affect her, as did certain sights and sounds. These feelings translated themselves to her in extreme melancholy. She thought of the death of newborn things, lonely roads, and strangers who appear out of nowhere simply to hold one's hand, woods in which the sun was always setting. In church especially did these dreams grow. The songs caressed her, and while she tried to hold her mind on the wages of sin, her body trembled for redemption, salvation, a mysterious rebirth that would simply happen, with no effort on her part. In none of her fantasies was she ever aggressive; she was usually idling by the river bank, or gathering berries in a field when a someone appeared, with gentle and penetrating eyes, who—with no exchange of words—understood; and before whose glance her foot straightened and her eyes dropped. The someone had no face, no form, no voice, no odor. He was a simple Presence, an all-embracing tenderness with strength and a promise of rest. It did not matter that she had no idea of what to do or say to the Presence—after the wordless knowing and the soundless touching, her dreams disintegrated. But the Presence would know what to do. She had only to lay her head on his chest and he would lead her away to the sea, to the city, to the woods ... forever.

There was a woman named Ivy who seemed to hold in her mouth all of the sounds of Pauline's soul. Standing a little apart from the choir, Ivy sang the dark sweetness that Pauline could not name; she sang the death-defying death that Pauline yearned for; she sang of the Stranger[167] who *knew* ...

Precious Lord take my hand

---

167 the Stranger: Cholly를 말함

Lead me on, let me stand
I am tired, I am weak, I am worn.
Through the storms, through the night
Lead me on to the light
Take my hand, precious Lord, lead me on.

When my way grows drear
Precious Lord linger near,
When my life is almost gone
Hear my cry hear my call
Hold my hand lest I fall
Take my hand, precious Lord, lead me on.

Thus it was that when the Stranger, the someone, did appear out of nowhere, Pauline was grateful but not surprised.

He came, strutting right out of a Kentucky sun on the hottest day of the year. He came big, he came strong, he came with yellow eyes, flaring nostrils, and he came with his own music.

Pauline was leaning idly on the fence, her arms resting on the cross rail between the pickets. She had just put down some biscuit dough and was cleaning the flour from under her nails. Behind her at some distance she heard whistling. One of these rapid, high-note riffs[168] that black boys make up as they go while sweeping, shoveling, or just walking along. A kind of city-street music where laughter belies anxiety, and joy is as short and straight as the blade of a pocketknife. She listened carefully to the music and let it pull her lips into a smile. The whistling got louder, and still she did not turn around, for she wanted it to last. While smiling to herself and holding fast to the break in somber thoughts,

---

168 riff: 재즈에서 짧게 반복되는 악절(樂節)을 말함. 두 마디 아니면 세 마디 짜리가 보통이다. 솔로 연주를 받쳐 주거나 대편성 오케스트라에서 긴장감을 자아내기 위해 동원되는 짧고 인상적인 악구.

she felt something tickling her broken foot. She laughed aloud and turned to see. The whistler was bending down tickling her broken foot and kissing her leg. She could not stop her laughter—not until he looked up at her and she saw the Kentucky sun drenching the yellow, heavy-lidded eyes of Cholly Breedlove.

"*When I first seed Cholly, I want you to know it was like all the bits of color from that time down home when all us chil'ren went berry picking after a funeral and I put some in the pocket of my Sunday dress, and they mashed up and stained my hips. My whole dress was messed with purple, and it never did wash out. Not the dress nor me. I could feel that purple deep inside me. And that lemonade Mama used to make when Pap came in out the fields. It be cool and yellowish, with seeds floating near the bottom. And that streak of green them june bugs made on the trees the night we left from down home. All of them colors was in me. Just sitting there. So when Cholly come up and tickled my foot, it was like them berries, that lemonade, them streaks of green the june bugs made, all come together. Cholly was thin then, with real light eyes. He used to whistle, and when I heerd him, shivers come on my skin.*"

Pauline and Cholly loved each other. He seemed to relish her company and even to enjoy her country ways and lack of knowledge about city things. He talked with her about her foot and asked, when they walked through the town or in the fields, if she were tired. Instead of ignoring her infirmity, pretending it was not there, he made it seem like something special and endearing. For the first time Pauline felt that her bad foot was an asset.

And he did touch her, firmly but gently, just as she had dreamed. But minus the gloom of setting suns and lonely river banks. She was secure and grateful; he was kind and lively. She had not known there was so much laughter in the world.

They agreed to marry and go 'way up north, where Cholly said steel mills were begging for workers. Young, loving, and full of energy, they came to Lorain, Ohio. Cholly found work in the steel mills right away, and Pauline started keeping house.

And then she lost her front tooth.[169] But there must have been a speck, a brown speck easily mistaken for food but which did not leave, which sat on the enamel for months, and grew, until it cut into the surface and then to the brown putty underneath, finally eating away to the root, but avoiding the nerves, so its presence was not noticeable or uncomfortable. Then the weakened roots, having grown accustomed to the poison, responded one day to severe pressure, and the tooth fell free, leaving a ragged stump behind. But even before the little brown speck, there must have been the conditions, the setting that would allow it to exist in the first place.

In that young and growing Ohio town whose side streets, even, were paved with concrete, which sat on the edge of a calm blue lake, which boasted an affinity with Oberlin, the underground railroad station, just thirteen miles away, this melting pot on the lip of America[170] facing the cold but receptive Canada—What could go wrong?

"*Me and Cholly was getting along good then. We come up north; supposed to be more jobs and all. We moved into two rooms up over a furniture store, and I set about housekeeping. Cholly was working at the steel plant, and everything was looking good. I don't know what all happened. Everything changed. It was hard to get to*

---

169 And then she lost her front tooth: 썩은 앞니가 빠지는 것은 그녀가 자신이 못생겼으며 가치 없다고 단정짓는 계기가 된다.

170 this melting pot on the lip of America. 미국의 변방에 위치한 용광로. (Melting pot: a place where a variety of races, cultures, or individuals assimilate into a cohesive whole.)

know folks up here, and I missed my people. I weren't used to so much white folks. The ones I seed before was something hateful, but they didn't come around too much. I mean, we didn't have too much truck with them. Just now and then in the fields, or at the commissary. But they want all over us. Up north they was everywhere—next door, downstairs, all over the streets—and colored folks few and far between. Northern colored folk was different too. Dicty-like.[171] *No better than whites for meanness. They could make you feel just as no-count, 'cept I didn't expect it from them. That was the lonesomest time of my life.*[172] *I 'member looking out them front windows just waiting for Cholly to come home at three o'clock. I didn't even have a cat to talk to.*"

In her loneliness, she turned to her husband for reassurance, entertainment, for things to fill the vacant places. Housework was not enough; there were only two rooms, and no yard to keep or move about in. The women in the town wore high-heeled shoes, and when Pauline tried to wear them, they aggravated her shuffle into a pronounced limp.[173] Cholly was kindness still, but began to resist her total dependence on him. They were beginning to have less and less to say to each other. He had no problem finding other people and other things to occupy him[174]—men were always climbing the stairs asking for him, and he was happy to accompany them, leaving her alone.

---

171 Dicty-like: 속물적인, 거만한, (여기서는) 잘난 척 하는(Black slang for snobbish, or haughty.)

172 ...Northern colored people...That was the lonesomest time of my life: 결혼하기로 결정한 이후 Cholly와 함께 이동한 Pauline은 가족이나 전통문화와 단절된 결과로 자기 부정에 빠지게 된다. 이는 McTear 부인과 건강한 삶을 살아가는 그녀의 가족의 모습과 대조적이며 Pecola의 비극과도 연결된다.

173 they aggravated her shuffle into a pronounced limp: 하이힐은 그녀의 지척거리는 걸음새를 더욱 눈에 띄게 절름거리게 했다.

174 He had no problem finding other people and other things to occupy him: Cholly는 그의 시간을 채워 줄 사람들과 일거리를 찾는 데는 문제가 없었다.

Pauline felt uncomfortable with the few black women she met. They were amused by her because she did not straighten her hair. When she tried to make up her face as they did, it came off rather badly. Their goading glances and private snickers at her way of talking (saying "chil'ren") and dressing developed in her a desire for new clothes. When Cholly began to quarrel about the money she wanted, she decided to go to work. Taking jobs as a day worker helped with the clothes, and even a few things for the apartment, but it did not help with Cholly. He was not pleased with her purchases and began to tell her so. Their marriage was shredded with quarrels. She was still no more than a girl, and still waiting for that plateau of happiness, that hand of a precious Lord who, when her way grew drear, would always linger near. Only now she had a clearer idea of what drear meant. Money became the focus of all their discussions, hers for clothes, his for drink. The sad thing was that Pauline did not really care for clothes and makeup. She merely wanted other women to cast favorable glances her way.

After several months of doing day work, she took a steady job in the home of a family of slender means and nervous, pretentious ways.

"*Cholly commenced to getting meaner and meaner and wanted to fight me all of the time. I give him as good as I got. Had to.*[175] *Look like working for that woman and fighting Cholly was all I did. Tiresome. But I holt on to my jobs, even though working for that woman was more than a notion. It wasn't so much her meanness as just simpleminded. Her whole family was. Couldn't get along with one another worth nothing. You'd think with a pretty house like that and all the money they could holt on to, they would enjoy one another. She haul off and cry over the*

---

175 I give him as good as I got. Had to: 내가 받은 만큼 확실히 갚았지. 그래야 했어.

leastest thing. If one of her friends cut her short on the telephone, she'd go to crying. She should of been glad she had a telephone. I ain't got one yet. I recollect oncet how her baby brother who she put through dentistry school didn't invite them to some big party he throwed. They was a big to-do about that. Everybody stayed on the telephone for days. Fussing and carrying on. She asked me, 'Pauline, what would you do if your own brother had a party and didn't invite you?' I said ifn I really wanted to go to that party, I reckoned I'd go anyhow. Never mind what he want. She just sucked her teeth a little and made out like what I said was dumb. All the while I was thinking how dumb she was. Whoever told her that her brother was her friend? Folks can't like folks just 'cause they has the same mama. I tried to like that woman myself. She was good about giving me stuff, but I just couldn't like her. Soon as I worked up a good feeling on her account, she'd do something ignorant and start in to telling me how to clean and do. If I left her on her own, she'd drown in dirt. I didn't have to pick up after Chicken and Pie the way I had to pick up after them. None of them knew so much as how to wipe their behinds. I know, 'cause I did the washing. And couldn't pee proper to save their lives. Her husband ain't hit the bowl yet.[176] *Nasty white folks is about the nastiest things they is. But I would have stayed on 'cepting for Cholly come over by where I was working and cut up so. He come there drunk wanting some money. When that white woman see him, she turned red. She tried to act strong-like, but she was scared bad. Anyway, she told Cholly to get out or she would call the police. He cussed her and started pulling on me. I would of gone upside his head, but I don't want no dealings with the police. So I taken my things and left. I tried to get back, but she didn't want me no more if I was going to stay with Cholly.*

---

176 Her husband ain't hit the bowl yet: 그 여자의 남편은 오줌도 제대로 조준 못하고 사방에 튀겼어.

She said she would let me stay if I left him. I thought about that. But later on it didn't seem none too bright for a black woman to leave a black man for a white woman. She didn't never give me the eleven dollars she owed me, neither. That hurt bad. The gas man had cut the gas off, and I couldn't cook none. I really begged that woman for my money. I went to see her. She was mad as a wet hen. Kept on telling me I owed her for uniforms and some old broken-down bed she give me. I didn't know if I owed her or not, but I needed my money. She wouldn't let up none, neither, even when I give her my word that Cholly wouldn't come back there no more. Then I got so desperate I asked her if she would loan it to me. She was quiet for a spell, and then she told me I shouldn't let a man take advantage over me. That I should have more respect, and it was my husband's duty to pay the bills, and if he couldn't, I should leave and get alimony. All such simple stuff. What was he gone give me alimony on? I seen she didn't understand that all I needed from her was my eleven dollars to pay the gas man so I could cook. She couldn't get that one thing through her thick head. 'Are you going to leave him, Pauline?' she kept on saying. I thought she'd give me my money if I said I would, so I said 'Yes, ma'am.' 'All right,' she said. 'You leave him, and then come back to work, and we'll let bygones be bygones.' 'Can I have my money today?' I said. 'No' she said. 'Only when you leave him. I'm only thinking of you and your future. What good is he, Pauline, what good is he to you?' How you going to answer a woman like that, who don't know what good a man is, and say out of one side of her mouth she's thinking of your future but won't give you your own money so you can buy you something besides baloney to eat? So I said, 'No good, ma'am. He ain't no good to me. But just the same, I think I'd best stay on.' She got up, and I left. When I got outside, I felt pains in my crotch, I had held my legs together so tight trying to make that woman understand. But I reckon now she couldn't understand. She married a man with a slash in his face instead of a mouth.[177] *So how could she understand?*"

One winter Pauline discovered she was pregnant. When she told Cholly, he surprised her by being pleased. He began to drink less and come home more often. They eased back into a relationship more like the early days of their marriage, when he asked if she were tired or wanted him to bring her something from the store. In this state of ease, Pauline stopped doing day work and returned to her own housekeeping. But the loneliness in those two rooms had not gone away. When the winter sun hit the peeling green paint of the kitchen chairs, when the smoked hocks were boiling in the pot, when all she could hear was the truck delivering furniture downstairs, she thought about back home, about how she had been all alone most of the time then too, but that this lonesomeness was different. Then she stopped staring at the green chairs, at the delivery truck; she went to the movies instead. There in the dark her memory was refreshed, and she succumbed to her earlier dreams. Along with the idea of romantic love, she was introduced to another—physical beauty. Probably the most destructive ideas in the history of human thought. Both originated in envy, thrived in insecurity, and ended in disillusion. In equating physical beauty with virtue, she stripped her mind, bound it, and collected self-contempt by the heap. She forgot lust and simple caring for. She regarded love as possessive mating, and romance as the goal of the spirit. It would be for her a well-spring from which she would draw the most destructive emotions, deceiving the lover and seeking to imprison the beloved, curtailing freedom in every way.

She was never able, after her education in the movies, to look at a

---

177 She married a man with a slash in his face instead of a mouth: (=a man who couldn't talk or communicate)

face and not assign it some category in the scale of absolute beauty, and the scale was one she absorbed in full from the silver screen. There at last were the darkened woods, the lonely roads, the river banks, the gentle knowing eyes. There the flawed became whole, the blind sighted, and the lame and halt threw away their crutches. There death was dead, and people made every gesture in a cloud of music. There the black-and-white images[178] came together, making a magnificent whole—all projected through the ray of light from above and behind.

It was really a simple pleasure, but she learned all there was to love and all there was to hate.

"*The onliest time I be happy seem like was when I was in the picture show. Every time I got, I went. I'd go early, before the show started. They'd cut off the lights, and everything be black. Then the screen would light up, and I'd move right on in them pictures. White men taking such good care of they women, and they all dressed up in big clean houses with the bathtubs right in the same room with the toilet.*[179] *Them pictures gave me a lot of pleasure, but it made coming home hard, and looking at Cholly hard. I don't know. I 'member one time I went to see Clark Gable*[180] *and Jean Harlow.*[181] *I fixed my hair up like I'd seen hers on a magazine. A part on the side, with one little curl on my forehead. It looked just like her. Well, almost just like. Anyway, I sat in that show with my hair done up that way and had a good*

---

178 the black-and-white images: 은막에서의 흑백 이미지

179 The onliest time....: Pauline은 영화를 보며 외로움과 소외감을 벗어나고 동시에 백인들이 풍요로운 삶을 산다는 백인 신화를 수용하게 된다(Peach 42).

180 Clark Gable(1901–1960): 미국 영화배우로 남성미 넘치는 배역들을 맡았으며, 영화 《바람과 함께 사라지다(Gone With the Wind)》 (1939)의 레트 버틀러 역할로 가장 유명하다.

181 Jean Harlow(1911–1937): 금발의 여배우로 1930년대 초 클라크 게이블의 상대역을 맡았다.

time. I thought I'd see it through to the end again, and I got up to get me some candy. I was sitting back in my seat, and I taken a big bite of that candy, and it pulled a tooth right out of my mouth. I could of cried. I had good teeth, not a rotten one in my head. I don't believe I ever did get over that. There I was, five months pregnant, trying to look like Jean Harlow, and a front tooth gone. Everything went then. Look like I just didn't care no more after that. I let my hair go back, plaited it up,[182] *and settled down to just being ugly. I still went to the pictures, though, but the meanness got worse. I wanted my tooth back. Cholly poked fun at me, and we started fighting again. I tried to kill him. He didn't hit me too hard, 'cause I were pregnant I guess, but the fights, once they got started up again, kept up. He begin to make me madder than anything I knowed, and I couldn't keep my hands off him.*[183] *Well, I had that baby—a boy—and after that got pregnant again with another one. But it weren't like I thought it was gone be. I loved them and all, I guess, but maybe it was having no money, or maybe it was Cholly, but they sure worried the life out of me.*[184] *Sometimes I'd catch myself hollering at them and beating them, and I'd feel sorry for them, but I couldn't seem to stop. When I had the second one, a girl, I 'member I said I'd love it no matter what it looked like. She looked like a black ball of hair. I don't recollect trying to get pregnant that first time. But that second time, I actually tried to get pregnant. Maybe 'cause I'd had one already and wasn't scairt to do it. Anyway, I felt good, and wasn't thinking on the carrying, just the baby itself. I used to talk to it whilst it be still in the womb. Like good friends we was. You know. I be hanging wash and I knowed lifting weren't good for it.*

---

182 plaited it up: 땋아 올리다: "To plait" is "to twist three long pieces of hair over and under each other to make one long piece"; braid

183 I couldn't keep my hands off him: 그에게 손찌검을 하지 않을 수 없었어.

184 they sure worried the life out of me: 아이들은 정말로 내 진을 다 뺐어.

I'd say to it holt on now I gone hang up these few rags, don't get froggy; it be over soon. It wouldn't leap or nothing. Or I be mixing something in a bowl for the other chile and I'd talk to it then too. You know, just friendly talk. On up til the end I felted good about that baby. I went to the hospital when my time come. So I could be easeful. I didn't want to have it at home like I done with the boy. They put me in a big room with a whole mess of women. The pains was coming, but not too bad. A little old doctor come to examine me. He had all sorts of stuff. He gloved his hand and put some kind of jelly on it and rammed it up between my legs. When he left off, some more doctors come. One old one and some young ones. The old one was learning the young ones about babies. Showing them how to do. When he got to me he said now these here women you don't have any trouble with. They deliver right away and with no pain. Just like horses. The young ones smiled it little. They looked at my stomach and between my legs. They never said nothing to me. Only one looked at me. Looked at my face, I mean. I looked right back at him. He dropped his eyes and turned red. He knowed, I reckon, that maybe I weren't no horse foaling. But them others. They didn't know. They went on. I seed them talking to them white women: 'How you feel? Gonna have twins?' Just shucking them, of course, but nice talk. Nice friendly talk. I got edgy, and when them pains got harder, I was glad. Glad to have something else to think about. I moaned something awful. The pains wasn't as bad as I let on, but I had to let them people know having a baby was more than a bowel movement. I hurt just like them white women. Just 'cause I wasn't hooping and hollering before didn't mean I wasn't feeling pain. What'd they think? That just 'cause I knowed how to have a baby with no fuss that my behind wasn't pulling and aching like theirs? Besides, that doctor don't know what he talking about. He must never seed no mare foal. Who say they don't have no pain?

Just 'cause she don't cry? 'Cause she can't say it, they think it ain't there? If they looks in her eyes and see them eyeballs lolling back, see the sorrowful look, they'd know. Anyways, the baby come. Big old healthy thing. She looked different from what I thought. Reckon I talked to it so much before I conjured up a mind's eye view of it. So when I seed it, it was like looking at a picture of your mama when she was a girl. You knows who she is, but she don't look the same. They give her to me for a nursing, and she liked to pull my nipple off right away. She caught on fast. Not like Sammy, he was the hardest child to feed. But Pecola look like she knowed right off what to do. A right smart baby she was. I used to like to watch her. You know they makes them greedy sounds. Eyes all soft and wet. A cross between a puppy and a dying man. But I knowed she was ugly. Head full of pretty hair, but Lord she was ugly."

When Sammy and Pecola were still young Pauline had to go back to work. She was older now, with no time for dreams and movies. It was time to put all of the pieces together, make coherence where before there had been none. The children gave her this need; she herself was no longer a child. So she became, and her process of becoming was like most of ours: she developed a hatred for things that mystified or obstructed her; acquired virtues that were easy to maintain; assigned herself a role in the scheme of things; and harked back to simpler times for gratification.

She took on the full responsibility and recognition of breadwinner and returned to church. First, however, she moved out of the two rooms into a spacious first floor of a building that had been built as a store. She came into her own with the women who had despised her, by being more moral than they; she avenged herself on Cholly by forcing him to indulge in the weaknesses she despised. She joined a church where shouting was frowned upon, served on

Stewardess Board No. 3,[185] and became a member of Ladies Circle No. 1.[186] At prayer meeting she moaned and sighed over Cholly's ways, and hoped God would help her keep the children from the sins of the father. She stopped saying "chil'ren" and said "childring" instead. She let another tooth fall, and was outraged by painted ladies who thought only of clothes and men. Holding Cholly as a model of sin and failure, she bore him like a crown of thorns, and her children like a cross.[187]

It was her good fortune to find a permanent job in the home of a well-to-do family whose members were affectionate, appreciative, and generous. She looked at their houses, smelled their linen, touched their silk draperies, and loved all of it. The child's pink nightie, the stacks of white pillow slips edged with embroidery, the sheets with top hems picked out with blue cornflowers. She became what is known as an ideal servant, for such a role filled practically all of her needs. When she bathed the little Fisher girl, it was in a porcelain tub with silvery taps running infinite quantities of hot, clear water. She dried her in fluffy white towels and put her in cuddly night clothes. Then she brushed the yellow hair, enjoying the roll and slip of it between her fingers. No zinc tub, no buckets of stove-heated water, no flaky, stiff, grayish towels washed in a kitchen sink, dried in a dusty backyard, no tangled black puffs of rough wool to comb. Soon she stopped trying to keep her own house. The things she could afford to buy did not last, had no beauty or style, and were absorbed by the dingy storefront. More and more she neglected her house, her children, her man—they were like the afterthoughts one has just before sleep, the

185 Stewardess Board No. 3: 제3지구 여신도 봉사단(Stewardess Board is a help serve communion and companion board to the Stewards. They are to help see that that the church has the proper finances.)

186 Ladies Circle No. 1: 제1지구 부녀회

187 she bore him like a crown of thorns, and her children like a cross: 그녀는 남편을 가시 면류관으로, 그리고 아이들을 십자가로 생각했다

early-morning and late-evening edges of her day, the dark edges that made the daily life with the Fishers lighter, more delicate, more lovely. Here she could arrange things, clean things, line things up in neat rows. Here her foot flopped around on deep pile carpets, and there was no uneven sound. Here she found beauty, order, cleanliness, and praise. Mr. Fisher said, "I would rather sell her blueberry cobblers than real estate." She reigned over cupboards stacked high with food that would not be eaten for weeks, even months; she was queen of canned vegetables bought by the case, special fondants and ribbon candy curled up in tiny silver dishes. The creditors and service people who humiliated her when she went to them on her own behalf respected her, were even intimidated by her, when she spoke for the Fishers. She refused beef slightly dark or with edges not properly trimmed. The slightly reeking fish that she accepted for her own family she would all but throw in the fish man's face if he sent it to the Fisher house. Power, praise, and luxury were hers in this household. They even gave her what she had never had—a nickname—Polly. It was her pleasure to stand in her kitchen at the end of a day and survey her handiwork. Knowing there were soap bars by the dozen, bacon by the rasher, and reveling in her shiny pots and pans and polished floors. Hearing, "We'll never let her go. We could never find anybody like Polly. She will *not* leave the kitchen until everything is in order. Really, she is the ideal servant."

Pauline kept this order, this beauty, for herself, a private world, and never introduced it into her storefront, or to her children. Them she bent toward respectability, and in so doing taught them fear: fear of being clumsy, fear of being like their father, fear of not being loved by God, fear of madness like Cholly's mother's. Into her son she beat a loud desire to run away, and into her daughter she beat a fear of growing up, fear of other people, fear of life.

All the meaningfulness of her life was in her work. For her

virtues were intact. She was an active church woman, did not drink, smoke, or carouse, defended herself mightily against Cholly, rose above him in every way, and felt she was fulfilling a mother's role conscientiously when she pointed out their father's faults to keep them from having them, or punished them when they showed any slovenliness, no matter how slight, when she worked twelve to sixteen hours a day to support them. And the world itself agreed with her.

It was only sometimes, sometimes, and then rarely, that she thought about the old days, or what her life had turned to. They were musings, idle thoughts, full sometimes of the old dreaminess, but not the kind of thing she cared to dwell on.

"I started to leave him once, but something came up. Once, after he tried to set the house on fire, I was all set in my mind to go. I can't even 'member now what held me. He sure ain't give me much of a life. But it wasn't all bad. Sometimes things wasn't all bad. He used to come easing into bed sometimes, not too drunk. I make out like I'm asleep, 'cause it's late, and he taken three dollars out of my pocketbook that morning or something. I hear him breathing, but I don't look around. I can see in my mind's eye his black arms thrown back behind his head, the muscles like great big peach stones sanded down, with veins running like little swollen rivers down his arms. Without touching him I be feeling those ridges on the tips of my fingers. I sees the palms of his hands calloused to granite, and the long fingers curled up and still. I think about the thick, knotty hair on his chest, and the two big swells his breast muscles make. I want to rub my face hard in his chest and feel the hair cut my skin. I know just where the hair growth slacks out—just above his navel—and how it picks up again and spreads out. Maybe he'll shift a little, and his leg will touch me, or I feel his flank just graze my behind. I don't move

even yet. Then he lift his head, turn over, and put his hand on my waist. If I don't move, he'll move his hand over to pull and knead my stomach. Soft and slow-like. I still don't move, because I don't want him to stop. I want to pretend sleep and have him keep on rubbing my stomach. Then he will lean his head down and bite my tit. Then I don't want him to rub my stomach anymore. I want him to put his hand between my legs. I pretend to wake up, and turn to him, but not opening my legs. I want him to open them for me. He does, and I be soft and wet where his fingers are strong and hard. I be softer than I ever been before. All my strength in his hand. My brain curls up like wilted leaves. A funny, empty feeling is in my hands. I want to grab holt of something, so I hold his head. His mouth is under my chin. Then I don't want his hand between my legs no more, because I think I am softening away. I stretch my legs open, and he is on top of me. Too heavy to hold, and too light not to. He puts his thing in me. In me. In me. I wrap my feet around his back so he can't get away. His face is next to mine. The bed springs sounds like them crickets used to back home. He puts his fingers in mine, and we stretches our arms outwise like Jesus on the cross. I hold on tight. My fingers and my feet hold on tight, because everything else is going, going. I know he wants me to come first. But I can't. Not until he does. Not until I feel him loving me. Just me. Sinking into me. Not until I know that my flesh is all that be on his mind. That he couldn't stop if he had to. That he would die rather than take his thing out of me. Of me. Not until he has let go of all he has, and give it to me. To me. To me. When he does, I feel a power. I be strong, I be pretty, I be young. And then I wait. He shivers and tosses his head. Now I be strong enough, pretty enough, and young enough to let him make me come. I take my fingers out of his and put my hands on his behind. My legs drop back onto the bed. I don't make no noise, because the chil'ren might hear. I begin to feel those little bits of color floating up into me—deep in me. That streak of green from the june-bug light, the purple from the berries trickling along my thighs, Mama's lemonade yellow runs sweet in me. Then I feel like I'm laughing between my legs, and the laughing gets all mixed up with the colors, and I'm afraid I'll come, and afraid I won't. But I know I will. And I do. And it be rainbow all inside. And it lasts and lasts and lasts. I want to thank him, but don't know how, so I pat him like you do a baby. He asks me if I'm all right. I say yes. He gets off me and lies down to sleep. I want to say something, but I don't. I don't want to take my mind offen the rainbow.[188] *I should get up and go to the toilet, but I don't. Besides, Cholly is asleep with his leg throwed over me. I can't move and don't want to.*

"But it ain't like that anymore. Most times he's thrashing away inside me before I'm woke, and through when I am. The rest of the time I can't even be next to his stinking drunk self. But I don't care 'bout it no more. My Maker[189] *will take care of me. I know He will. I know He will. Besides, it don't make no difference about this old earth. There is sure to be a glory. Only thing I miss sometimes is that rainbow. But like I say, I don't recollect it much anymore."*

---

188 I don't want to take my mind offen(=off of) the rainbow: 나는 무지개를 놓치고 싶지 않았던 거지 (☞ Take my mind off ~~: ~에서 마음을 돌리다, ~을 잊다.)
189 My Maker: 조물주

SEEFATHERHEISBIGANDSTRONGFATH ERWILLYOUPLAYWITHJANEFATHER ISSMILINGSMILEFATHERSMILESMILE [190]

When Cholly was four days old, his mother wrapped him in two blankets and one newspaper and placed him on a junk heap by the railroad. His Great Aunt Jimmy, who had seen her niece carrying a bundle out of the back door, rescued him. She beat his mother with a razor strap and wouldn't let her near the baby after that. Aunt Jimmy raised Cholly herself, but took delight sometimes in telling him of how she had saved him. He gathered from her that his mother wasn't right in the head.[191] But he never had a chance to find out, because she ran away shortly after the razor strap, and no

---

190 "딕과 제인" 이야기 중 아버지에 초점을 맞춘 부분을 인용함. 제인의 아버지는 제인과 놀아주고 웃음을 띈 자상한 모습이다. 독자들은 스토리를 읽어 내려가면서 제인의 아버지와는 대조적인 Pecola의 아버지를 만나게 되며, 이 인용 부분이 띄어쓰기 없이 혼란스러운 이유를 알게된다.

191 wasn't right in the head: 분별력이 없었다. 정상이 아니다. 미쳤다.("Not right in the head" means informally "(of a person) not completely sane.")

one had heard of her since.

Cholly was grateful for having been saved. Except sometimes. Sometimes when he watched Aunt Jimmy eating collards with her fingers, sucking her four gold teeth, or smelled her when she wore the asafetida[192] bag around her neck, or when she made him sleep with her for warmth in winter and he could see her old, wrinkled breasts sagging in her nightgown—then he wondered whether it would have been just as well to have died there. Down in the rim of a tire under a soft black Georgia sky.

He had four years of school before he got courage enough to ask his aunt who and where his father was.

"That Fuller boy, I believe it was," his aunt said. "He was hanging around then, but he taken off pretty quick before you was born. I think he gone to Macon. Him or his brother. Maybe both. I hear old man Fuller say something 'bout it once."

"What name he have?" asked Cholly.

"Fuller, Foolish."

"I mean what his given name?"

"Oh." She closed her eyes to think, and sighed. "Can't recollect nothing no more. Sam, was it? Yeh. Samuel. No. No, it wasn't. It was Samson. Samson Fuller."

"How come you all didn't name me Samson?" Cholly's voice was low.

"What for? He wasn't nowhere around when you was born. Your mama didn't name you nothing. The nine days wasn't up before she throwed you on the junk heap. When I got you I named you myself on the ninth day. You named after my dead brother. Charles Breedlove. A good man. Ain't no Samson never come to no good end."

192 asafetida: 아위 수지(阿魏 樹脂). 진경제(鎭痙劑) 용으로 사용한다. (A fetid resinous gum obtained from the roots of a herbaceous plant, used in herbal medicine and Indian cooking)

Cholly didn't ask anything else.

Two years later he quit school to take a job at Tyson's Feed and Grain Store. He swept up, ran errands, wighed bags, and lifted them onto the drays. Sometimes they let him ride with the drayman. A nice old man called Blue Jack. Blue used to tell him old-timey stories about how it was when Emancipation Proclamation came. How the black people hollered, cried, and sang. And ghost stories about how a white man cut off his wife's head and buried her in the swamp, and the headless body came out at night and went stumbling around the yard, knocking over stuff because it couldn't see, and crying all the time for a comb. They talked about the women Blue had had, and the fights he'd been in when he was younger, about how he talked his way out of getting lynched once, and how others hadn't.

Cholly loved Blue. Long after he was a man, he remembered the good times they had had. How on a July 4 at a church picnic a family was about to break open a watermelon. Several children were standing around watching. Blue was hovering about on the periphery of the circle—a faint smile of anticipation softening his face. The father of the family lifted the melon high over his head—his big arms looked taller than the trees to Cholly, and the melon blotted out the sun. Tall, head forward, eyes fastened on a rock, his arms higher than the pines, his hands holding a melon bigger than the sun, he paused an instant to get his bearing and secure his aim. Watching the figure etched against the bright blue sky, Cholly felt goose pimple popping along his arms and neck. He wondered if God looked like that. No. God was a nice old white man, with long white hair, flowing white beard, and little blue eyes that looked sad when people died and mean when they were bad. It must be the devil who looks like that—holding the world in his hands, ready to dash it to the ground and spill the red guts so niggers could eat the sweet, warm insides. If the devil did look like that, Cholly preferred him. He never felt anything thinking about God, but just the idea of the devil excited him. And now the strong, black devil was blotting out the sun and getting ready to split open the world.

Far away somebody was playing a mouth organ; the music slithered over the cane fields and into the pine grove; it spiraled around the tree trunks and mixed itself with the pine scent, so Cholly couldn't tell the difference between the sound and the odor that hung about the heads of the people.

The man swung the melon down to the edge of a rock. A soft cry of disappointment accompanied the sound of smashed rind. The break was a bad one. The melon was jagged, and hunks of rind and red meat scattered on the grass.

Blue jumped. "Aw—awww," he moaned, "dere go da heart." His voice was both sad and pleased. Everybody looked to see the big red chunk from the very center of the melon, free of rind and sparse of seed, which had rolled a little distance from Blue's feet. He stooped to pick it up. Blood red, its planes dull and blunted with sweetness, its edges rigid with juice. Too obvious, almost obscent, in the joy it promised.

"Go 'head, Blue," the father laughed. "You can have it."

Blue smile and walked away. Little children scrambled for the pieces on the ground. Women picked out the seeds for the smallest ones and broke off little bits of the meat for themselves. Blue's eye caught Cholly's. He motioned to him. "Come on, boy. Le's you and me eat the heart."

Together the old man and the boy sat on the grass and shared the heart of the watermelon. The nasty-sweet guts of the earth.

It was in the spring, a very chilly spring, that Aunt Jimmy died of peach cobbler. She went to a camp meeting that took place after a rainstorm, and the damp wood of the benches was bad for her. For four or five days afterward, she felt poorly. Friends came to see about her. Some made camomile[193] tea; others rubbed her with liniment.[194] Miss Alice, her closest friend, read the Bible to her. Still she was declining. Advice was prolific, if contradictory.

"Don't eat no whites of eggs."

"Drink new milk."

"Chew on this root."

Aunt Jimmy ignored all but Miss Alice's Bible reading. She nodded in drowsy appreciation as the words from First Corinthians droned over her. Sweet amens fell from her lips as she was chastised for all her sins. But her body would not respond.

Finally it was decided to fetch M'Dear. M'Dear was a quiet woman who lived in a shack near the woods. She was a competent midwife and decisive diagnostician. Few could remember when M'Dear was not around. In any illness that could not be handled by ordinary means—known cures, intuition, or endurance—the word was always, "Fetch M'Dear."

When she arrived at Aunt Jimmy's house, Cholly was amazed at the sight of her. He had always pictured her as shriveled and hunched over, for he knew she was very, very old. But M'Dear loomed taller than the preacher who accompanied her. She must have been over six feet tall. Four big white knots of hair gave power and authority to her soft black face. Standing straight as a poker, she seemed to need her hickory stick not for support but for communication. She tapped it lightly on the floor as she looked down at Aunt Jimmy's wrinkled face. She stroked the knob with the thumb of her right hand while she ran her left one over Aunt Jimmy's body. The backs of her long fingers she placed on

---

193 camomile (or chamomile): The name of a composite plant, Anthemis nobilis, an aromatic creeping herb, found on dry sandy commons in England, with downy leaves, and flowers white in the ray and yellow in the disk, but in cultivation often all white like a double daisy. The flowers are employed in medicine for their bitter and tonic properties.

194 liniment: 도찰제(塗擦劑), 도포제(A liquid or lotion, esp. one made with oil, for rubbing on the body to relieve pain)

the patient's cheek, then placed her palm on the forehead. She ran her fingers through the sick woman's hair, lightly scratching the scalp, and then looking at what the fingernails revealed. She lifted Aunt Jimmy's hand and looked closely at it—fingernails, back skin, the flesh of the palm she pressed with three fingertips. Later she put her ear on Aunt Jimmy's chest and stomach to listen. At M'Dear's request, the women pulled the slop jar[195] from under the bed to show the stools. M'Dear tapped her stick while looking at them.

"Bury the slop jar and everything in it," she said to the women. To Aunt Jimmy she said, "You done caught cold in your womb. Drink pot liquor and nothing else."

"Will it pass?" asked Aunt Jimmy. "Is I'm gone be all right?"

"I reckon."

M'Dear turned and left the room. The preacher put her in his buggy to take her home.

That evening the women brought bowls of pot liquor from black-eyed peas, from mustards, from cabbage, from kale, from collards, from turnips, from beets, from green beans. Even the juice from a boiling hog jowl.

Two evenings later Aunt Jimmy had gained much strength. When Miss Alice and Mrs. Gaines stopped in to check on her, they remarked on her improvement. The three women sat talking about various miseries they had had, their cure or abatement, what had helped. Over and over again they returned to Aunt Jimmy's condition. Repeating its cause, what could have been done to prevent the misery from taking hold, and M'Dear's infallibility. Their voices blended into a threnody[196] of nostalgia about pain.

---

195 slop jar: 부엌의 구정물통; 침실용 변기, 요강 (An indoor container that takes the place of toilets, especially for night use or for people too ill to walk outside to an outhouse)

196 threnody: A song of lamentation; spec. a lament for the dead, a dirge.

Rising and falling, complex in harmony, uncertain in pitch, but constant in the recitative of pain. They hugged the memories of illnesses to their bosoms. They licked their lips and clucked their tongues in fond remembrance of pains they had endured—childbirth, rheumatism, croup,[197] sprains, backaches, piles.[198] All of the bruises they had collected from moving about the earth—harvesting, cleaning, hoisting, pitching, stooping, kneeling, picking—always with young ones underfoot.

But they had been young once. The odor of their armpits and haunches had mingled into a lovely musk; their eyes had been furtive, their lips relaxed, and the delicate turn of their heads on those slim black necks had been like nothing other than a doe's. Their laughter had been more touch than sound.

Then they had grown. Edging into life from the back door. Becoming. Everybody in the world was in a position to give them orders. White women said, "Do this." White children said, "Give me that." White men said, "Come here." Black men said, "Lay down." The only people they need not take orders from were black children and each other. But they took all of that and re-created it in their own image. They ran the houses of white people, and knew it. When white men beat their men, they cleaned up the blood and went home to receive abuse from the victim. They beat their children with one hand and stole for them with the other. The hands that felled trees also cut umbilical cords; the hands that wrung the necks of chickens and butchered hogs also nudged African violets into bloom; the arms that loaded sheaves, bales, and sacks rocked babies into sleep. They patted biscuits into flaky ovals of innocence—and shrouded the dead. They plowed all day and came home to nestle like plums under the limbs of their men. The legs that straddled a mule's back were the same ones that straddled

---

197 croup: (병리) 크루프, 후두염증(어린이의 후두나 기관의 염증)
198 piles: (병리) 치질, 치핵

their men's hips. And the difference was all the difference there was.

Then they were old. Their bodies honed, their odor sour. Squatting in a cane field, stooping in a cotton field, kneeling by a river bank, they had carried a world on their heads. They had given over the lives of their own children and tendered their grandchildren. With relief they wrapped their heads in rags, and their breasts in flannel; eased their feet into felt. They were through with lust and lactation[199], beyond tears and terror. They alone could walk the roads of Mississippi, the lanes of Georgia, the fields of Alabama unmolested. They were old enough to be irritable when and where they chose, tired enough to look forward to death, disinterested enough to accept the idea of pain while ignoring the presence of pain. They were, in fact and at last, free. And the lives of these old black women were synthesized in their eyes—purée[200] of tragedy and humor, wickedness and serenity, truth and fantasy.

They chattered far into the night. Cholly listened and grew sleepy. The lullaby of grief enveloped him, rocked him, and at last numbed him. In his sleep the foul odor of an old woman's stools turned into the healthy smell of horse shit, and the voices of the three women were muted into the pleasant notes of a mouth organ. He was aware, in his sleep, of being curled up in a chair, his hands tucked between his thighs. In a dream his penis changed into a long hickory stick, and the hands caressing it were the hands of M'Dear.

On a wet Saturday night, before Aunt Jimmy felt strong enough to get out of the bed, Essie Foster brought her a peach cobbler. The old lady ate a piece, and the next morning when Cholly went to

---

199 lactation: 젖의 분비, 젖의 분비기(期), 포유기(간)

200 purée: A smooth, creamy substance made of liquidized or crushed fruit of vegetables

empty the slop jar, she was dead. Her mouth was a slackened O, and her hands, those long fingers with a man's hard nails, having done their laying by, could now be dainty on the sheet. One open eye looked at him as if to say, "Mind how you take holt of that jar, boy." Cholly stared back, unable to move, until a fly settled at the corner of her mouth. He fanned it away angrily, looked back at the eye, and did its bidding.

Aunt Jimmy's funeral was the first Cholly had ever attended. As a member of the family, one of the bereaved, he was the object of a great deal of attention. The ladies had cleaned the house, aired everything out, notified everybody, and stitched together what looked like a white wedding dress for Aunt Jimmy, a maiden lady, to wear when she met Jesus. They even produced a dark suit, white shirt, and tie for Cholly. The husband of one of them cut his hair. He was enclosed in fastidious tenderness. Nobody talked to him; that is, they treated him like the child he was, never engaging him in serious conversation; but they anticipated wishes he never had: meals appeared, hot water for the wooden tub, clothes laid out. At the wake[201] he was allowed to fall asleep, and arms carried him to bed. Only on the third day after the death—the day of the funeral—did he have to share the spotlight.[202] Aunt Jimmy's people came from nearby towns and farms. Her brother O. V., his children and wife, and lots of cousins. But Cholly was still the major figure, because he was "Jimmy's boy, the last thing she loved," and "the one who found her." The solicitude of the women, the head pats of the men, pleased Cholly, and the creamy conversations fascinated him.

"What'd she die from?"

"Essie's pie."

---

201 wake: 경야(經夜); 죽은 사람을 장사 지내기 전에 근친지기(近親知己)들이 널(棺) 곁에서 밤새도록 지키는 일.

202 did he have to share the spotlight = attract attention

"Don't say?"

"Uh-huh. She was doing fine, I saw her the very day before. Said she wanted me to bring her some black thread to patch some things for the boy. I should of known just from her wanting black thread that was a sign."

"Sure was."

"Just like Emma. 'Member? She kept asking for thread. Dropped dead that very evening."

"Yeah. Well, she was determined to have it. Kept on reminding me. I told her I had some to home, but naw, she wanted it new. So I sent Li'l June[203] to get some that very morning when she was laying dead. I was just fixing to bring it over, 'long with a piece of sweet bread. You know how she craved my sweet bread."

"Sure did. Always bragged on it. She was a good friend to you."

"I believe it. Well, I had no more got my clothes on when Sally bust in the door hollering about how Cholly here had been over to Miss Alice saying she was dead. You could have knocked me over, I tell you."

"Guess Essie feels mighty bad."

"Oh, Lord, yes. But I told her the Lord giveth and the Lord taketh away. Wasn't her fault none. She makes good peach pies. But she bound to believe it was the pie did it, and I 'spect she right."

"Well, she shouldn't worry herself none 'bout that. She was just doing what we all would of done."[204]

"Yeah. 'Cause I was sure wrapping up that sweet bread, and that could of done it too."

"I doubts that. Sweet bread is pure. But a pie is the worse thing to give anybody ailing. I'm surprised Jimmy didn't know better."

"If she did, she wouldn't let on. She would have tried to please. You know how she was. So good."

---

203 Li'l June: Little June

204 we all would of done: = we all would have done

"I'll say. Did she leave anything?"

"Not even a pocket handkerchief. The house belongs to some white folks in Clarksville."

"Oh, yeah? I thought she owned it."

"May have at one time. But not no more. I hear the insurance folks been down talking to her brother."

"How much do it come to?"[205]

"Eighty-five dollars, I hear."

"That all?"

"Can she get in the ground on that?"[206]

"Don't see how. When my daddy died last year this April it costed one hundred and fifty dollars. 'Course, we had to have everything just so. Now Jimmy's people may all have to chip in. That undertaker that lays out black folks ain't none too cheap."

"Seems a shame. She been paying on that insurance all her life."

"Don't I know?"

"Well, what about the boy? What he gone do?"

"Well, caint nobody find that mama, so Jimmy's brother gone take him back to his place. They say he got a nice place. Inside toilet and everything."

"That's nice. He seems like a good Christian man. And the boy need a man's hand."

"What time's the funeral?"

"Two clock. She ought to be in the ground by four."

"Where's the banquet? I heard Essie wanted it at her house."

"Naw, it's at Jimmy's. Her brother wanted it so."

"Well, it will be a big one. Everybody liked old Jimmy. Sure will miss her in the pew."

The funeral banquet was a peal of joy after the thunderous beauty of the funeral. It was like a street tragedy with spontaneity tucked

---

205 How much do it come to?: 보험금은 얼마나 될까?

206 Can she get in the ground on that?: 그 돈으로 장례가 될까?

softly into the corners of a highly formal structure. The deceased was the tragic hero, the survivors the innocent victims; there was the omnipresence of the deity, strophe and antistrophe[207] of the chorus of mourners led by the preacher. There was grief over the waste of Life, the stunned wonder at the ways of God, and the restoration of order in nature at the graveyard.

Thus the banquet was the exultation, the harmony, the acceptance of physical frailty, joy in the termination of misery. Laughter, relief, a steep hunger for food.

Cholly had not yet fully realized his aunt was dead. Everything was so interesting. Even at the graveyard he felt nothing but curiosity, and when his turn had come to view the body at the church, he had put his hand out to touch the corpse to see if it were really ice cold like everybody said. But he drew his hand back quickly. Aunt Jimmy looked so private, and it seemed wrong somehow to disturb that privacy. He had trudged back to his pew dry-eyed amid tearful shrieks and shouts of others, wondering if he should try to cry.

Back in his house, he was free to join in the gaiety and enjoy what he really felt—a kind of carnival spirit. He ate greedily and felt good enough to try to get to know his cousins. There was some question, according to the adults, as to whether they were his real cousins or not, since Jimmy's brother O. V. was only a half-brother, and Cholly's mother had been the daughter of Jimmy's sister, but that sister was from the second marriage of Jimmy's father, and O. V. was from the first marriage.

One of these cousins interested Cholly in particular. He was about fifteen or sixteen years old. Cholly went outside and found the boy standing with some others near the tub where Aunt Jimmy used to boil her clothes.

---

207 strophe and antistrophe: 조문객들의 응답송(應答頌). (고대 그리스의) 합창 무용단의 노래에서 유래.

He ventured a tentative "Hey." They responded with another. The fifteen-year-old named Jake offered Cholly a rolled-up cigarette. Cholly took it, but when he held the cigarette at arm's length and stuck the tip of it into the match flame, instead of putting it in his mouth and drawing on it, they laughed at him. Shamefaced, he threw the cigarette down. He felt it important to do something to reinstate himself with Jake. So when he asked Cholly if he knew any girls, Cholly said, "Sure."

All the girls Cholly knew were at the banquet, and he pointed to a cluster of them standing, hanging, draping on the back porch. Darlene too. Cholly hoped Jake wouldn't pick her.

"Let's get some and walk around," said Jake.

The two boys sauntered over to the porch. Cholly didn't know how to begin. Jake wrapped his legs around the rickety porch rail and just sat there staring off into space as though he had no interest in them at all. He was letting them look him over, and guardedly evaluating them in return.

The girls pretended they didn't see the boys and kept on chattering. Soon their talk got sharp; the gentle teasing they had been engaged in with each other changed to bitchiness, a serious kind of making fun. That was Jake's clue; the girls were reacting to him. They had gotten a whiff of his manhood and were shivering for a place in his attention.

Jake left the porch rail and walked right up to a girl named Suky, the one who had been most bitter in her making fun.

"Want to show me 'round?" He didn't even smile.

Cholly held his breath, waiting for Suky to shut Jake up. She was good at that, and well known for her sharp tongue. To his enormous surprise, she readily agreed, and even lowered her lashes. Taking courage, Cholly turned to Darlene and said, "Come on 'long. We just going down to the gully." He waited for her to screw up her face and say no, or what for, or some such thing. His feelings about her were mostly fear—fear that she would not like him, and fear that she would.

His second fear materialized. She smiled and jumped down the three leaning steps to join him. Her eyes were full of compassion, and Cholly remembered that he was the bereaved.

"If you want to," she said, "but not too far. Mama said we got to leave early, and it's getting dark."

The four of them moved away. Some of the other boys had come to the porch and were about to begin that partly hostile, partly indifferent, partly desperate mating dance. Suky, Jake, Darlene, and Cholly walked through several backyards until they came to an open field. They ran across it and came to a dry riverbed lined with green. The object of the walk was a wild vineyard where the muscadine[208] grew. Too new, too tight to have much sugar, they were eaten anyway. None of them wanted—not then—the grape's easy relinquishing of all its dark juice. The restraint, the holding off, the promise of sweetness that had yet to unfold, excited them more than full ripeness would have done. At last their teeth were on edge, and the boys diverted themselves by pelting the girls with the grapes. Their slim black boy wrists made G clefs[209] in the air as they executed the tosses. The chase took Cholly and Darlene away from the lip of the gully, and when they paused for breath, Jake and Suky were nowhere in sight. Darlene's white cotton dress was stained with juice. Her big blue hair bow had come undone, and the sundown breeze was picking it up and fluttering it about her head. They were out of breath and sank down in the green-and-purple grass on the edge of the pine woods.

Cholly lay on his back panting. His mouth full of the taste of muscadine, listening to the pine needles rustling loudly in their anticipation of rain. The smell of promised rain, pine, and

---

208 muscadine: 포도의 일종(미국 남동부산)

209 G clef: 높은 《사》 음자리표, 고음부 기호

muscadine made him giddy. The sun had gone and pulled away its shreds of light. Turning his head to see where the moon was, Cholly caught sight of Darlene in moonlight behind him. She was huddled into a D[210]—arms encircling drawn-up knees, on which she rested her head. Cholly could see her bloomers and the muscles of her young thighs.

"We bed' get on back," he said.

"Yeah." She stretched her legs flat on the ground and began to retie her hair ribbon. "Mama gone whup[211] me."

"Naw she ain't."

"Uh-huh. She told me she would if I get dirty."

"You ain't dirty."

"I am too. Looka that." She dropped her hands from the ribbon and smoothed out a place on her dress where the grape stains were heaviest.

Cholly felt sorry for her; it was just as much his fault. Suddenly he realized that Aunt Jimmy was dead, for he missed the fear of being whipped. There was nobody to do it except Uncle O. V., and he was the bereaved too.

"Let me," he said. He rose to his knees facing her and tried to tie her ribbon. Darlene put her hands under his open shirt and rubbed the damp tight skin. When he looked at her in surprise, she stopped and laughed. He smiled and continued knotting the bow. She put her hands back under his shirt.

"Hold still," he said. "How I gone get this?"

She tickled his ribs with her fingertips. He giggled and grabbed his rib cage. They were on top of each other in a moment. She corkscrewing her hands into his clothes. He returning the play, digging into the neck of her dress, and then under her dress. When he got his hand in her bloomers, she suddenly stopped

210 She was huddled into a D: 그녀는 D자 모양으로 허리를 굽히고 있었다.

211 whup = whop: to strike with heavy blows; to beat soundly, flog

laughing and looked serious. Cholly, frightened, was about to take his hand away, but she held his wrist so he couldn't move it. He examined her then with his fingers, and she kissed his face and mouth. Cholly found her muscadine-lipped mouth distracting. Darlene released his head, shifted her body, and pulled down her pants. After some trouble with the buttons, Cholly dropped his pants down to his knees. Their bodies began to make sense to him, and it was not as difficult as he had thought it would be. She moaned a little, but the excitement collecting inside him made him close his eyes and regard her moans as no more than pine sighs over his head. Just as he felt an explosion threaten, Darlene froze and cried out. He thought he had hurt her, but when he looked at her face, she was staring wildly at something over his shoulder. He jerked around.

There stood two white men. One with a spirit lamp, the other with a flashlight. There was no mistake about their being white; he could smell it. Cholly jumped, trying to kneel, stand, and get his pants up all in one motion. The men had long guns.

"Hee hee hee heeeee." The snicker was a long asthmatic cough.

The other raced the flashlight all over Cholly and Darlene.

"Get on wid it, nigger,"[212] said the flashlight one.

"Sir?" said Cholly, trying to find a buttonhole.

"I said, get on wid it. An' make it good, nigger, make it good."

There was no place for Cholly's eyes to go. They[213] slid about furtively searching for shelter, while his body remained paralyzed. The flashlight man lifted his gun down from his shoulder, and Cholly heard the clop of metal. He dropped back to his knees. Darlene had her head averted, her eyes staring out of the lamplight into the surrounding darkness and looking almost unconcerned, as though they had no part in the drama taking place

---

212 Get on wid (=with) it, nigger

213 They (=Cholly's eyes)

around them. With a violence born of total helplessness, he pulled her dress up, lowered his trousers and underwear.

"Hee hee hee hee heeeeee."

Darlene put her hands over her face as Cholly began to simulate what had gone on before. He could do no more than make-believe. The flashlight made a moon on his behind.[214]

"Hee hee hee hee heeee."

"Come on, coon.[215] Faster. You ain't doing nothing for her."

"Hee hee hee hee heeee."

Cholly, moving faster, looked at Darlene. He hated her. He almost wished he could do it—hard, long, and painfully, he hated her so much. The flashlight wormed its way into his guts and turned the sweet taste of muscadine into rotten fetid bile. He stared at Darlene's hands covering her face in the moon and lamplight. They looked like baby claws.

"Hee hee hee hee heee."

Some dogs howled. "Thas them. Thas them. I know thas Old Honey."[216]

"Yep," said the spirit lamp.

"Come on." The flashlight turned away, and one of them whistled to Honey.

"Wait," said the spirit lamp, "the coon ain't comed yet."

"Well, he have to come on his own time. Good luck, coon baby."

They crushed the pine needles underfoot. Cholly could hear them whistling for a long time, and then the dogs' answer no longer a howl, but warm excited yelps of recognition.

Cholly raised himself and in silence buttoned his trousers. Darlene did not move. Cholly wanted to strangle her, but instead

---

214 The flashlight made a moon on his behind: 회중전등의 빛이 그의 엉덩이에 둥그런 불빛을 만들었다.

215 coon: (경멸적) 흑인

216 Old Honey: 개 이름

he touched her leg with his foot. "We got to get, girl. Come on!"

She reached for her underwear with her eyes closed, and could not find them. The two of them patted about in the moonlight for the panties. When she found them, she put them on with the movements of an old woman. They walked away from the pine woods toward the road. He in front, she plopping along behind. It started to rain. "That's good," Cholly thought. "It will explain away our clothes."

When they got back to the house, some ten or twelve guests were still there. Jake was gone, Suky too. Some people had gone back for more helpings of food—potato pie, ribs. All were engrossed in early-night reminiscences about dreams, figures, premonitions. Their stuffed comfort was narcotic and had produced recollections and fabrications of hallucinations.

Cholly and Darlene's entrance produced only a mild stir.

"Ya'll soaked, ain't you?"

Darlene's mother was only vaguely fussy. She had eaten and drunk too much. Her shoes were under her chair, and the side snaps of her dress were opened. "Girl. Come on in here. Thought I told you ..."

Some of the guests thought they would wait for the rain to slacken. Others, who had come in wagons, thought they'd best leave now. Cholly went into the little storeroom which had been made into a bed room for him. Three infants were sleeping on his cot. He took off his rain-and pine-soaked clothes and put on his coveralls.[217] He didn't know where to go. Aunt Jimmy's room was out of the question, and Uncle O. V. and his wife would be using it later anyway. He took a quilt from a trunk, spread it on the floor, and lay down. Somebody was brewing coffee, and he had a sharp craving for it, just before falling asleep.

---

217 coveralls: coverall은 (상의와 하의가 붙은) 헐거운 작업복 (a full-length protective outer garment often zipped up the front)

The next day was cleaning-out day,[218] settling accounts, distributing Aunt Jimmy's goods. Mouths were set in downward crescents, eyes veiled, feet tentative.

Cholly floated about aimlessly, doing chores as he was told. All the glamour and warmth the adults had given him on the previous day were replaced by a sharpness that agreed with his mood. He could think only of the flashlight, the muscadines, and Darlene's hands. And when he was not thinking of them, the vacancy in his head was like the space left by a newly pulled tooth still conscious of the rottenness that had once filled it. Afraid of running into Darlene, he would not go far from the house, but neither could he endure the atmosphere of his dead Aunt's house. The picking through her things, the comments on the "condition" of her goods. Sullen, irritable, he cultivated his hatred of Darlene. Never did he once consider directing his hatred toward the hunters. Such an emotion would have destroyed him. They were big, white, armed men. He was small, black, helpless. His subconscious knew what his conscious mind did not guess—that hating them would have consumed him, burned him up like a piece of soft coal, leaving only flakes of ash and a question mark of smoke. He was, in time, to discover that hatred of white men—but not now. Not in impotence but later, when the hatred could find sweet expression. For now, he hated the one who had created the situation, the one who bore witness to his failure, his impotence. The one whom he had not been able to protect, to spare, to cover from the round moon glow of the flashlight. The hee-hee-hee's. He recalled Darlene's dripping hair ribbon, flapping against her face as they walked back in silence in the rain. The loathing that galloped through him made him tremble. There was no one to talk to. Old Blue was too drunk too often these days to make sense. Besides, Cholly doubted if he could reveal his shame to Blue. He would have

---

218 cleaning-out day: 모든 것을 정리하는 날

to lie a little to tell Blue, Blue the woman-killer. It seemed to him that lonely was much better than alone.

The day Cholly's uncle was ready to leave, when everything was packed, when the quarrels about who gets what had seethed down to a sticking gravy on everybody's tongue, Cholly sat on the back porch waiting. It had occurred to him that Darlene might be pregnant. It was a wildly irrational, completely uninformed idea, but the fear it produced was complete enough.

He had to get away. Never mind the fact that he was leaving that very day. A town or two away was not far enough, especially since he did not like or trust his uncle, and Darlene's mother could surely find him, and Uncle O. V. would turn him over to her. Cholly knew it was wrong to run out on a pregnant girl, and recalled, with sympathy, that his father had done just that. Now he understood. He knew then what he must do—find his father. His father would understand. Aunt Jimmy said he had gone to Macon.

With no more thought than a chick leaving its shell, he stepped off the porch. He had gotten a little way when he remembered the treasure; Aunt Jimmy had left something, and he had forgotten all about it. In a stove flue[219] no longer used, she had hidden a little meal bag which she called her treasure. He slipped into the house and found the room empty. Digging into the flue, he encountered webs and soot, and then the soft bag. He sorted the money; fourteen one-dollar bills, two two-dollar bills, and lots of silver change ... twenty-three dollars in all. Surely that would be enough to get to Macon. What a good, strong-sounding word, *Macon*.

Running away from home for a Georgia black boy was not a great problem. You just sneaked away and started walking. When night came you slept in a barn, if there were no dogs, a cane field, or an empty sawmill. You ate from the ground and bought root beer and

---

219 flue: (In early use) chimney; subsequently a smoke-duct in a chimney.

licorice[220] in little country stores. There was always an easy tale of woe to tell inquiring black adults, and whites didn't care, unless they were looking for sport.

When he was several days away, he could go to the back door of nice houses and tell the black cook or white mistress that he wanted a job weeding, plowing, picking, cleaning, and that he lived nearby. A week or more there, and he could take off. He lived this way through the turn of summer, and only the following October did he reach a town big enough to have a regular bus station. Dry-mouthed with excitement and apprehension, he went to the colored side of the counter to buy his ticket.

"How much to Macon, sir?"

"Eleven dollars. Five-fifty for children under twelve."

Cholly had twelve dollars and four cents.

"How old you be?"

"Just on twelve, sir, but my mama only give me ten dollars."

"You jest about the biggest twelve I ever seed."

"Please, sir, I got to get to Macon. My mama's sick."

"Thought you said you mama give you ten dollars."

"That's my play mama. My real mama is in Macon, sir."

"I reckon I knows a lying nigger when I sees one, but jest in case you ain't, jest in case one of them mammies is really dyin' and wants to see her little old smoke before she meets her maker, I gone do it."

Cholly heard nothing. The insults were part of the nuisances of life, like lice. He was happier than he had ever remembered being, except that time with Blue and the watermelon. The bus wasn't leaving for four hours, and the minutes of those hours struggled

---

220 감초(甘草); 말린 감초 뿌리, 그 추출물(약용, 감미료). 여기서는 감초 캔디. (Licorice is a sweet, chewy, aromatic black substance made by evaporation from the juice of a root and used as a candy and in medicine.)

like gnats on fly paper[221]—dying slow, exhausted with the fight to stay alive. Cholly was afraid to stir, even to relieve himself. The bus might leave while he was gone. Finally, rigid with constipation, he boarded the bus to Macon.

He found a window seat in the back all to himself, and all of Georgia slid before his eyes, until the sun shrugged out of sight. Even in the dark, he hungered to see, and only after the fiercest fight to keep his eyes open did he fall asleep. When he awoke it was very well into day, and a fat black lady was nudging him with a biscuit gashed with cold bacon. With the taste of bacon still in his teeth, they sidled into Macon.

At the end of the alley he could see men clustered like grapes. One large whooping voice spiraled over the heads of the bended forms. The kneeling forms, the leaning forms, all intent on one ground spot. As he came closer, he inhaled a rife and stimulating man smell. The men were gathered, just as the man in the pool hall had said, for and about dice and money. Each figure was decorated some way with the slight pieces of green.[222] Some of them had separated their money, folded the bills around their fingers, clenched the fingers into fists, so the neat ends of the money stuck out in a blend of daintiness and violence. Others had stacked their bills, creased them down the middle, and held the wad as though they were about to deal cards. Still others had left their money in loosely crumpled balls. One man had money sticking out from under his cap. Another stroked his bills with a thumb and forefinger. There was more money in those black hands than Cholly had ever seen before. He shared their excitement, and the dry-mouthed apprehension on meeting his father gave way to the saliva flow of excitement. He glanced at the faces, looking for

---

221 fly paper: 파리 잡는 끈끈이 종이
222 green: 지폐(a greenback: a dollar bill)

the one who might be his father. How would he know him? Would he look like a larger version of himself? At that moment Cholly could not remember what his own self looked like. He only knew he was fourteen years old, black, and already six feet tall. He searched the faces and saw only eyes, pleading eyes, cold eyes, eyes gone flat with malice, others laced with fear—all focused on the movement of a pair of dice that one man was throwing, snatching up, and throwing again. Chanting a kind of litany to which the others responded, rubbing the dice as though they were two hot coals, he whispered to them. Then with a whoop the cubes flew from his hand to a chorus of amazements and disappointments. Then the thrower scooped up money, and someone shouted, "Take it and crawl, you water dog,[223] you, the best I know." There was some laughter, and a noticeable release of tension, during which some men exchanged money.

Cholly tapped an old white-haired man on the back.

"Can you tell me is Samson Fuller 'round here somewhere?"

"Fuller?" The name was familiar to the man's tongue. "I don't know, he here somewhere. They he is. In the brown jacket." The man pointed.

A man in a light-brown jacket stood at the far end of the group. He was gesturing in a quarrelsome, agitated manner with another man. Both of them had folded their faces in anger. Cholly edged around to where they stood, hardly believing he was at the end of his journey. There was his father, a man like any other man, but there indeed were his eyes, his mouth, his whole head. His shoulders lurked beneath that jacket, his voice, his hands—all real. They existed, really existed, somewhere. Right here. Cholly had always thought of his father as a giant of a man, so when he was

223 Take it and crawl, you water dog: Water dog은 북미산 도롱뇽, 혹은 물에 길든 개나 사냥용 개를 지칭하기도 하며, 여기서는 노련한 노름꾼을 말한다. "다 긁어가시지."

very close it was with a shock that he discovered that he was taller than his father. In fact, he was staring at a balding spot on his father's head, which he suddenly wanted to stroke. While thus fascinated by the pitiable clean space hedged around by neglected tufts of wool, the man turned a hard, belligerent face to him.

"What you want, boy?"

"Uh. I mean ... is you Samson Fuller?"

"Who sent you?"

"Huh?"

"You Melba's boy?"

"No, sir, I'm ..." Cholly blinked. He could not remember his mother's name. Had he ever known it? What could he say? Whose boy was he? He couldn't say, "I'm your boy." That sounded disrespectful.

The man was impatient. "Something wrong with your head? Who told you to come after me?"

"Nobody." Cholly's hands were sweating. The man's eyes frightened him. "I just thought ... I mean, I was just wandering around, and, uh, my name is Cholly...."

But Fuller had turned back to the game that was about to begin anew. He bent down to toss a bill on the ground, and waited for a throw. When it was gone, he stood up and in a vexed and whiny voice shouted at Cholly, "Tell that bitch she get her money. Now, get the fuck outta my face!"

Cholly was a long time picking his foot up from the ground. He was trying to back up and walk away. Only with extreme effort could he get the first muscle to cooperate. When it did, he walked back up the alley, out of its shade, toward the blazing light of the street. As he emerged into the sun, he felt something in his legs give way. An orange crate with a picture of clasping hands pasted on its side was upended on the sidewalk. Cholly sat down on it. The sunshine dropped like honey on his head. A horse-drawn fruit wagon went by, its driver singing: "Fresh from the vine, sweet as sugar, red as wine."

Noises seemed to increase in volume. The clic-cloc of the women's heels, the laughter of idling men in doorways. There was a streetcar somewhere. Cholly sat. He knew if he was very still he would be all right. But then the trace of pain edged his eyes, and he had to use everything to send it away. If he was very still, he thought, and kept his eyes on one thing, the tears would not come. So he sat in the dripping honey sun, pulling every nerve and muscle into service to stop the fall of water from his eyes. While straining in this way, focusing every erg of energy on his eyes, his bowels suddenly opened up, and before he could realize what he knew, liquid stools were running down his legs. At the mouth of the alley where his father was, on an orange crate in the sun, on a street full of grown men and women, he had soiled himself like a baby.

In panic he wondered should he wait there, not moving until nighttime? No. His father would surely emerge and see him and laugh. Oh, Lord. He would laugh. Everybody would laugh. There was only one thing to do.

Cholly ran down the street, aware only of silence. People's mouths moved, their feet moved, a car jugged by—but with no sound. A door slammed in perfect soundlessness. His own feet made no sound. The air seemed to strangle him, hold him back. He was pushing through a world of invisible pine sap that threatened to smother him. Still he ran, seeing only silent moving things, until he came to the end of buildings, the beginning of open space, and saw the Ocmulgee River winding ahead. He scooted down a gravelly slope to a pier jutting out over the shallow water. Finding the deepest shadow under the pier, he crouched in it, behind one of the posts. He remained knotted there in fetal position, paralyzed, his fists covering his eyes, for a long time. No sound, no sight, only darkness and heat and the press of his knuckles on his eyelids. He even forgot his messed-up trousers.

Evening came. The dark, the warmth, the quiet, enclosed Cholly like the skin and flesh of an elderberry protecting its own seed.

Cholly stirred. The ache in his head was all he felt. Soon, like bright bits of glass, the events of that afternoon cut into him. At first he saw only money in black fingers, then he thought he was sitting on an uncomfortable chair, but when he looked, it turned out to be the head of a man, a head with a bald spot the size of an orange. When finally these bits merged into full memory, Cholly began to smell himself. He stood up and found himself weak, trembling, and dizzy. He leaned for a moment on the pier post, then took off his pants, underwear, socks, and shoes. He rubbed handfuls of dirt on his shoes; then he crawled to the river edge. He had to find the water's beginning with his hands, for he could not see it clearly. Slowly he swirled his clothes in the water and rubbed them until he thought they were clean. Back near his post, he took off his shirt and wrapped it around his waist, then spread his trousers and underwear on the ground. He squatted down and picked at the rotted wood of the pier. Suddenly he thought of his Aunt Jimmy, her asafetida bag, her four gold teeth, and the purple rag she wore around her head. With a longing that almost split him open, he thought of her handing him a bit of smoked hock out of her dish. He remembered just how she held it—clumsy-like, in three fingers, but with so much affection. No words, just picking up a bit of meat and holding it out to him. And then the tears rushed down his cheeks, to make a bouquet under his chin.

Three women are leaning out of two windows. They see the long clean neck of a new young boy and call to him. He goes to where they are. Inside, it is dark and warm. They give him lemonade in a Mason jar. As he drinks, their eyes float up to him through the bottom of the jar, through the slick sweet water. They give him back his manhood, which he takes aimlessly.

The pieces of Cholly's life could become coherent only in the head of a musician. Only those who talk their talk through the gold of curved metal, or in the touch of black-and-white rectangles and taut skins and strings echoing from wooden corridors, could give true form to his life. Only they would know how to connect the heart of a red watermelon to the asafetida bag to the muscadine to the flashlight on his behind to the fists of money to the lemonade in a Mason jar to a man called Blue and come up with what all of that meant in joy, in pain, in anger, in love, and give it its final and pervading ache of freedom. Only a musician would sense, know, without even knowing that he knew, that Cholly was free. Dangerously free. Free to feel whatever he felt—fear, guilt, shame, love, grief, pity. Free to be tender or violent, to whistle or weep. Free to sleep in doorways or between the white sheets of a singing woman. Free to take a job, free to leave it. He could go to jail and not feel imprisoned, for he had already seen the furtiveness in the eyes of his jailer, free to say, "No, suh," and smile, for he had already killed three white men. Free to take a woman's insults, for his body had already conquered hers. Free even to knock her in the head, for he had already cradled that head in his arms. Free to be gentle when she was sick, or mop her floor, for she knew what and where his maleness was. He was free to drink himself into a silly helplessness, for he had already been a gandy dancer,[224] done thirty days on a chain gang,[225] and picked a woman's bullet out of the calf of his leg. He was free to live his

---

224 a gandy dancer: (美 속어) (철로의 구간) 선로공, 육체 노동자; 혹은 계절 노동자 (Track maintenance workers on a railroad section gang; they are probably named because of the movements made while using tools from the Gandy Manufacturing Company.)

225 a chain gang: (美) 한 쇠사슬에 묶인 죄수들 (a group of convicts chained together while working outside the prison)

fantasies, and free even to die, the how and the when of which held no interest for him. In those days, Cholly was truly free. Abandoned in a junk heap by his mother, rejected for a crap game by his father, there was nothing more to lose. He was alone with his own perceptions and appetites, and they alone interested him.

It was in this godlike state that he met Pauline Williams. And it was Pauline, or rather marrying her, that did for him what the flashlight did not do. The constantness, varietylessness, the sheer weight of sameness drove him to despair and froze his imagination. To be required to sleep with the same woman forever was a curious and unnatural idea to him; to be expected to dredge up enthusiasms for old acts, and routine ploys; he wondered at the arrogance of the female. When he had met Pauline in Kentucky, she was hanging over a fence scratching herself with a broken foot. The neatness, the charm, the joy he awakened in her made him want to nest with her. He had yet to discover what destroyed that desire. But he did not dwell on it. He thought rather of whatever had happened to the curiosity he used to feel. Nothing, nothing, interested him now. Not himself, not other people. Only in drink was there some break, some floodlight, and when that closed, there was oblivion.

But the aspect of married life that dumbfounded him and rendered him totally disfunctional was the appearance of children. Having no idea of how to raise children, and having never watched any parent raise himself, he could not even comprehend what such a relationship should be. Had he been interested in the accumulation of things, he could have thought of them as his material heirs; had he needed to prove himself to some nameless "others," he could have wanted them to excel in his own image and for his own sake. Had he not been alone in the world since he was thirteen, knowing only a dying old woman who felt responsible for him, but whose age, sex, and interests were so remote from his own, he might have felt a stable connection between himself and the children. As it was, he reacted to them, and his reactions were based on what he felt at the moment.

So it was on a Saturday afternoon, in the thin light of spring, he staggered home reeling drunk and saw his daughter in the kitchen.

She was washing dishes. Her small back hunched over the sink. Cholly saw her dimly and could not tell what he saw or what he felt. Then he became aware that he was uncomfortable; next he felt the discomfort dissolve into pleasure. The sequence of his emotions was revulsion, guilt, pity, then love. His revulsion was a reaction to her young, helpless, hopeless presence. Her back hunched that way; her head to one side as though crouching from a permanent and unrelieved blow. Why did she have to look so whipped? She was a child—unburdened—why wasn't she happy? The clear statement of her misery was an accusation. He wanted to break her neck—but tenderly. Guilt and impotence rose in a bilious duet.[226] What could he do for her—ever? What give her? What say to her? What could a burned-out[227] black man say to the hunched back of his eleven-year-old daughter? If he looked into her face, he would see those haunted, loving eyes. The hauntedness would irritate him—the love would move him to fury. How dare she love him? Hadn't she any sense at all? What was he supposed to do about that? Return it? How? What could his calloused hands produce to make her smile? What of his knowledge of the world and of life could be useful to her? What could his heavy arms and befuddled brain accomplish that would earn him his own respect, that would in turn allow him to accept her love? His hatred of her slimed in his stomach and threatened to become vomit. But just before the puke moved from

---

226 Guilt and...in a bilious duet: 죄책감과 무능함에 대한 인식이 구토하듯이 함께 솟아올랐다.

227 burnt-out(=burned-out): 녹초가 되다: Widely used "(of a person) in a state of physical or mental collapse caused by overwork or stress."

anticipation to sensation, she shifted her weight and stood on one foot scratching the back of her calf with her toe. It was a quiet and pitiful gesture. Her hands were going around and around a frying pan, scraping flecks of black into cold, greasy dishwater. The timid, tucked-in look of the scratching toe—that was what Pauline was doing the first time he saw her in Kentucky. Leaning over a fence staring at nothing in particular. The creamy toe of her bare foot scratching a velvet leg. It was such a small and simple gesture, but it filled him then with a wondering softness. Not the usual lust to part tight legs with his own, but a tenderness, a protectiveness. A desire to cover her foot with his hand and gently nibble away the itch from the calf with his teeth. He did it then, and startled Pauline into laughter. He did it now.

The tenderness welled up in him, and he sank to his knees, his eyes on the foot of his daughter. Crawling on all fours toward her, he raised his hand and caught the foot in an upward stroke. Pecola lost her balance and was about to careen to the floor. Cholly raised his other hand to her hips to save her from falling. He put his head down and nibbled at the back of her leg. His mouth trembled at the firm sweetness of the flesh. He closed his eyes, letting his fingers dig into her waist. The rigidness of her shocked body, the silence of her stunned throat, was better than Pauline's easy laughter had been. The confused mixture of his memories of Pauline and the doing of a wild and forbidden thing excited him, and a bolt of desire ran down his genitals, giving it length, and softening the lips of his anus. Surrounding all of this lust was a border of politeness. He wanted to fuck her—tenderly. But the tenderness would not hold. The tightness of her vagina was more than he could bear. His soul seemed to slip down to his guts and fly out into her, and the gigantic thrust he made into her then provoked the only sound she made—a hollow suck of air in the back of her throat. Like the rapid loss of air from a circus balloon.

Following the disintegration—the falling away—of sexual desire, he was conscious of her wet, soapy hands on his wrists, the fingers clenching, but whether her grip was from a hopeless but stubborn struggle to be free, or from some other emotion, he could not tell.

Removing himself from her was so painful to him he cut it short and snatched his genitals out of the dry harbor of her vagina. She appeared to have fainted. Cholly stood up and could see only her grayish panties, so sad and limp around her ankles. Again the hatred mixed with tenderness. The hatred would not let him pick her up, the tenderness forced him to cover her.

So when the child regained consciousness, she was lying on the kitchen floor under a heavy quilt, trying to connect the pain between her legs with the face of her mother looming over her.

SEETHEDOGBOWWOWGOESTHEDOG DOYOUWANTTOPLAYDOYOUWANT TOPLAYWITHJANESEETHEDOGRUNR

Once there was an old man who loved things, for the slightest contact with people produced in him a faint but persistent nausea. He could not remember when this distaste began, nor could he remember ever being free of it. As a young boy he had been greatly disturbed by this revulsion which others did not seem to share, but having got a fine education, he learned, among other things, the word "misanthrope." Knowing his label provided him with both comfort and courage, he believed that to name an evil was to neutralize if not annihilate it. Then, too, he had read several books and made the acquaintance of several great misanthropes of the ages, whose spiritual company soothed him and provided him with yardsticks for measuring his whims, his yearnings, and his antipathies. Moreover, he found misanthropy an excellent means of developing character: when he subdued his revulsion and occasionally touched, helped, counseled, or befriended somebody, he was able to think of his behavior as generous and his intentions as noble. When he was enraged by some human effort or flaw, he was able to regard himself as discriminating, fastidious, and full of nice scruples.

As in the case of many misanthropes, his disdain for people led him into a profession designed to serve them. He was engaged in a line of work that was dependent solely on his ability to win the trust of others, and one in which the most intimate relationships were necessary. Having dallied with the priesthood in the Anglican Church, he abandoned it to become a caseworker. Time and misfortune, however, conspired against him, and he settled finally on a profession that brought him both freedom and satisfaction. He became a "Reader, Adviser, and Interpreter of Dreams." It was a profession that suited him well. His hours were his own, the competition was slight, the clientele was already persuaded and therefore manageable, and he had numerous opportunities to witness human stupidity without sharing it or being compromised by it, and to nurture his fastidiousness by viewing physical decay.[228] Although his income was small, he had no taste for luxury—his experience in the monastery had solidified his natural asceticism while it developed his preference for solitude. Celibacy was a haven, silence a shield.

All his life he had a fondness for things—not the acquisition of wealth or beautiful objects, but a genuine love of worn objects: a coffee pot that had been his mother's, a welcome mat[229] from the door of a rooming house[230] he once lived in, a quilt from a Salvation Army[231] store counter. It was as though his disdain of human

---

228 by viewing physical decay: 늙어가는 자신의 육신을 바라보면서

229 a welcome mat: (현관의) welcome이라는 글이 새겨진 도어 매트(구두 흙 터는 매트), 신발 털개

230 a rooming house: 《美, 캐나다》 (식사를 제공하지 않는) 하숙집(a private house in which rooms are rented for living or staying temporarily)

231 Salvation Army: 구세군

contact had converted itself into a craving for things humans had touched. The residue of the human spirit smeared on inanimate objects was all he could withstand of humanity. To contemplate, for example, evidence of human footsteps on the mat—absorb the smell of the quilt and wallow in the sweet certainty that many bodies had sweated, slept, dreamed, made love, been ill, and even died under it. Wherever he went, he took along his things, and was always searching for others. This thirst for worn things led to casual but habitual examinations of trash barrels in alleys and wastebaskets in public places....

All in all, his personality was an arabesque: intricate, symmetrical, balanced, and tightly constructed[232]—except for one flaw. The careful design was marred occasionally by rare but keen sexual cravings.

He could have been an active homosexual but lacked the courage. Bestiality did not occur to him, and sodomy was quite out of the question, for he did not experience sustained erections and could not endure the thought of somebody else's. And besides, the one thing that disgusted him more than entering and caressing a woman was caressing and being caressed by a man. In any case, his cravings, although intense, never relished physical contact. He abhorred flesh on flesh. Body odor, breath odor, overwhelmed him. The sight of dried matter in the corner of the eye,[233] decayed or missing teeth, ear wax, blackheads,[234] moles, blisters, skin crusts—all the natural excretions and protections the body was capable of—disquieted him. His attentions therefore gradually settled on those humans whose bodies were least offensive—children. And since he was too diffident to confront homosexuality, and since little boys were

---

232 His personality was an arabesque: intricate, symmetrical, balanced, and tightly constructed: 그의 성격은 복잡하고 뒤얽히고, 대칭적이며, 균형이 잡히고, 견고하게 구성된 아라비아풍의 장식 무늬였다.

233 dried matter in the corner of the eye: 눈곱

234 blackheads: (=comedo) 여드름(small, dark spots on someone's skin caused by blocked pores)

insulting, scary, and stubborn, he further limited his interests to little girls. They were usually manageable and frequently seductive. His sexuality was anything but lewd; his patronage of little girls smacked of innocence and was associated in his mind with cleanliness. He was what one might call a very clean old man.

A cinnamon-eyed West Indian with lightly browned skin.

Although his given name was printed on the sign in his kitchen window, and on the business cards he circulated, he was called by the townspeople Soaphead Church. No one knew where the "Church" part came from—perhaps somebody's recollection of his days as a guest preacher—those reverends who had been called but who had no flock or coop,[235] and were constantly visiting other churches, sitting on the altar with the host preacher. But everybody knew what "Soaphead" meant—the tight, curly hair that took on and held a sheen and wave when pomaded with soap lather. A sort of primitive process.

He had been reared in a family proud of its academic accomplishments and its mixed blood—in fact, they believed the former was based on the latter. A Sir Whitcomb, some decaying British nobleman, who chose to disintegrate under a sun more easeful than England's, had introduced the white strain into the family in the early 1800's. Being a gentleman by order of the King, he had done the civilized thing for his mulatto bastard—provided it with three hundred pounds sterling, to the great satisfaction of the bastard's mother, who felt that fortune had smiled on her. The bastard too was grateful, and regarded as his life's goal the hoarding of this white strain.[236] He bestowed his favors on a fifteen-year-old girl of similar parentage. She, like a good Victorian parody,[237] learned from her husband all that was

---

235 coop: a fenced-off area

236 the hoarding of the white strain: 백인 가문의 혈통을 지키는 일

237 like a good Victorian parody: 빅토리아 시대를 꽤나 모방하여

worth learning—to separate herself in body, mind, and spirit from all that suggested Africa; to cultivate the habits, tastes, preferences that her absent father-in-law[238] and foolish mother-in-law would have approved.

They transferred this Anglophilia[239] to their six children and sixteen grandchildren. Except for an occasional and unaccountable insurgent who chose a restive black,[240] they married "up,"[241] lightening the family complexion and thinning out the family features.[242]

With the confidence born of a conviction of superiority, they performed well at schools. They were industrious, orderly, and energetic, hoping to prove beyond a doubt De Gobineau's hypothesis[243] that "all civilizations derive from the white race, that none can exist without its help, and that a society is great and brilliant only so far as it preserves the blood of the noble group that created it." Thus, they were seldom overlooked by schoolmasters who recommended promising students for study abroad. The men studied medicine, law, theology, and emerged repeatedly in the powerless government offices available to the native population. That they were corrupt in public and private practice, both lecherous and lascivious, was considered their noble

---

238 her absent father-in-law: 그녀의 부재(不在)한 시아버지. 여기서는 Sir Whitlock을 지칭함

239 Anglophilia: 잉글랜드(영국) 숭배 (a term applied to someone who has an enormous admiration for and devotion to things British)

240 Except for an occasional and unaccountable insurgent who chose a restive black: 이따금 알 수 없는 이유로 반항하며, 고집스런 흑인을 배우자로 선택하는 경우를 제외하고는.

241 They married "up": 그들은 결혼을 통해 신분을 상승시켰다.

242 lightening the family complexion and thinning out the family features: 얼굴 피부색을 점점 하얗게 하고 가계의 외모를 희석해 가면서

243 De Gobineau's hypothesis: 아르튀르 드 고비노(Arthur de Gobineau, 1816～1882). 19세기의 프랑스 인종학자, 사회이론가이자 백인우월주의자. 『인종 불평등론(Essay on the Inequality of Human Races)』(1854)등의 저서가 있다. 인종주의 이론의 선구자로 유명하며 그의 이론은 나치의 이념에 영향을 끼쳤다.

right, and thoroughly enjoyed by most of the less gifted population.

As the years passed, due to the carelessness of some of the Whitcomb brothers, it became difficult to maintain their whiteness, and some distant and some not so distant relatives married each other. No obviously bad effects were noticed from these ill-advised unions, but one or two old maids or gardener boys marked a weakening of faculties and a disposition toward eccentricity in some of the children. Some flaw outside the usual alcoholism and lechery. They blamed the flaw on intermarriage with the family, however, not on the original genes of the decaying lord. In any case, there were flukes.[244] No more than in any other family, to be sure, but more dangerous because more powerful. One of them was a religious fanatic who founded his own secret sect and fathered four sons, one of whom became a schoolmaster known for the precision of his justice and the control in his violence. This schoolmaster married a sweet, indolent half-Chinese girl for whom the fatigue of bearing a son was too much. She died soon after childbirth. Her son, named Elihue Micah Whitcomb, provided the schoolmaster with ample opportunity to work out his theories of education, discipline, and the good life. Little Elihue learned everything he needed to know well, particularly the fine art of self-deception. He read greedily but understood selectively, choosing the bits and pieces of other men's ideas that supported whatever predilection he had at the moment. Thus he chose to remember Hamlet's abuse of Ophelia,[245] but not Christ's love of Mary

---

244 fluke: 플루크(우연히 맞기) A successful stroke made by accident or chance in billiards-playing. Hence generally. a lucky stroke, an unexpected success; a piece of good luck.

245 Hamlet's abuse of Ophelia: 햄릿은 자신을 사랑하는 오필리아를 혼란스럽게 만들며, 우발적으로 그녀의 아버지 폴로니어스를 죽이게 됨으로써 그녀가 실성하여 물에 빠져 사망하게 만든다.

Magdalene;[246] Hamlet's frivolous politics, but not Christ's serious anarchy. He noticed Gibbon's[247] acidity, but not his tolerance, Othello's love for the fair Desdemona, but not Iago's perverted love of Othello.[248] The works he admired most were Dante's[249]; those he despised most were Dostoyevsky's.[250] For all his exposure to the best minds of the Western world, he allowed only the narrowest interpretation to touch him. He responded to his father's controlled violence by developing hard habits and a soft imagination. A hatred of, and fascination with, any hint of disorder or decay.

At seventeen, however, he met his Beatrice,[251] who was three years his senior. A lovely, laughing big-legged girl who worked as a clerk in a Chinese department store. Velma. So strong was her affection and zest for life, she did not eliminate the frail, sickly Elihue from it. She found his fastidiousness and complete lack of humor touching and longed to introduce him to the idea of delight. He resisted the introduction, but she married him anyway, only to discover that he was suffering from and enjoying an invincible

---

246 Christ's love of Mary Magdalene: 막달라 마리아에 대한 예수의 사랑

247 Gibbon, Edward(1737-1794): 『로마제국 쇠망사(*History of the Decline and Fall of the Roman Empire*)』로 유명하다. 로마의 멸망이 기독교 정신의 융성과 관련이 있다고 봄.

248 Othello's love for the fair Desdemona, but not Iago's perverted love of Othello: 오셀로가 아름다운 데스데모나를 사랑한 것은 이해했지만 이아고가 오셀로에 대해 왜곡된 감정을 품었던 것은 놓쳤다는 뜻. 무어(Moor)인 장군 오셀로는 젊고 아름다운 데스데모나와 결혼하지만 이아고의 모함으로 질투심에 빠져 그녀를 죽인다.

249 Dante(1265–1321): 이탈리아 시인. 피렌체 출생. <지옥>, <연옥>, <천당>으로 구성된 대작 『신곡(*Divine Comedy*)』을 통해 중세의 정신을 종합하여 문예부흥의 선구자가 되어 인류문화가 지향할 목표를 제시하였다.

250 Fyodor (Mikhailovich) Dostoevsky (1821–1881): 러시아의 소설가. 모스크바 출생. 톨스토이와 함께 19세기 러시아 문학을 대표하는 세계적인 문호이다. 인간의 내면을 추구하여 근대소설의 새로운 가능성을 열어놓았다.

251 Beatrice: 단테가 열 아홉 살에 만나 사랑한 연인으로, 그는 유럽인들이 삶의 교과서로 여기는 『신곡』에서 그녀를 신에 버금가는 신성하고 고귀한 존재로 격상시켰다.

melancholy. When she learned two months into the marriage how important his melancholy was to him, that he was very interested in altering her joy to a more academic gloom, that he equated lovemaking with communion and the Holy Grail,[252] she simply left. She had not lived by the sea all those years, listened to the wharfman's songs all that time, to spend her life in the soundless cave of Elihue's mind.

He never got over her desertion. She was to have been the answer to his unstated, unacknowledged question—where was the life to counter the encroaching nonlife? Velma was to rescue him from the nonlife he had learned on the flat side of his father's belt.[253] But he resisted her with such skill that she was finally driven out to escape the inevitable boredom produced by such a dainty life.

Young Elihue was saved from visible shattering by the steady hand of his father, who reminded him of the family's reputation and Velma's questionable one. He then pursued his studies with more vigor than before and decided at last to enter the ministry. When he was advised that he had no avocation, he left the island, came to America to study the then budding field of psychiatry. But the subject required too much truth, too many confrontations, and offered too little support to a failing ego. He drifted into sociology, then physical therapy. This diverse education continued for six years, when his father refused to support him any longer, until he "found" himself. Elihue, not knowing where to look, was thrown back on his own devices, and "found" himself quite unable to earn money. He began to sink into a rapidly fraying gentility, punctuated with a few of the white-collar occupations available to black people, regardless of their noble bloodlines, in America: desk

---

252 the Holy Grail: 성배(聖杯) (그리스도가 최후의 만찬에서 사용했다고 전해지는 술잔)

253 the nonlife he had learned on the flat side of his father's belt: 아버지에게서 배운 활기없는 삶

clerk at a colored hotel in Chicago, insurance agent, traveling salesman for a cosmetics firm catering to blacks. He finally settled in Lorain, Ohio, in 1931, palming himself off as a minister, and inspiring awe with the way he spoke English. The women of the town early discovered his celibacy, and not being able to comprehend his rejection of them, decided that he was supernatural rather than unnatural.

Once he understood their decision, he quickly followed through, accepting the name (Soaphead Church) and the role they had given him. He rented a kind of back-room[254] apartment from a deeply religious old lady named Bertha Reese. She was clean, quiet, and very close to total deafness. The lodgings were ideal in every way but one. Bertha Reese had an old dog, Bob, who, although as deaf and quiet as she, was not as clean. He slept most of his days away on the back porch, which was Elihue's entrance. The dog was too old to be of any use, and Bertha Reese had not the strength or presence of mind to care for him properly. She fed him, and watered him, left him alone. The dog was mangy; his exhausted eyes ran with a sea-green matter around which gnats and flies clustered.[255] Soaphead was revolted by Bob and wished he would hurry up and die. He regarded this wish for the dog's death as humane, for he could not bear, he told himself, to see anything suffer. It did not occur to him that he was really concerned about his own suffering, since the dog had adjusted himself to frailty and old age. Soaphead finally determined to put an end to the animal's misery, and bought some poison with which to do it. Only the horror of having to go near him had prevented Soaphead from completing his mission. He waited for rage or blinding revulsion to

---

254 back-room: a room at the back of a house or other building.

255 The dog was mangy; his exhausted eyes ran with a sea-green matter around which gnats and flies clustered. 그 개는 옴 투성이였고, 지친 눈은 푸르스름한 것이 흘러내리고 주위에는 각다귀와 파리들이 달라붙었다.

spur him.

Living there among his worn things, rising early every morning from dreamless sleeps, he counseled those who sought his advice.

His business was dread. People came to him in dread, whispered in dread, wept and pleaded in dread. And dread was what he counseled.

Singly they found their way to his door, wrapped each in a shroud stitched with anger, yearning, pride, vengeance, loneliness, misery, defeat, and hunger. They asked for the simplest of things: love, health, and money. Make him love me. Tell me what this dream means. Help me get rid of this woman. Make my mother give me back my clothes. Stop my left hand from shaking. Keep my baby's ghost off the stove. Break so-and-so's fix.[256] To all of these requests he addressed himself. His practice was to do what he was bid—not to suggest to a party that perhaps the request was unfair, mean, or hopeless.

With only occasional, and increasingly rare, encounters with the little girls he could persuade to be entertained by him, he lived rather peaceably among his things, admitting to no regrets. He was aware, of course, that something was awry in his life, and all lives, but put the problem where it belonged, at the foot of the Originator of Life.[257] He believed that since decay, vice, filth, and disorder were pervasive, they must be in the Nature of Things. Evil existed because God had created it. He, God, had made a sloven and unforgivable error in judgment: designing an imperfect universe. Theologians justified the presence of corruption as a means by which men strove, were tested, and triumphed. A triumph of cosmic neatness. But this neatness, the neatness of Dante, was in the orderly sectioning and segregating of all levels of evil and decay. In the world it was not so. The most exquisite-

---

256 Break so-and-so's fix: 누구에게 씌워진 주술을 풀어달라고.

257 the Originator of Life: 만물의 창조자인 조물주

looking ladies sat on toilets, and the most dreadful-looking had pure and holy yearnings. God had done a poor job, and Soaphead suspected that he himself could have done better. It was in fact a pity that the Maker had not sought his counsel.

Soaphead was reflecting once again on these thoughts one late hot afternoon when he heard a tap on his door. Opening it, he saw a little girl, quite unknown to him. She was about twelve or so, he thought, and seemed to him pitifully unattractive. When he asked her what she wanted, she did not answer, but held out to him one of his cards advertising his gifts and services: "If you are overcome with trouble and conditions that are not natural, I can remove them; Overcome Spells, Bad Luck, and Evil Influences. Remember, I am a true Spiritualist and Psychic Reader, born with power, and I will help you. Satisfaction in one visit. During many years of practice I have brought together many in marriage and reunited many who were separated. If you are unhappy, discouraged, or in distress, I can help you. Does bad luck seem to follow you? Has the one you love changed? I can tell you why. I will tell you who your enemies and friends are, and if the one you love is true or false. If you are sick, I can show you the way to health. I locate lost and stolen articles. Satisfaction guaranteed."

Soaphead Church told her to come in.

"What can I do for you, my child?"

She stood there, her hands folded across her stomach, a little protruding pot of tummy. "Maybe. Maybe you can do it for me."

"Do what for you?"

"I can't go to school no more. And I thought maybe you could help me."

"Help you how? Tell me. Don't be frightened."

"My eyes."

"What about your eyes?"

"I want them blue."

Soaphead pursed his lips, and let his tongue stroke a gold inlay. He thought it was at once the most fantastic and the most logical petition he had ever received. Here was an ugly little girl asking for beauty. A surge of love and understanding swept through him, but was quickly replaced by anger. Anger that he was powerless to help her. Of all the wishes people had brought him—money, love, revenge—this seemed to him the most poignant and the one most deserving of fulfillment. A little black girl who wanted to rise up out of the pit of her blackness and see the world with blue eyes. His outrage grew and felt like power. For the first time he honestly wished he could work miracles. Never before had he really wanted the true and holy power—only the power to make others believe he had it. It seemed so sad, so frivolous, that mere mortality, not judgment, kept him from it. Or did it?

With a trembling hand he made the sign of the cross over her. His flesh crawled; in that hot, dim little room of worn things, he was chilled.

"I can do nothing for you, my child. I am not a magician. I work only through the Lord. He sometimes uses me to help people. All I can do is offer myself to Him as the instrument through which he works. If He wants your wish granted, He will do it."

Soaphead walked to the window, his back to the girl. His mind raced, stumbled, and raced again. How to frame the next sentence? How to hang on to the feeling of power. His eye fell on old Bob sleeping on the porch.

"We must make, ah, some offering, that is, some contact with nature. Perhaps some simple creature might be the vehicle through which He will speak. Let us see."

He knelt down at the window, and moved his lips. After what seemed a suitable length of time, he rose and went to the icebox that stood near the other window. From it he removed a small packet wrapped in pinkish butcher paper. From a shelf he took a small brown bottle and sprinkled some of its contents on the substance inside the paper. He put the packet, partly opened, on the table.

"Take this food and give it to the creature sleeping on the porch. Make sure he eats it. And mark well how he behaves. If nothing happens, you will know that God has refused you. If the animal behaves strangely, your wish will be granted on the day following this one."

The girl picked up the packet; the odor of the dark, sticky meat made her want to vomit. She put a hand on her stomach.

"Courage. Courage, my child. These things are not granted to faint hearts."

She nodded and swallowed visibly, holding down the vomit. Soaphead opened the door, and she stepped over the threshold.

"Good-bye, God bless," he said and quickly shut the door. At the window he stood watching her, his eyebrows pulled together into waves of compassion, his tongue fondling the worn gold in his upper jaw. He saw the girl bending down to the sleeping dog, who, at her touch, opened one liquid eye, matted in the corners with what looked like green glue. She reached out and touched the dog's head, stroking him gently. She placed the meat on the floor of the porch, near his nose. The odor roused him; he lifted his head, and got up to smell it better. He ate it in three or four gulps. The girl stroked his head again, and the dog looked up at her with soft triangle eyes. Suddenly he coughed, the cough of a phlegmy old man[258]—and got to his feet. The girl jumped. The dog gagged, his mouth chomping the air, and promptly fell down. He tried to raise himself, could not, tried again, and half-fell down the steps. Choking, stumbling, he moved like a broken toy around the yard. The girl's mouth was open, a little petal of tongue showing. She made a wild, pointless gesture with one hand and then covered her

---

258 the cough of a phlegmy old man: 가래가 많은 노인의 기침소리 같았다.

mouth with both hands. She was trying not to vomit. The dog fell again, a spasm jerking his body. Then he was quiet. The girl's hands covering her mouth, she backed away a few feet, then turned, ran out of the yard and down the walk.

Soaphead Church went to the table. He sat down, with folded hands balancing his forehead on the balls of his thumbs. Then he rose and went to a tiny night table with a drawer, from which he took paper and a fountain pen. A bottle of ink was on the same shelf that held the poison. With these things he sat again at the table. Slowly, carefully, relishing his penmanship, he wrote the following letter:

Att: TO HE WHO GREATLY ENNOBLED HUMAN NATURE BY CREATING IT

Dear God:

The Purpose of this letter is to familiarize you with facts which either have escaped your notice, or which you have chosen to ignore.

Once upon a time I lived greenly and youngish on one of your islands. An island of the archipelago in the South Atlantic between North and South America, enclosing the Caribbean Sea and the Gulf of Mexico: divided into the Greater Antilles,[259] the Lesser Antilles, and the Bahama Islands. Not the Windward or Leeward Island colonies, mark you, but within, of course, the Greater of the two Antilles (while the precision of my prose may be, at times, laborious, it is necessary that I identify myself to you clearly).

Now.

We in this colony took as our own the most dramatic, and the most obvious, of our white master's characteristics, which were, of course, their worst. In retaining the identity of our race, we held fast to those characteristics most gratifying to sustain and least

---

259 Antilles: the islands forming the greater part of the West Indies in the Caribbean

troublesome to maintain. Consequently we were not royal but snobbish, not aristocratic but class-conscious; we believed authority was cruelty to our inferiors, and education was being at school. We mistook violence for passion, indolence for leisure, and thought recklessness was freedom. We raised our children and reared our crops; we let infants grow, and property develop. Our manhood was denned by acquisitions. Our womanhood by acquiescence. And the smell of your fruit and the labor of your days we abhorred.

This morning, before the little black girl came, I cried—for Velma. Oh, not aloud. There is no wind to carry, bear, or even refuse to bear, a sound so heavy with regret. But in my silent own lone way, I cried—for Velma. You need to know about Velma to understand what I did today.

She (Velma) left me the way people leave a hotel room. A hotel room is a place to be when you are doing something else. Of itself it is of no consequence to one's major scheme. A hotel room is convenient. But its convenience is limited to the time you need it while you are in that particular town on that particular business; you hope it is comfortable, but prefer, rather, that it be anonymous. It is not, after all, where you *live*.

When you no longer need it, you pay a little something for its use; say, "Thank you, sir," and when your business in that town is over, you go away from that room. Does anybody regret leaving a hotel room? Does anybody, who has a home, a real home somewhere, want to stay there? Does anybody look back with affection, or even disgust, at a hotel room when they leave it? You can only love or despise whatever *living* was done in that room. But the room itself? But you take a souvenir. Not, oh, not, to remember the room. To remember, rather, the time and the place of your business, your adventure. What can anyone feel for a hotel room? One doesn't any more feel for a hotel room than one expects a hotel room to feel for its occupant.

That, heavenly, heavenly Father, was how she left me; or rather, she never left me, because she was never ever there.

You remember, do you, how and of what we are made? Let me tell you now about the breasts of little girls. I apologize for the inappropriateness (is that it?), the imbalance of loving them at awkward times of day, and in awkward places, and the tastelessness of loving those which belonged to members of my family. Do I have to apologize for loving strangers?

But you too are amiss here, Lord. How, why, did you allow it to happen? How is it I could lift my eyes from the contemplation of Your Body and fall deeply into the contemplation of theirs? The buds. The buds on some of these saplings. They were mean, you know, mean and tender. Mean little buds resisting the touch, springing like rubber. But aggressive. Daring me to touch. Commanding me to touch. Not a bit shy, as you'd suppose. They stuck out at me, oh yes, at me. Slender-chested, finger-chested lassies. Have you ever seen them, Lord? I mean, really seen them? One could not see them and not love them. You who made them must have considered them lovely even as an idea—how much more lovely is the manifestation of that idea. I couldn't, as you must recall, keep my hands, my mouth, off them. Salt-sweet. Like not quite ripe strawberries covered with the light salt sweat of running days and hopping, skipping, jumping hours.

The love of them—the touch, taste, and feel of them—was not just an easy luxurious human vice; they were, for me, A Thing To Do Instead.[260] Instead of papa, instead of the Cloth, instead of Velma, and I *chose* not to do without them. But I didn't go into the church. At least I didn't do that. As to what I did do? I told people I knew all about You. That I had received Your Powers. It was not a complete *lie*; but it was a *complete* lie. I should never

260 A Thing to Do Instead: 대신 마땅히 할 일.

have, I admit, I should never have taken their money in exchange for well-phrased, well-placed, well-faced lies. But, mark you, I hated it. Not for a moment did I love the lies or the money.

But consider: The woman who left the hotel room.

Consider: The greentime, the noontime of the archipelago.

Consider: Their hopeful eyes that were outdone only by their hoping breasts.

Consider: How I needed a comfortable evil to prevent my knowing what I could not bear to know.

Consider: How I hated and despised the money.

And now, consider: Not according to my just deserts, but according to *my* mercy, the little black girl that came a-looning at me today. Tell me, Lord, how could you leave a lass so long so lone that she could find her way to me? How could you? I weep for you, Lord. And it is because I weep for You that I had to do your work for You.

Do you know what she came for? Blue eyes. New, blue eyes, she said. Like she was buying shoes. "I'd like a pair of new blue eyes." She must have asked you for them for a very long time, and you hadn't replied. (A habit, I could have told her, a long-ago habit broken for Job[261]—but no more.) She came to *me* for them. She had one of my cards. (Card enclosed.) By the way, I added the Micah—Elihue Micah Whitcomb. But I am called Soaphead Church. I cannot remember how or why I got the name. What makes one name more a person than another? Is the name the real thing, then? And the person only what his name says? Is that why to the simplest and friendliest of questions: "What is your name?" put to you by Moses,[262] You would not say, and said instead "I am

261 Job: 구약성서 《욥기》의 주인공으로 잇따른 재난으로 재산과 열 명의 자녀를 모두 잃고 건강마저 잃었지만 이 모든 혹한 시련을 견뎌내고 하느님에 대한 믿음을 굳게 지킨 인물.

262 Moses: 《출애굽기》 3:14. And God said unto Moses, I AM THAT I AM: and he said, Thus shalt thou say unto the children of Israel.

who I am." Like Popeye?[263] I Yam What I Yam? Afraid you were, weren't you, to give out your name? Afraid they would know the name and then know you? Then they wouldn't fear you? It's quite all right. Don't be vexed. I mean no offense. I understand. I have been a bad man too, and an unhappy man too. But someday *I* will die. I was always so kind. Why do I have to die? The little girls. The little girls are the only things I'll miss. Do you know that when I touched their sturdy little tits and bit them—just a little—I felt I was being friendly? I didn't want to kiss their mouths or sleep in the bed with them or take a child bride for my own. Playful, I felt, and friendly. Not like the newspapers said. Not like the people whispered. And they didn't mind at all. Not at all. Remember how so many of them came back? No one would even try to understand that. If I'd been hurting them, would they have come back? Two of them, Doreen and Sugar Babe, they'd come together. I gave them mints, money, and they'd eat ice cream with their legs open while I played with them. It was like a party. And there wasn't nastiness, and there wasn't any filth, and there wasn't any odor, and there wasn't any groaning—just the light white laughter of little girls and me. And there wasn't any look—any long funny look—any long funny Velma look afterward. No look that makes you feel dirty afterward. That makes you want to die. With little girls it is all clean and good and friendly.

You have to understand that, Lord. You said, "Suffer little children to come unto me, and harm them not."[264] Did you forget? Did you forget about the children? Yes. You forgot. You let them go wanting, sit on road shoulders, crying next to their dead mothers.

---

263 Popeye: I YAM WHAT I YAM (1933) was the first official Popeye cartoon released by Max Fleischer's animation studio.

264 Suffer the little children to come unto me, and harm [orig. forbid] them not: 《마가복음》 10:14.

I've seen them charred, lame, halt. You forgot, Lord. You forgot how and when to be God.

That's why I changed the little black girl's eyes for her, and I didn't touch her; not a finger did I lay on her. But I gave her those blue eyes she wanted. Not for pleasure, and not for money. I did what You did not, could not, would not do: I looked at that ugly little black girl, and I loved her. I played You.[265] And it was a very good show!

I, I have caused a miracle. I gave her the eyes. I gave her the blue, blue, two blue eyes. Cobalt blue. A streak of it right out of your own blue heaven. No one else will see her blue eyes. But *she* will. And she will live happily ever after. I, I have found it meet and right so to do.[266]

Now you are jealous. You are jealous of me.

You see? I, too, have created. Not aboriginally, like you, but creation is a heady wine,[267] more for the taster than the brewer.

Having therefore imbibed, as it were, of the nectar,[268] I am not afraid of You, of Death, not even of Life, and it's all right about Velma; and it's all right about Papa; and it's all right about the Greater and the Lesser Antilles. Quite all right. Quite.

---

265 I played You. 내가 당신 [즉 하나님] 노릇을 했소.

266 meet and right so to do: (Hymn 221)

MEET and right it is to sing,
In every time and place,
Glory to our heavenly King,
The God of truth and grace;
Join we then with sweet accord,
All in one thanksgiving join,
Holy, holy, holy Lord,
Eternal praise be thine!

267 a heady wine: In simple terms, a heady wine would be one that is high in alcohol. To the taster, this occurs on the first sniff and sends one's head backward to mentally re-group before the second evaluation.

268 Having. . . imbibed. . . of the nectar (=the drink of the gods): For the Yogi who has imbibed the Delightful Nectar of God Enjoys Immortality.

With kindest regards, I remain,

Your,

Elihue Micah Whitcomb

Soaphead Church folded the sheets of paper into three equal parts and slipped them into an envelope. Although he had no seal, he longed for sealing wax. He removed a cigar box from under the bed and rummaged about in it. There were some of his most precious things: a sliver of jade that had dislodged from a cuff link at the Chicago hotel; a gold pendant shaped like a Y with a piece of coral attached to it that had belonged to the mother he never knew; four large hairpins that Velma had left on the rim of the bathroom sink; a powder blue grosgrain[269] ribbon from the head of a little girl named Precious Jewel; a blackened faucet head from the sink in a jail cell in Cincinnati; two marbles he had found under a bench in Morningside Park[270] on a very fine spring day; an old Lucky Hart[271] catalog that smelled still of nut-brown and mocha face powder, and lemon vanishing cream. Distracted by his things, he forgot what he had been looking for. The effort to recall was too great; there was a buzzing in his head, and a wash of fatigue overcame him. He closed his box, eased himself out on the bed, and slipped into an ivory sleep from which he could not hear the tiny yelps of an old lady who had come out of her candy store and found the still carcass of an old dog named Bob.

---

269 grosgrain: 그로그렝 (비단, 또는 인조견으로 이랑 무늬지게 짠 천) A heavy, ribbed fabric, typically of silk or rayon.

270 Morningside Park: a New York City public park in northern Manhattan.

271 Lucky Hart: a brand name

Summer

I have only to break into the tightness of a strawberry, and I see summer—its dust and lowering skies. It remains for me a season of storms. The parched days and sticky nights are undistinguished in my mind, but the storms, the violent sudden storms, both frightened and quenched me. But my memory is uncertain; I recall a summer storm in the town where we lived and imagine a summer my mother knew in 1929. There was a tornado that year, she said, that blew away half of south Lorain. I mix up her summer with my own. Biting the strawberry, thinking of storms, I see her. A slim young girl in a pink crepe dress. One hand is on her hip; the other lolls about her thigh—waiting. The wind swoops her up, high above the houses, but she is still standing, hand on hip. Smiling. The anticipation and promise in her lolling hand are not altered by the holocaust. In the summer tornado of 1929, my mother's hand is unextinguished. She is strong, smiling, and relaxed while the world falls down about her. So much for memory. Public fact becomes private reality, and the seasons of a Midwestern town become the *Moirai*[272] of our small lives.

The summer was already thick when Frieda and I received our seeds. We had waited since April for the magic package containing the packets and packets of seeds we were to sell for five cents each, which would entitle us to a new bicycle. We believed it, and spent a major part of every day trooping about the town selling them. Although Mama had restricted us to the homes of people she knew or the neighborhoods familiar to us, we knocked on all doors, and floated in and out of every house that opened to us: twelve-room houses that sheltered half as many families, smelling of grease and urine; tiny wooden four-room houses tucked into bushes near the railroad tracks; the up-over places—apartments up over fish markets, butcher shops, furniture stores, saloons, restaurants; tidy brick houses with flowered carpets and glass bowls with fluted edges.

During that summer of the seed selling we thought about the money, thought about the seeds, and listened with only half an ear to what people were saying. In the houses of people who knew us we were asked to come in and sit, given cold water or lemonade; and while we sat there being refreshed, the people continued their conversations or went about their chores. Little by little we began to piece a story together, a secret, terrible, awful story. And it was only after two or three such vaguely overheard conversations that we realized that the story was about Pecola. Properly placed, the fragments of talk ran like this:

"Did you hear about that girl?"

"What? Pregnant?"

"Yas. But guess who?"

---

272 Moirai: 《그리스 신화》 모이라(운명의 여신): individual destiny; the will of the gods ; fate

"Who? I don't know all these little old boys."

"That's just it. Ain't no little old boy. They say it's Cholly."

"Cholly? Her daddy?"

"Uh-huh"

"Lord. Have mercy. That dirty nigger."

" 'Member that time he tried to burn them up? I knew he was crazy for sure then."

"What's she gone do? The mama?"

"Keep on like she been, I reckon. He taken off."

"County ain't gone let her keep that baby, is they?"

"Don't know."

"None of them Breedloves seem right anyhow. That boy is off somewhere every minute, and the girl was always foolish."

"Don't nobody know nothing about them anyway. Where they come from or nothing. Don't seem to have no people."

"What you reckon make him do a thing like that?"

"Beats me.[273] Just nasty."

"Well, they ought to take her out of school."

"Ought to. She carry some of the blame."

"Oh, come on. She ain't but twelve or so."

"Yeah. But you never know. How come she didn't fight him?"

"Maybe she did."

"Yeah? You never know."

"Well, it probably won't live. They say the way her mama beat her she lucky to be alive herself."

"She be lucky if it don't live. Bound to be the ugliest thing walking."

"Can't help but be. Ought to be a law: two ugly people doubling up like that to make more ugly. Be better off in the ground."

"Well, I wouldn't worry none. It be a miracle if it live."

Our astonishment was short-lived, for it gave way to a curious

---

273 Beats me: I do not know or understand.

kind of defensive shame; we were embarrassed for Pecola, hurt for her, and finally we just felt sorry for her. Our sorrow drove out all thoughts of the new bicycle. And I believe our sorrow was the more intense because nobody else seemed to share it. They were disgusted, amused, shocked, outraged, or even excited by the story. But we listened for the one who would say, "Poor little girl," or, "Poor baby," but there was only head-wagging where those words should have been. We looked for eyes creased with concern, but saw only veils.

I thought about the baby that everybody wanted dead, and saw it very clearly. It was in a dark, wet place, its head covered with great O's of wool,[274] the black face holding, like nickels, two clean black eyes, the flared nose, kissing-thick lips, and the living, breathing silk of black skin. No synthetic yellow bangs suspended over marble-blue eyes, no pinched nose and bowline mouth. More strongly than my fondness for Pecola, I felt a need for someone to want the black baby to live—just to counteract the universal love of white baby dolls, Shirley Temples, and Maureen Peals. And Frieda must have felt the same thing. We did not think of the fact that Pecola was not married; lots of girls had babies who were not married. And we did not dwell on the fact that the baby's father was Pecola's father too; the process of having a baby by any male was incomprehensible to us—at least she knew her father. We thought only of this overwhelming hatred for the unborn baby. We remembered Mrs. Breedlove knocking Pecola down and soothing the pink tears of the frozen doll baby that sounded like the door of our icebox. We remembered the knuckled eyes of schoolchildren under the gaze of Meringue Pie and the eyes of these same children when they looked at Pecola. Or maybe we didn't remember; we just knew. We had defended ourselves since memory against everything and

---

274 Great O's of wool: great curls

everybody, considered all speech a code to be broken by us, and all gestures subject to careful analysis; we had become headstrong, devious, and arrogant. Nobody paid us any attention, so we paid very good attention to ourselves. Our limitations were not known to us—not then. Our only handicap was our size; people gave us orders because they were bigger and stronger. So it was with confidence, strengthened by pity and pride, that we decided to change the course of events and alter a human life.

"What we gone do, Frieda?"

"What can we do? Miss Johnson said it would be a miracle if it lived."

"So let's make it a miracle."

"Yeah, but how?"

"We could pray."

"That's not enough. Remember last time with the bird?"

"That was different; it was half-dead when we found it."

"I don't care, I still think we have to do something really strong this time."

"Let's ask Him to let Pecola's baby live and promise to be good for a whole month."

"O.K. But we better give up something so He'll know we really mean it this time."

"Give up what? We ain't got nothing. Nothing but the seed money, two dollars."

"We could give that. Or, you know what? We could give up the bicycle. Bury the money and ... plant the seeds."

"All of the money?"

"Claudia, do you want to do it or not?"

"O.K. I just thought ... O.K."

"We have to do it *right*, now. We'll bury the money over by her house so we can't go back and dig it up, and we'll plant the seeds out back of our house so we can watch over them. And when they come up, we'll know everything is all right. All right?"

"All right. Only let me sing this time. You say the magic words."

LOOKLOOKHERECOMESAFRIENDTHE
FRIENDWILLPLAYWITHJANETHEYWI
LLPLAYAGOODGAMEPLAYJANEPLAY [275]

How many times a minute are you going to look inside that old thing?

I didn't look in a long time.

You did too—

So what? I can look if I want to.

I didn't say you couldn't. I just don't know why you have to look every minute. They [276] *aren't going anywhere.*

I know it. I just like to look.

You scared they might go away?

Of course not. How can they go away?

---

275 이 섹션은 Pecola가 마침내 정신분열을 일으켜 자문자답하고 있음을 보인다. 두개의 자아가 명조체와 이탤릭체로 구분되어 표기되고 있다.

276 두 눈을 가리킴

The others[277] *went away.*

They didn't go away. They changed.

Go away. Change. What's the difference?

A lot. Mr. Soaphead said they would last forever.

Forever and ever Amen?[278]

Yes, if you want to know.

You don't have to be so smarty when you talk to me.

I'm not being smarty. You started it.

I'd just like to do something else besides watch you stare in that mirror.

You're just jealous.

I am not.

You are. You wish you had them.

Ha. What would I look like with blue eyes?

Nothing much.

If you're going to keep this up, I may as well go on off by myself.

No. Don't go. What you want to do?

We could go outside and play, I guess.

But it's too hot.

You can take your old mirror. Put it in your coat pocket, and you can look at yourself up and down the street.

Boy! I never would have thought you'd be so jealous.

Oh, come on!

You are.

Are what?

Jealous.

O.K. So I'm jealous.

See. I told you.

No. I told you.

Are they[279] really nice?

---

277 전에 있던 까만 눈

278 기독교에서 기도문의 마지막 구절로 흔히 사용됨.

Yes. Very nice.

Just "very nice"?

Really, truly, very nice.

Really, truly, bluely nice?

Oh, God. You are crazy.

I am not!

I didn't mean it that way.

Well, what did you mean?

Come on. It's too hot in here.

Wait a minute. I can't find my shoes.

Here they are.

Oh. Thank you.

Got your mirror?

Yes dearie....

Well, let's go then.... Ow!

What's the matter?

The sun is too bright. It hurts my eyes.

Not mine. I don't even blink. Look. I can look right at the sun.

Don't do that.

Why not? It doesn't hurt. I don't even have to blink.

Well, blink anyway. You make me feel funny, staring at the sun like that.

Feel funny how?

I don't know.

Yes, you do. Feel funny how?

I told you, I don't know.

Why don't you look at me when you say that? You're looking drop-eyed[280] like Mrs. Breedlove.

Mrs. Breedlove look drop-eyed at you?

Yes. Now she does. Ever since I got my blue eyes, she look away

---

279 Pecola 자신의 눈

280 look drop-eyed: 맘에 들지 않아 눈을 내리깔고 외면하는 모습.

from me all of the time. Do you suppose she's jealous too?

Could be. They are pretty, you know.

I know. He really did a good job. Everybody's jealous. Every time I look at somebody, they look off.

Is that why nobody has told you how pretty they are?

Sure it is. Can you imagine? Something like that happening to a person, and nobody but nobody saying anything about it? They all try to pretend they don't see them. Isn't that funny? ... I said, isn't that funny?

Yes.

You are the only one who tells me how pretty they are.

Yes.

You are a real friend. I'm sorry about picking on you before. I mean, saying you were jealous and all.

That's all right.

No. Really. You are my very best friend. Why didn't I know you before?

You didn't need me before.

Didn't need you?

I mean ... you were so unhappy before. I guess you didn't notice me before.

I guess you're right. And I was so lonely for friends. And you were right here. Right before my eyes.

No, honey. Right after your eyes.

What?

What does Maureen think about your eyes?

She doesn't say anything about them. Has she said anything to you about them?

No. Nothing.

Do you like Maureen?

Oh. She's all right. For a half-white girl, that is.

I know what you mean. But would you like to be her friend? I mean, would you like to go around with her or anything?

No.

Me neither. But she sure is popular.

Who wants to be popular?

Not me.

Me neither.

But you couldn't be popular anyway. You don't even go to school.

You don't either.

I know. But I used to.

What did you stop for?

They made me.

Who made you?

I don't know. After that first day at school when I had my blue eyes. Well, the next day they had Mrs. Breedlove come out. Now I don't go anymore. But I don't care.

You don't?

No, I don't. They're just prejudiced, that's all.

Yes, they sure are prejudiced.

Just because I got blue eyes, bluer than theirs, they're prejudiced.

That's right.

They are bluer, aren't they?

Oh, yes. Much bluer.

Bluer than Joanna's?

Much bluer than Joanna's.

And bluer than Michelena's?

Much bluer than Michelena's.

I thought so. Did Michelena say anything to you about my eyes?

No. Nothing.

Did you say anything to her?

No.

How come?

How come what?

How come you don't talk to anybody?

I talk to you.

Besides me.

I don't like anybody besides you.

Where do you live?

I told you once.

What is your mother's name?

Why are you so busy meddling me?

I just wondered. You don't talk to anybody. You don't go to school. And nobody talks to you.

How do you know nobody talks to me?

They don't. When you're in the house with me, even Mrs. Breedlove doesn't say anything to you. Ever. Sometimes I wonder if she even sees you.

Why wouldn't she see me?

I don't know. She almost walks right over you.

Maybe she doesn't feel too good since Cholly's gone.

Oh, yes. You must be right.

She probably misses him.

I don't know why she would. All he did was get drunk and beat her up.

Well, you know how grown-ups are.

Yes. No. How are they?

Well, she probably loved him anyway.

HIM?

Sure. Why not? Anyway, if she didn't love him, she sure let him do it to her a lot.

That's nothing.

How do you know?

I saw them all the time. She didn't like it.

Then why'd she let him do it to her?

Because he made her.

How could somebody make you do something like that?

Easy.

Oh, yeah? How easy?

They just make you, that's all.

I guess you're right. And Cholly could make anybody do anything.

He could not.

He made you, didn't he? [281]

Shut up!

I was only teasing.

Shut up!

O.K. O.K.

He just tried, see? He didn't do anything. You hear me?

I'm shutting up.

You'd better. I don't like that kind of talk.

I said I'm shutting up.

You always talk so dirty. Who told you about that, anyway?

I forget.

Sammy?

No. You did.

I did not.

You did. You said he tried to do it to you when you were sleeping on the couch.

See there! You don't even know what you're talking about. It was when I was washing dishes.

Oh, yes. Dishes.

By myself. In the kitchen.

Well, I'm glad you didn't let him.

Yes.

Did you?

Did I what?

Let him.

---

281 Cholly의 Pecola에 대한 성폭행 행위를 암시하고 있음

Now who's crazy?

I am, I guess.

You sure are.

Still ...

Well. Go ahead. Still what?

I wonder what it would be like.

Horrible.

Really?

Yes. Horrible.

Then why didn't you tell Mrs. Breedlove?

I did tell her!

I don't mean about the first time. I mean about the second time, when you were sleeping on the couch.

I wasn't sleeping! I was reading!

You don't have to shout.

You don't understand anything, do you? She didn't even believe me when I told her.

So that's why you didn't tell her about the second time?

She wouldn't have believed me then either.

You're right. No use telling her when she wouldn't believe you.

That's what I'm trying to get through your thick head.

O.K. I understand now. Just about.

What do you mean, just about?

You sure are mean today.

You keep on saying mean and sneaky things. I thought you were my friend.

I am. I am.

Then leave me alone about Cholly.

O.K.

There's nothing more to say about him, anyway. He's gone, anyway.

Yes. Good riddance.[282]

---

282 Yes, good riddance: 그래, 잘 사라졌어. ("Good riddance" is said to express relief

Yes. Good riddance.

And Sammy's gone too.

And Sammy's gone too.

So there's no use talking about it. I mean them.

No. No use at all.

It's all over now.

Yes.

And you don't have to be afraid of Cholly coming at you anymore.

No.

That was horrible, wasn't it?

Yes.

The second time too?

Yes.

Really? The second time too?

Leave me alone! You better leave me alone.

Can't you take a joke? I was only funning.

I don't like to talk about dirty things.

Me neither. Let's talk about something else.

What? What will we talk about?

Why, your eyes.

Oh, yes. My eyes. My blue eyes. Let me look again.

See how pretty they are.

Yes. They get prettier each time I look at them.

They are the prettiest I've ever seen.

Really?

Oh, yes.

Prettier than the sky?

Oh, yes. Much prettier than the sky.

Prettier than Alice-and-Jerry Storybook[283] eyes?

---

at being free of a troublesome or unwanted person or thing.)

283 Alice-Jerry Storybook: Dick-and-Jane Storybook과 같은 계열의 이야기책으로 pre-primer.

Oh, yes. Much prettier than Alice-and-Jerry Storybook eyes.

And prettier than Joanna's?

Oh, yes. And bluer too.

Bluer than Michelena's?

Yes.

Are you sure?

Of course I'm sure.

You don't sound sure....

Well, I am sure. Unless....

Unless what?

Oh, nothing. I was just thinking about a lady I saw yesterday. Her eyes sure were blue. But no. Not bluer than yours.

Are you sure?

Yes. I remember them now. Yours are bluer.

I'm glad.

Me too. I'd hate to think there was anybody around with bluer eyes than yours. I'm sure there isn't. Not around here, anyway.

But you don't know, do you? You haven't seen everybody, have you?

No. I haven't.

So there could be, couldn't there?

Not hardly.

But maybe. Maybe. You said "around here." Nobody "around here" probably has bluer eyes. What about someplace else? Even if my eyes are bluer than Joanna's and bluer than Michelena's and bluer than that lady's you saw, suppose there is somebody way off somewhere with bluer eyes than mine?

Don't be silly.

There could be. Couldn't there?

Not hardly.

But suppose. Suppose a long way off. In Cincinnati, say, there is somebody whose eyes are bluer than mine? Suppose there are *two* people with bluer eyes?

So what? You asked for blue eyes. You got blue eyes.

He should have made them bluer.

Who?

Mr. Soaphead.

Did you say what color blue you wanted them?

No. I forgot.

Oh. Well.

Look. Look over there. At that girl. Look at her eyes. Are they bluer than mine?

No, I don't think so.

Did you look real good?

Yes.

Here comes someone. Look at his. See if they're bluer.

You're being silly. I'm not going to look at everybody's eyes.

You have to.

No I don't.

Please. If there is somebody with bluer eyes than mine, then maybe there is somebody with the bluest eyes. The bluest eyes in the whole world.

That's just too bad, isn't it?

Please help me look.

No.

But suppose my eyes aren't blue enough?

Blue enough for what?

Blue enough for ... I don't know. Blue enough for something. Blue enough ... for you!

I'm not going to play with you anymore.

Oh. Don't leave me.

Yes. I am.

Why? Are you mad at me?

Yes.

Because my eyes aren't blue enough? Because I don't have the bluest eyes?

No. Because you're acting silly.

Don't go. Don't leave me. Will you come back if I get them?

Get *what?*

The bluest eyes. Will you come back then?

Of course I will. I'm just going away for a little while.

You promise?

Sure. I'll be back. Right before your very eyes.

So it was.

A little black girl yearns for the blue eyes of a little white girl, and the horror at the heart of her yearning is exceeded only by the evil of fulfillment.

We saw her sometimes, Frieda and I—after the baby came too soon and died. After the gossip and the slow wagging of heads. She was so sad to see. Grown people looked away; children, those who were not frightened by her, laughed outright.

The damage done was total. She spent her days, her tendril, sap-green days, walking up and down, up and down, her head jerking to the beat of a drummer so distant only she could hear. Elbows bent, hands on shoulders, she flailed her arms like a bird in an eternal, grotesquely futile effort to fly. Beating the air, a winged but grounded bird, intent on the blue void it could not reach—could not even see—but which filled the valleys of the mind.

We tried to see her without looking at her, and never, never went near. Not because she was absurd, or repulsive, or because we were frightened, but because we had failed her. Our flowers never grew. I was convinced that Frieda was right, that I had planted them too deeply. How could I have been so sloven? So we avoided Pecola Breedlove—forever.

And the years folded up like pocket handkerchiefs. Sammy left town long ago; Cholly died in the workhouse; Mrs. Breedlove still does housework. And Pecola is somewhere in that little brown house she and her mother moved to on the edge of town, where you can see her even now, once in a while. The birdlike gestures are worn away to a mere picking and plucking her way between the tire rims and the sunflowers, between Coke bottles and milkweed, among all the waste and beauty of the world—which is what she herself was. All of our waste which we dumped on her and which she absorbed. And all of our beauty, which was hers first and which she gave to us. All of us—all who knew her—felt so wholesome after we cleaned ourselves on her. We were so beautiful when we stood astride her ugliness. Her simplicity decorated us, her guilt sanctified us, her pain made us glow with health, her awkwardness made us think we had a sense of humor. Her inarticulateness made us believe we were eloquent. Her poverty kept us generous. Even her waking dreams we used—to silence our own nightmares. And she let us, and thereby deserved our contempt. We honed our egos on her, padded our characters with her frailty, and yawned in the fantasy of our strength.

And fantasy it was, for we were not strong, only aggressive; we were not free, merely licensed; we were not compassionate, we were polite; not good, but well behaved. We courted death in order to call ourselves brave, and hid like thieves from life. We substituted good grammar for intellect; we switched habits to simulate maturity; we rearranged lies and called it truth, seeing in the new pattern of an old idea the Revelation[284] and the Word.

She, however, stepped over into madness, a madness which protected her from us simply because it bored us in the end.

Oh, some of us "loved" her. The Maginot Line. And Cholly loved

---

284 the Revelation: 계시(啓示) (something that is considered to be a sign or message from God)

her. I'm sure he did. He, at any rate, was the one who loved her enough to touch her, envelop her, give something of himself to her. But his touch was fatal, and the something he gave her filled the matrix of her agony with death. Love is never any better than the lover. Wicked people love wickedly, violent people love violently, weak people love weakly, stupid people love stupidly, but the love of a free man is never safe. There is no gift for the beloved. The lover alone possesses his gift of love. The loved one is shorn, neutralized, frozen in the glare of the lover's inward eye.

And now when I see her searching the garbage—for what? The thing we assassinated? I talk about how I did *not* plant the seeds too deeply, how it was the fault of the earth, the land, of our town. I even think now that the land of the entire country was hostile to marigolds that year. This soil is bad for certain kinds of flowers. Certain seeds it will not nurture, certain fruit it will not bear, and when the land kills of its own volition, we acquiesce and say the victim had no right to live. We are wrong, of course, but it doesn't matter. It's too late. At least on the edge of my town, among the garbage and the sunflowers of my town, it's much, much, much too late.

Afterword

We had just started elementary school. She said she wanted blue eyes. I looked around to picture her with them and was violently repelled by what I imagined she would look like if she had her wish. The sorrow in her voice seemed to call for sympathy, and I faked it for her, but, astonished by the desecration she proposed, I "got mad" at her instead.

Until that moment I had seen the pretty, the lovely, the nice, the ugly, and although I had certainly used the word "beautiful," I had never experienced its shock—the force of which was equaled by the knowledge that no one else recognized it, not even, or especially, the one who possessed it.

It must have been more than the face I was examining: the silence of the street in the early afternoon, the light, the atmosphere of confession. In any case it was the first time I knew beautiful. Had imagined it for myself. Beauty was not simply something to behold; it was something one could *do*.

The Bluest Eye was my effort to say something about that; to say something about why she had not, or possibly ever would have, the experience of what she possessed and also why she prayed for so radical an alteration. Implicit in her desire was racial self-loathing. And twenty years later I was still wondering about how one learns that. Who told her? Who made her feel that it was better to be a freak than what she was? Who had looked at her and found her so wanting, so small a weight on the beauty scale? The novel pecks away at the gaze that condemned her.

The reclamation of racial beauty in the sixties stirred these thoughts, made me think about the necessity for the claim. Why, although reviled by others, could this beauty not be taken for granted within the community? Why did it need wide public articulation to exist? These are not clever questions. But in 1962 when I began this story, and in 1965 when it began to be a book, the answers were not as obvious to me as they quickly became and are now. The assertion of racial beauty was not a reaction to the self-mocking, humorous critique of cultural/racial foibles common in all groups, but against the damaging internalization of assumptions of immutable inferiority originating in an outside gaze. I focused, therefore, on how something as grotesque as the demonization of an entire race could take root inside the most delicate member of society: a child; the most vulnerable member: a female. In trying to dramatize the devastation that even casual racial contempt can cause, I chose a unique situation, not a representative one. The extremity of Pecola's case stemmed largely from a crippled and crippling family—unlike the average black family and unlike the narrator's. But singular as Pecola's life was, I believed some aspects of her woundability were lodged in all young girls. In exploring the social and domestic aggression that could cause a child to literally fall apart, I mounted a series of rejections, some routine, some exceptional, some monstrous, all the while trying hard to avoid complicity in the demonization process Pecola was subjected to. That is, I did not want to dehumanize the characters, who trashed Pecola and contributed to her collapse.

One problem was centering: the weight of the novel's inquiry on so delicate and vulnerable a character could smash her and lead readers into the comfort of pitying her rather than into an interrogation of themselves for the smashing. My solution—break the narrative into parts that had to be reassembled by the reader—seemed to me a good idea, the execution of which does not satisfy me now. Besides, it didn't work: many readers remain touched but not moved.

The other problem, of course, was language. Holding the despising glance while sabotaging it was difficult. The novel tried to hit the raw nerve of racial self-contempt, expose it, then soothe it not with narcotics but with language that replicated the agency I discovered in my first experience of beauty. Because that moment was so racially infused (my revulsion at what my school friend wanted: very blue eyes in a very black skin; the harm she was doing to *my* concept of the beautiful), the struggle was for writing that was indisputably black. I don't yet know quite what that is, but neither that nor the attempts to disqualify an effort to find out keeps me from trying to pursue it.

Some time ago I did the best job I could of describing strategies for grounding my work in race-specific yet race-free prose. Prose free of racial hierarchy and triumphalism. Parts of that description are as follows.

The opening phrase of the first sentence, "Quiet as it's kept," had several attractions for me. First, it was a familiar phrase, familiar to me as a child listening to adults; to black women conversing with one another, telling a story, an anecdote, gossip about some one or event within the circle, the family, the neighborhood. The words are conspiratorial. "Shh, don't tell anyone else," and "No one is allowed to know this." It is a secret between us and a secret that is being kept from us. The conspiracy is both held and withheld, exposed and sustained. In some sense it was precisely what the act of writing the book was: the public exposure of a private confidence. In order to comprehend fully the duality of that position, one needs to be reminded of the political climate in which the writing took place, 1965-69, a time of great social upheaval in the lives of black people. The publication (as opposed to the writing) involved the exposure; the writing was the disclosure of secrets, secrets "we" shared and those withheld from us by ourselves and by the world outside the community.

"Quiet as it's kept" is also a figure of speech that is written, in this instance, but clearly chosen for how speakerly it is, how it speaks and bespeaks a particular world and its ambience. Further, in addition to its "back fence" connotation, its suggestion of illicit gossip, of thrilling revelation, there is also, in the "whisper," the assumption (on the part of the reader) that the teller is on the inside, knows something others do not, and is going to be generous with this privileged information. The intimacy I was aiming for, the intimacy between the reader and the page, could start up immediately because the secret is being shared, at best, and eavesdropped upon, at the least. Sudden familiarity or instant intimacy seemed crucial to me. I did not want the reader to have time to wonder, "What do I have to do, to give up, in order to read this? What defense do I need, what distance maintain?" Because I know (and the reader does not—he or she has to wait for the second sentence) that this is a terrible story about things one would rather not know anything about.

What, then, is the Big Secret about to be shared? The thing we (reader and I) are "in" on? A botanical aberration. Pollution, perhaps. A skip, perhaps, in the natural order of things: a September, an autumn, a fall without marigolds. Bright, common, strong and sturdy marigolds. When? In 1941, and since that is a momentous year (the beginning of World War II for the United States), the "fall" of 1941, just before the declaration of war, has a "closet" innuendo. In the temperate zone where there is a season known as "fall" during which one expects marigolds to be at their peak, in the months before the beginning of U.S. participation in World War II, something grim is about to be divulged. The next sentence will make it clear that the sayer, the one who knows, is a child speaking, mimicking the adult black women on the porch or in the backyard. The opening phrase is an effort to be grown-up about this shocking information. The point of view of a child alters the priority an adult would assign the information. "We thought ... it was because Pecola was having her father's baby that the marigolds did not grow" foregrounds the flowers, backgrounds illicit, traumatic, incomprehensible sex coming to its dreaded fruition. This forgrounding of "trivial" information and backgrounding of shocking knowledge secures the point of view but gives the reader pause about whether the voice of children can be trusted at all or is more trustworthy than an adult's. The reader is thereby protected from a confrontation too soon with the painful details, while simultaneously provoked into a desire to know them. The novelty, I thought, would be in having this story of female violation revealed from the vantage point of the victims or could-be victims of rape—the persons no one inquired of (certainly not in 1965): the girls themselves. And since the victim does not have the vocabulary to understand the violence or its context, gullible, vulnerable girlfriends, looking back as the knowing adults they pretended to be in the beginning, would have to do that for her, and would have to fill those silences with their own reflective lives. Thus, the opening provides the stroke that announces something more than a secret shared, but a silence broken, a void filled, an unspeakable thing spoken at last. And it draws the connection between a minor destabilization in seasonal flora and the insignificant destruction of a black girl. Of course "minor" and "insignificant" represent the outside world's view—for the girls, both phenomena are earthshaking depositories of information they spend that whole year of childhood (and afterward) trying to fathom, and cannot. If they have any success, it will be in transferring the problem of fathoming to the presumably adult reader, to the inner circle of listeners. At the least they have distributed the weight of these problematical questions to a larger constituency, and justified the public exposure of a privacy. If the conspiracy that the opening words announce is entered into by the reader, then the book can be seen to open with its close: a speculation on the disruption of "nature" as being a social disruption wpith tragic individual consequences in which the reader, as part of the population of the text, is implicated.

However, a problem lies in the central chamber of the novel. The shattered world I built (to complement what is happening to Pecola), its pieces held together by seasons in childtime and commenting at every turn on the incompatible and barren white-family primer, does not in its present form handle effectively the silence at its center: the void that is Pecola's "unbeing." It should have had a shape—like the emptiness left by a boom or a cry. It required a sophistication unavailable to me, and some deft manipulation of the voices around her. She is not *seen* by herself until she hallucinates a self. And the fact of her hallucination becomes a kind of outside-the-book conversation.

Also, although I was pressing for a female expressiveness, it eluded me for the most part, and I had to content myself with female personae because I was not able to secure throughout the work the feminine subtext that is present in the opening sentence (the women gossiping, eager and aghast in "Quiet as it's kept"). The shambles this struggle became is most evident in the section on Pauline Breedlove, where I resorted to two voices, hers and the urging narrator's, both of which are extremely unsatisfactory to me. It is interesting to me now that where I thought I would have the most difficulty subverting the language to a feminine mode, I had the least: connecting Cholly's "rape" by the whitemen to his own of his daughter. This most masculine act of aggression becomes feminized in my language, "passive," and, I think, more accurately repellent when deprived of the male "glamour of shame" rape is (or once was) routinely given.

My choices of language (speakerly, aural, colloquial), my reliance for full comprehension on codes embedded in black culture, my effort to effect immediate co-conspiracy and intimacy (without any distancing, explanatory fabric), as well as my attempt to shape a silence while breaking it are attempts to transfigure the complexity and wealth of Black American culture into a language worthy of the culture.

Thinking back now on the problems expressive language presented to me, I am amazed by their currency, their tenacity. Hearing "civilized" languages debase humans, watching cultural exorcisms debase literature, seeing oneself preserved in the amber of disqualifying metaphors—I can say that my narrative project is as difficult today as it was thirty years ago.

With very few exceptions, the initial publication of *The Bluest Eye* was like Pecola's life: dismissed, trivialized, misread. And it has taken twenty-five years to gain for her the respectful publication this edition is.

Princeton, New Jersey
November, 1993

Essays in Criticism

Layered Rhythms: Virginia Woolf and Toni Morrison*

Barbara T. Christian

> Writing and reading are not all that distinct for a writer. Both exercises require being alert and ready for unaccountable beauty, for the intricateness or simple elegance of the writer's imagination, for the world that imagination evokes. Both require being mindful of the places where imagination sabotages itself, locks its own gates, pollutes its vision. Writing and reading mean being aware of the writer's notions of risk and safety, the serene achievement of, or sweaty fight for, meaning and response-ability.
>
> – Toni Morrison, *Playing in the Dark*

I SEE YOUR FACE, TONI MORRISON, possibly the best novelist in America today, when people ask, "What does it mean that you wrote your M.A. thesis in the early fifties on *suicide* in the works of William Faulkner and Virginia Woolf?"[1] Do such people want to inflict the "anxiety of influence" on you? Or perhaps is it that they want to be sure that your writing will be seen as a part of the Great Western tradition? What is the purpose of securing a link between you and William Faulkner, as Harold Bloom did in his introduction

---

* Source: Peterson, Nancy J. Ed. *Toni Morrison: Critical and Theoretical Approaches*. Baltimore, London: The Johns Hopkins UP, 1997. 19-36. Permission granted. © Modern Fiction Studies, 2007.

to an edition of collected essays on your work? Or between you and Virginia Woolf, as the program of the Third Annual Conference on Virginia Woolf suggests?[2] Why must you be studied in relation to such writers, icons of twentieth-century European and Anglo-American literature? Is it that as an African American woman writer, clearly a "genius," you must have a Western white literary father and mother? Not just any white father, but one such as Faulkner, who, as Ralph Ellison has put it in *Shadow and Act*, was one of the few Anglo-American writers to fight out "the moral problem [of Negroes in America] which was repressed after the nineteenth century" (43) Not just any white mother, but one such as Virginia Woolf, who is now clearly situated in the canon: as modernist, satisfying the twentieth-century Great Books requirement;[3] as feminist, satisfying the needs of twentieth-century women scholars.[4] You have commented on this tendency among critics. Your own words are a cautionary preface to our project:

> My general disappointment in some of the criticism that my work has received has nothing to do with approval. It has something to do with the vocabulary used in order to describe these things. I don't like to find my books condemned or embraced as good, when that condemnation or that praise is based on criteria from other paradigms. I would much prefer that they were dismissed or embraced based on the success of their accomplishment within the culture out of which I write. ("Rootedness" 342)

I am an African American woman critic who wrote about your work before you were celebrated and who has, despite critical trends, maintained my sense of your writing as an African American woman. Please allow me to invent a fiction as you do in your novels—in this case, a fiction about you and Virginia Woolf

—for fictions can be beneficial, imaginative, even transforming. Because I know this is an invention and I worry about "notions of risk and safety," I will rely primarily on your words and Virginia's in the charting of my invention. I am inspired by your and Virginia's different, yet related projects—layered rhythms I call them.

I see you in the early fifties, a colored graduate student when colored meant black, pacing yourself through Cornell, squinting your eye at that famous suicide point on the campus where too may students took their lives. I see you, a colored girl who, a few years before, had changed her name from Chloe (a name in America associated with blacks) to Toni (an androgynous name), because even folks at Howard University had trouble pronouncing it. I find that an instance of serendipity, for Virginia Woolf used the name Chloe in her fictional representation of Mary Carmichael's novel in *A Room of One's Own*—"Chloe liked Olivia," pointing to Shakespearean characters, even as she disrupted bourgeois heterosexuality (86).

Yes, yes, I do see you, assessing the wintry whiteness at Cornell. But you are used to whiteness. You are from Lorain, Ohio, where possibly your father, like Claudia's daddy in your first novel, *The Bluest Eye* (1970), became, in the winter, a "Wolf killer turned hawk fighter, [who] worked night and day to keep one from the door and the other from under the windowsills" (47). Yet how different this wintry whiteness is in this New England enclave of privilege. A graduate student, a black graduate student, a black female graduate student—what was there for you at Cornell? Years later, you would say about your stay there that "if [your] ancestors could go through slavery, you guessed you could get through that" ("Interview").

I understand what you mean. For I went to one of those graduate schools in English. But at least Columbia was in New York City, with its many colored folk, and I was there in the mid-sixties. Still I was one of a few blacks, possibly the only black woman (oh no, a black female West Indian, are you from Jamaica? No—from the Virgin Islands) graduate student. So I can see you pondering wintry Cornell. What do we want in these places to which we came, so far away from home—from Lorain Ohio, from St. Thomas Virgin Islands, from wherever, a black wherever.

Why are you, in 1953, majoring in English? I can see your parents asking you, "What are you going to do with that degree? To study English? At Cornell? You're so bright. Why don't you become a doctor, a lawyer, a Credit to Your Race?" But on some visceral level, you can't explain, you love language—the shapes of stories, the inheritance from your parents, who were great storytellers, but did not necessarily understand themselves as artists, nor what they bequeathed to you (*Toni Morrison*).

You want—what do you desire? Chaucer, Shakespeare certainly, but where do you dwell in their words? You'd certainly heard of African American writers. You'd taken a course at Howard during your undergraduate years with Alain Locke, that elder African American critic, who'd helped to make the Harlem Renaissance, who'd seen the beginnings of the Richard Wright era.[5] You would say, in one of your interviews, that reading much of the African American literature you encountered in classrooms had left you feeling bereft, for it did not seem to be directed to you, a black person, but seemed to be addressed to an other. You felt "bereft" (*Toni Morrison*). You "needed yourself" in language. How else to fulfill that need, and still be a Credit to The Race, except to go to graduate school in English?

Nineteen-fifty-three is New Criticism at its height: the text is all. No world lies outside the text. The text has nothing to do with race or even cultural specificity. You are reading not only Chaucer and

Shakespeare, those ancient venerables from Europe, but also American writers—Hawthorne, Melville—for the American academy is finally admitting American writers into the canon. Even Faulkner, though he is still alive, might just have made it into the curriculum. Like so many of the few African Americans in literature, you will focus on Faulkner's works, a code even ten years later in the 1960s for those of us who wanted to study blacks in literature. There was no such thing as African American literature—studying Faulkner was what they call in the music business, a cover. Still, although blacks appeared to be absent from "American" literature, you sensed the ways in which the African presence in America erupted In the works, of Hawthorne and Melville, a subject you would write about in 1992, in your book of literary criticism *Playing in the Dark'*.

But what about Virginia Woolf? Not an American who was confronted with a black presence, whether she repressed it or not (although her antics in the Abyssinian Debacle so much discussed by Woolf scholars needs to be thought about from a black perspective).[6] Not a venerable British ancient, but an early twentieth century British woman who, after all, had insisted in an essay that the reason why there was no female Shakespeare was because Shakespeare's sister did not have 500 pounds a year and a room of her own. Mrs. Woolf did not come to a writing career easily. As was true of her times, her so-educated father, Leslie Stephen, discriminated between her and her brothers. While they were allowed to go to Oxford, she had to stay at home. But you, Toni Morrison, in the tradition of black families, precisely because you were a daughter, were encouraged to go to college. How else might you survive, without the brawn of a black man, the sentiment that circumscribed white women?[7] Like so many black women, "[you] had nothing to fall back on; not maleness, not whiteness, not ladyhood, not anything. And out of the profound desolation of [your] reality [you] may well have invented [your]self" (Morrison, qtd. in Giddings 15)

Unlike Virginia, you would become a mother, and for much of your adult life a single mother, who would write, not in a room of your own, but with the interruptions of children and the jobs necessary for your and their survival, writing on scraps of paper at subway stops ("Interview"). You would see motherhood as "liberating," as your "best" self, for your children respected those parts of you that had little to do with society's demands, since they were fresh, not quite yet socialized. And through their eyes, you could see the world through an imagination not yet tainted by stereotypes ("Toni Morrison", Moyers 60). So different from the Virginia you would meet in 1953, who because of the incest she experienced in childhood was concerned that having children would stifle her creativity and exacerbate her bouts of depression. One of the major themes of your work would be the complexities of motherhood, the liberation and restrictions of that role for African American women: how thick that mother love was, yet how complex, how beautiful, even monumental that role could be. So different from Virginia, who was living everyday with her fecund sister, Vanessa, a source some sibling conflict.[8]

Although from different cultures and times, you and Virginia did face problem as women writers. While Virginia had to "kill the angel in the house" (Gilbert and Gubar 17), you, Toni, had to "kill the mammy in the Big House." Virginia was responding to the fact that women were not expected to write, and when they did write, their tone admitted that [they] were only women or protesting that [they] were as good as any man (Woolf, *Room* 80). When women wrote, they were still expected to write in specific ways about specific themes—that is, within the romance genre—about love, marriage, manners. Virginia did have some woman writers to whom she could refer: Jane Austen, for example, who had brought the comedy of manners to a peak of perfection. But you, Toni Morrison, could not in 1953, in spite of society's stereotype of the black woman as as mammy, know about any African American women writers of any substance. Before the 1970s few scholars even of African American women literature, saw women as writers or even knew that there existed a strong line of African American women. In fact, it is unlikely that you read inside or outside the classroom any African American women of the past except, perhaps, Gwendolyn Brooks, who won a Pulitzer in 1951. You had not read the domestic allegories, as Claudia Tate calls them, in the sentimental fiction of nineteenth century African American writers like Frances Harper and Pauline Hopkins, or that great African American romance, Zora Neale Hurston's *Their Eyes Were Watching God* (1937). You could claim no maternal ancestors, although, of course, the stereotype of black women when they did appear would be as mammies in white fiction, "mammies" of a sort, in the black fiction of Du Bois, Wright or Ellison.[9]

What did Virginia mean when she used the term, "woman writer"? Was she speaking about you? No wonder, in order to write as a woman, you would focus so much on the subject of motherlove, while Virginia, because of her specific cultural inheritance, had to disrupt the European script of romance imposed on women.[10] Because of your folk's history, you did not have the same need as Virginia did to "kill the angel in the house." In contrast to Virginia's deconstruction of the nuclear family, your novels usually include a three-woman household recalling an older mythic familial structure. Thus, you would say in an interview that

> It seems to me that there's an enormous difference in the writing of black and white women. . . . Black women seem able to combine the nest and the adventure. They don't see conflicts in certain areas as do white women. They are both safe harbor and

> ship; they are both inn and trail. We, black women, do both. We don't find these places, these roles, mutually exclusive. That's one of the differences. ("Toni Morrison," Tate 122)

How to find a sentence for that difference in representing gender and race would become one of your abiding theoretical concerns.

But I've gone ahead of myself. What I want to know is how you got to know Virginia. Today everyone reads her. But this is 1994, 20 years after the Virginia Woolf fever of the 1970s. And you went to graduate school in the 1950s. Did someone just happen to mention her? Did you have one of those crazy teachers who insisted on exposing his students to odd writers? How would I know? I'm reaching across time from 1994 to you in 1953. Even in 1965, some 10 years later when I was a graduate student at Columbia, Virginia Woolf was still a suspect writer. Certainly her books were, mostly, out of print in the early fifties and were included in few college syllabi (Wilson 294). Yet, in 1955, you completed a thesis on an aspect of her work.

You are in graduate school at Cornell in 1953. That was the year that Eric Auerbach's classic *Mimesis* was translated into English. In it he included a long critique of an out-of-print book called *To the Lighthouse* by Virginia Woolf, an upper-class British woman who killed herself. Maybe one of your teachers' discussions of Auerbach's book in one of your classes led you to Virginia Woolf's book. After all, a twentieth-century woman writer was a relatively unusual item in your curriculum.

But what did you want with the work of a woman who killed herself? You know the way black people feel about suicide. As your narrator commented in your novel *Sula*, the black people of the Bottom feel that suicide is "beneath them"(9). Yet you were obviously intrigued by the idea of suicide, for that's what you focused on in your thesis. You'd clearly read *Mrs. Dalloway* which was published in 1925 and in which Septimus Warren Smith kill himself, a victim of shell shock from World War I. So like, yet unlike, Shadrack in your novel *Sula*, published some 50 years after, who too is suffering from World War I shell shock. But your Shadrack does not kill himself. Rather "Blasted and permanently astonished by the events of 1917, he had returned to Medallion, handsome but ravaged" (7):

> It was not death or dying that frightened him, but the unexpectedness of both. In sorting it all out, he hit on the notion that if one day a year were devoted to it, everybody could get it out of the way and the rest of the year would be safe and free. In this manner he instituted National Suicide Day. (14)

Shadrack turns shell shock and the possibility of suicide into a rite, which in turn is adopted by his community so that "they absorbed it into their thoughts, into their language, into their lives" (15). While the inhabitants of the Bottom might not understand Shadrack's experience in the war, ironically a misrecognition that will ultimately result in their extinction as community, they do understand the workings of rituals in staving off irrational catastrophic events like racism and war.

Like Virginia's works, your novels are bracketed by war—in your case the major wars in which America engaged—the Civil War in *Beloved*, World War I in *Sula* and *Jazz*, World War II in *The Bluest Eye* and *Sula*. Neither your works nor Virginia's are specifically about the action of war itself so much as they are about the effects, of such tumult on the psyches of your respective communities. Virginia was an adult during World War I and experienced firsthand the devastating effects on her generation—on dazzling young men like Andrew Ramsey in *To the Lighthouse* (1927), whose death from an exploded shell she literally recorded in brackets (201). You were not born until 1931, but you must have known early on about the Civil War which changed the very status of your black being. Your childhood memories must have included stories you heard about World War I , and the War to end all Wars, a war that ushered in a new period in African American history, the Jazz Age, when a flood of blacks migrated North to work at those jobs the soldiers had left. Your narrator in *Jazz* experiences the effects of the war quite differently from Virginia's characters, for that War is followed in America by the development of this whole new feeling among African Americans about themselves—that of experiencing the freedom and danger of the City, where one might be

> Alone, yes, but top-notch and indestructible—like the City in 1926 when all the wars are over and there will never be another one. The people down there in the shadow are happy about that. At last, at last, everything's ahead. The smart ones say so and people listening to them and reading what they write agree: Here comes the new. Look out. There goes the sad stuff. The bad stuff. The things-nobody-could-help stuff. The way everybody was then and there. Forget that. History is over, you all, and everything's ahead at last. (*Jazz* 7)

How wrong your narrator is, as Virginia Woolf would come to know in 1941, when partially as a result of depression about the news of World War II she took her life

But perhaps Virginia Woolf's works were not included in any of your classes. Maybe you, Toni, ran into her works in an avant-garde bookstore, and someone told you that her grandfather was a staunch abolitionist who married the sister of Wilberforce, the major speaker in the House of Commons against the slave trade (Bell 1: 3-4). Here your two apparently disparate cultures and histories cross, and you are not as distant from one another as it might seem. Or perhaps some crazy, too advanced graduate student who'd been to England talked incessantly about this innovative, what is the word, *experimental*, woman writer—check her out—not like those too old guys you're reading in class

In an interview published in 1983, you made an observation: "My sense of the novel is that it has always functioned for the class group that wrote it. The history of the novel as a form began when there was a new class, a middle class to read it, it was an art form that they needed" ("Rootedness" 340). You see your writing of novels as related to the needs of your group, African Americans. An English major, you knew the novel came out of an historical context that as a form like any other that is not "natural," it was constructed in relation to the needs of a class. So you would state in that same interview that "the novel is needed by African Americans now in a way that it was not needed before," since "we don't live in places we can hear those stories anymore, parents don't sit around and tell their children those classical mythological archetypal stories that we heard years ago" (430). In order to create a novel that would accomplish these goals, that would be not only beautiful and powerful but would also "work," one needed to incorporate "unorthodox novelistic characteristics" ("Rootedness" 342). You did not "regard Black literature as simply books written *by* Black People, or simply as literature written *about* Black people, or simply as literature that uses a certain mode of language in which you just sort of drop *g*'s" (342). You saw your endeavor as the "struggle to *find* that elusive but identifiable style" that is Black art (342).

Virginia Woolf would seem to be coming from the other side of that problem. But she too had to define what she was doing—what it meant, assured as she was of the British tradition, to be a woman writer. She saw the British tradition of novel writing as being so fixed, so focused on the conventions of her ancestral class, the class which had created it for different purposes precisely because it was a different time, that the genre had not adapted to the catastrophic changes that her generation was experiencing in the early twentieth century. Freud's theory of the unconscious brought into question the nineteenth-century European idea of characters who had total control over their knowledge of themselves. The Great War had wiped away any sense of European cultural coherence. The Bolshevik Revolution had transformed world politics. Woolf would speak for a whole generation when she asserted, in her essay "How It Strikes A Contemporary," that in contrast to the novelists of the nineteenth century, contemporary writers are beset by the dilemma that they "cannot make a world," "cannot generalise": "They cannot tell stories because they do not believe the stories are true" (244). Yet as Ralph Freedman points out in his book *The Lyrical Novel*, Virginia Woolf saw that in order to write lasting, generally accessible works, the writer needed to find appropriate avenues of escape. "[Woolf's] attempt to translate the traditional forms of the novel into organized explorations of consciousness represents her contribution to this task" (187-188). But her concerns were not only and precisely with the traditional forms of novel, but with what these forms meant for a woman writer in that tradition. So Virginia saw that women writers, as she knew them in 1925, needed to "[break] the sentence . . . [break] the sequence" (*Room* 85).[11]

You, Toni, would also see the need for inventing "unorthodox novelistic characteristics." Your reasons; though related to Virginia's, were also different from hers, as indicated by your differing use of the concept of "stories," your inheritance from quite different cultures. For Woolf's contemporaries, it is novelists who tell stories; the novel as a genre developed out of a particular class in Europe as a means to creating a sense of coherence. For you, however, stories refer to a racial group who have maintained coherence by passing on stories, generally opposed to the dominant group. While Virginia's stories are print and class-based, your stories, Toni, are oral- and folk-based. Early twentieth-century British novelists were stifled by the novel of manners that Jane Austen had mastered, a construct of conventions that had been wiped away by the intellectual and social events of early twentieth-century European societies. But African American writers had been stifled by the necessity to write primarily to audiences other than themselves, restricted as they were by an American master narrative. So Virginia would question the existence of a coherent narrative, while you would feel "bereft" when you read literature that was supposedly about yourself.

As was true of Virginia's context in the 1920s, monumental social events in your time opened up a space for your development of "unorthodox novelistic characteristics" ("Rootedness" 342). As a result of the African American political movements of the 1960s, African American culture would begin to be conceptualized as a vital culture by intellectuals rather than a pathology of or a deviation from Euro-American culture, as it was characterized in the works of possibly the most visible of pre-1960s African American writer, Richard Wright. Increasingly African American writers would characterize their primary audience as that of African Americans. Oral storytelling, which had been one basis of the persistence of that culture, was increasingly recognized as having "legitimate" conventions capable of being refigured in literary genres such as the novel. So while Virginia could redefine the traditional concepts of British fiction in the 1920s, you could, in the 1970s, recuperate traditional concepts of African American linguistic expression, considered "unorthodox" in the Euro-American novel.

For while you saw the novel as valuable for its ability to carry on the tradition of African American oral storytelling, that it could be "both print and oral literature," that the novel could harken back to an older communal tradition even as it was very much of the I modern world ("Rootedness" 341), Virginia doubted the "truthfulness" of stories. While your writing is clearly concerned with expressing the communal quality of African American life, its myths, beliefs, dreams, Virginia wondered about the idea of a communal narrative.

Yet, although your and Virginia's views of the novel might seem to be worlds apart, both of your writings are riveted on the relationship between the inner life of your characters and the world within which they find themselves, the object in fact of their consciousness. In this regard, I remember the talk you gave at Berkeley about your novel *Beloved* in 1987, when it had just been published. You stressed that one of your interests in writing it was that much of what had been written about American slavery ignored—rerpressed—the inner lives of slaves, sometimes for very good reasons, such as the fact that nineteenth-century African American writers had to be primarily concerned with the *institution* of slavery, with the abolishment of that institution, a concern which often precluded the exploration of their characters' psyches. Slave narratives used a formula based on the biblical story of the Fall and the Resurrection to engage the largely Christian white audience. Slave narrators had to hold back memories which might alienate their white readers.[12] But you were not so much interested in what happened: you already knew the Margaret Garner story. In fact, in every one of your novels, the reader knows what has happened or will happen on practically the first page. What you wanted to do was to fill those silences and to involve yourself and the reader in such a way as to feel the experience, both viscerally and as an idea.

As Virginia's works so amply demonstrate, memory is a central aspect of the inner life, one means by which we interpret the present as well as remember the past. How does one express that inner life without completely losing sense of the world in which characters in a novel must move, that is, losing the specificities of time and place? Virginia solved that tension between the inner and the outer life in the construction of her novels by using soliloquies, what Ralph Freedman calls "*dramatic* monologues in which psychological drama and common speech are replaced by lyrical drama and inner speech" (203). Unlike the stream of consciousness technique of writers such as Joyce, which Woolf criticized as being too "centered in a self which, in spite of its tremor of susceptibility, never embraces or creates what is outside itself or beyond" ("Modern Fiction" 156), her monologues were carefully crafted to reveal not only the quality of that particular character's mind, but also his or her ways of perceiving the world. In *Mrs. Dalloway*, we are in the minds of Clarissa Dalloway, Septimus Smith, Mr. Dalloway, Peter Walsh, during one day, a day framed by the tolling of Big Ben, clearly situating us in high society London. Even as the reader is experiencing reality in terms of the characters' inner lives, we are anchored in some time and place.

As a reader of Virginia Woolf, you, Toni, were clearly alert to the world evoked by her imagination. As a writer, you were confronted with some of the same issues of narrative technique with which she had to contend. In your first novel, *The Bluest Eye*, you would use soliloquies as she had, in order to capture the inner lives of your characters. However, you had to deal with an additional problem, for readers were not used to focusing on the inner lives of black characters. Racism, after all, affected the social lives of African Americans in such a way that the external social world had taken precedence over the inner lives of characters. How stunned I was when I first read Pauline Breedlove's soliloquy in *The Bluest Eye*, possibly the first evocation of a black domestic's inner voice. Although the omniscient narrator focuses on Pauline's social situation, her inner voice allows the reader to feel her specific dreams, her intense use of images of color, her individual way of perceiving the world in images of color even as it is rooted in her rural southern upbringing. You established for her a love of order, a sense of design which would have served her well, if she had had the opportunity to become an artist. It was from the African tradition of storytelling, where playing with images is as important as it is in a Woolf novel, that Pauline acquired her voice.

Perhaps your most characteristic transformation of the narrator is your different uses of a chorus, a community that includes the reader, in every one of your novels, since as you have said, "[your] audience is always the people in the book [you're] writing at the time" ("Toni Morrison," Tate 122). So there is the choral "I" narrator of *The Bluest Eye:* the town functioning as a character in *Sula;* the neighborhood and the community that responds in the two parts of town in *Song of Solomon;* all of nature thinking and feeling and watching and responding to the action going on in *Tar Baby;* the chorus of the community, living and dead, in *Beloved;* the City in *Jazz.* In your most recent novel, your unnamed narrator admits that she/he does not know everything about the characters in much the same way we do not know everything about someone by looking at a photograph, an aesthetic form that emerged in the 1920s, which seems to mimic life even as it freezes it: "When I see them now they are not sepia, still, losing their edges to the light of a future afternoon. Caught midway between was and must be. For me they are real. Sharply in focus and clicking" (*Jazz* 226). In her last novels, Virginia too began to use the concept of the chorus, especially in her last work, *Between the Acts,* in which she devises what Rachel Blau DuPlessis calls "a communal protagonist," "where no character in the plot stands above any other" (163-164). There are real differences between your respective uses of the chorus, however, for while both of you are insisting that there is a communal protagonist, your novels, Toni, still insist upon the tension between individuals, the experimental ones and their relationship to the community, to which, in your work, they return, as a means of testing out the extent to which difference is allowed and might even triumph.

Although you used soliloquy to express the inner voice, a choral note to express community, both social and mythic, you also needed an omniscient narrator in much of your work, for unlike Virginia, you were not usually writing about characters in the present. Part of your task had to be a remapping of the historical terrain for African Americans, a terrain that had been previously charted by a master narrative from the outside, rather than from the inside of their experiences, a history that even African American communities might have begun to forget, or might not want to remember. So, for example, although *The Bluest Eye* is set in 1941, so that the reader might understand Pauline and Cholly Breedlove, you had to move back in time to the 1920s of their southern youth. Even *Tar Baby*, your novel set primarily in the present, draws power from the mythic past of the island on which it is set. As critic Wahneema Lubiano has said about your work, because it "remaps the terrain of African American cultural and social history and allows for a community of the imagination, it interrupts the ideology that produces the kind of world we inhabit" (321).

But while your writing remaps American history, it is not historical in the usual sense of that word; linear progression is not its goal, for as you have so beautifully captured in your rendition of the inner voices of your characters, whatever we consider reality to be, we do not experience it either individually or communally as a march of years. Rather there is both inner time and outer time.

Virginia expressed a similar sentiment, when in her essay "Modern Fiction" she critiqued the thirty-two perfectly balanced chapters of the Victorian novel which emphasized the material world as the real world. "Is life like this?" For "life is not a series of gig lamps symmetrically arranged; but a luminous halo, a semi-transparent envelope surrounding us from the beginning of consciousness to the end" ("Modern Fiction" 154). Virginia experimented with the formal monologue as a way of fusing inner and outer time, honing it from novel to novel until in *The Waves* (1931), no narrator intrudes, and the juxtaposition of the characters' inner voices produces its own design of the interrelatedness and separateness of the characters, the waves of lives being the intersections of the private inner voice, the continuity of the seasons with their mythic significance, the traditions and shifts of society. What Virginia wanted to do in *The Waves* was "to saturate every atom. . . to eliminate all waste, deadness, superfluity: to give the moment whole; whatever it includes. Say that the moment is a combination of thought; sensation; the voice of the sea" ("Nov. 28, 1928" 139). In *The Waves*, she eliminated the narrator, the external movement of the narrative being delineated by her juxtaposition of her characters' formal monologues. In contrast, Toni, you wanted

> to make the story appear oral, meandering, effortless, spoken—to have the reader *feel* the narrator without *identifying* that narrator or hearing him or her knock about, and to have the reader work with the author in the construction of the book.... What is left out is as important as what is there. ("Rootedness " 341)

In your work, as in Virginia's, inner time is always transforming outer time through memory. But since memory is not only individual, but merges with others to create a communal memory, outer time also transforms inner time. It is that reciprocity between the individual inner and the communal outer which your work seeks. The folk's time, however, is not mechanical time, the march of years, which your chapter titles in *Sula* mock, but time as it marks an event in human society and in nature, which for you includes the folk as much as the seasons. The mythic quality of your worlds seems to be in opposition to many conceptions of human history, when in fact history and myth have always been related, myth being a central part of any people's history, history itself creating myth, time and timelessness in dialogue. In your work there is a deep relationship between your characters' belief system and their view of nature. Thus Baby Suggs preaches in "the Clearing"; in *Sula*, Eva can read the signs of nature. And in *Song of Solomon*, Milkman learns about "what there was before language. Before things were written down. Language in the time when men and animals did talk to one another..." (280).

Nature in its many aspects is central to your work, I believe, because nature is one constant, in time and space, for all human societies. So *The Bluest Eye* is structurally arranged in terms of the seasons; nature responds to the action in *Tar Baby*; Sethe has got a "chokecherry tree" inscribed upon her back in *Beloved*. Virginia too felt that deep connection with nature, that it is a crucial element of that "luminous halo" and is inside ourselves, even as it appears to be outside, thus her desire to fuse "thought, sensation, the sea"

But myth, Toni, in your work means not only a recognition of the power of primal natural forces, but also the presence of an ancestor. For African Americans, who were torn from their homeland and for whom migrations have been a constant, the ancestor female and male, rather than a particular homeland, is the ground of wisdom, the timeless presence. Art, for you, becomes one means by which that ancestor can be invoked. How does Virginia relate to an ancestor figure? Her evocation in *A Room of One's Own* of her father's favorite poet, Milton, not only critiques that male lineage, but also insists on creating a specifically female lineage. Thus she turns to the aunt who willed her money: "My aunt's legacy unveiled the sky to me, and substituted for the large and imposing figure of a gentleman, which Milton commended for my perpetual adoration, a view of the open sky" (39).[13]

Toni, you have described your own works in terms of rhythmic shapes: *Sula* as a spiral, for example, *Song of Solomon* as "a train picking up speed," for "every life to [you] has a rhythm, a shape," whose contours" "you can't see... all at once" ("Toni Morrison," Tate 124). Virginia wanted to capture "the moment," which reveals that life; you want to revel in the rhythm of that life: related temperaments yet different in their approach to language and to the imagination. You see the need "to clean the language up and give words back their original meaning" ("Toni Morrison," Tate 126) so that "the language... [does] not sweat" ("Language" 24). In an interview, you set a new goal for yourself—to write novels in which you do not have to indicate that your characters are black or white by the use of modifiers—but that the reader knows because of the context, your use of language ("Toni Morrison," Moyers 56-57). What, you wondered, would that mean for you as a writer?

Like Virginia, writing novels for you is decidedly an experimental act, a creative one—so that you are always pushing against what you have already learned to do. Increasingly, as in the prose poems of *Beloved* and the painterly prose of the narrator's observations in *Jazz*, your language is symbolic, just as Virginia's language in her last works became more formal, more like poetic drama.

Novelists, you have said, are always influenced by the moral currents of their world. It is not surprising, then, that because you and Virginia come from different cultural cosmologies, the moral questions you pose in your work are somewhat different, even as women. While you both clearly acknowledge the imagination as central to your temperament, while you have used some similar narrative strategies, what strikes me as the major difference is your relationship to the idea of love in your novels. You have so many times said that love is your major theme: life is poor, uninteresting, without being able to love somebody; but love is also a dilemma for human beings because, like the elements of nature, it can run so quickly to excess. All of your novels deal with that dilemma. Virginia, on the other hand, was concerned that women were expected to write about love—love here meaning romantic love; she insisted that women also wanted poetry, dreams, imagination. Without question, so do you, though in a different context. You have said that you are "not interested in indulging [your]self in some private, closed exercise of [your] imagination that fulfills only the obligation of [your] personal dreams—which is to say yes, the work must be political" ("Rootedness" 344). Virginia, I believe, would have held to that same sentiment, while questioning whether the imagination can be anything but private.

Perhaps, Toni, because you are an African American woman writing in the latter part of the twentieth century, you can now write about expanded definitions of love, rooted in a tradition of a people who, from their beginnings in this country, had been denied the right to express love, and thus have invented their particular strategies to hold onto it. In your world, love is not so much romance as it is primal "risk" and freedom," incapable of being completely contained.

In keeping with the open endings of your novels, I hesitate to bring any resolution to my invention. For your work is not yet finished, while Virginia's is there for you to contemplate. In being aware of "her notions of risk and safety," you may well have expanded your own—creating layered rhythms in your fiction, that is both your own personal voice and that of the folk. I see you, Toni, continuing to write and read, read and write in layered rhythms.

NOTES

1 Blake mentions this detail on page 189.

2 This essay was first presented at the Third Annual Conference on Virginia Woolf, Lincoln University, Jefferson City, Missouri, 10-13 June 1993.

3 For example, see Spender.

4 See, for example, Marcus.

5 A sister student of Toni Morrison who works at Sacramento State University told me this.

6 For a discussion of the Dreadnaught Hoax, in which Virginia Woolf and friends darkened their faces and dressed as Abyssinian men in a protest against British policy in North Africa, see Wilson 297.

7 See Lemer (especially 220-221) for a discussion of the reasons why African American families, in contrast to much of American society in the early part of the twentieth century, felt it necessary that their daughters, even more than their sons, needed higher education.

8 Episodes of competition and rivalry recur in Virginia's and Vanessa's relationship. See, for example, Bell 1: 22-24, 88-90, 132-136, 164-169; 2: 89, 110, 147, 218-219.

9 See Christian, "Shadows Uplifted."

10 See DuPlessis, 47-65.

11 This is the subject of DuPlessis' study.

12 For a discussion of this point, see Christian, "'Somebody Forgot to Tell Somebody Something.'"

13 I owe this insight to Stanford instructor Cheri Ross's lecture, "A Room of One's Own and the Revaluation of Space," 25 May 1993.

WORKS CITED

Bell, Quentin. *Virginia Woolf: A Biography.* 2 vols. New York: Harcourt. Brace, Jovanovich, 1972.

Blake, Susan. "Toni Morrison." *Dictionary of Literary Biography: African American Fiction Writers after 1955.* Vol. 33. Ed. Thadious Davis and Trudier Harris. Detroit: Gale, 1984.

Bloom, Harold. Introduction. *Toni Morrison.* Ed. Harold Bloom. New York: Chelsea House, 1990. 1-5.

Christian, Barbara. "Shadows Uplifted." *Black Women Novelists.* Westport: Greenwood, 1980. 3-34.

___. "'Somebody Forgot to Tell Somebody Something': African-American Women's Historical Novels." *Wild Women of the Whirlwind.* Ed. Joanne Braxton and André McLaughlin. New Brunswick: Rutgers UP, 1990. 326-341.

DuPlessis, Rachel Blau. *Writing Beyond the Ending: Narrative Strategies of Twentieth Century Women Writers.* Bloomington: Indiana UP, 1985.

Ellison, Ralph. *Shadow and Act.* New York: Random House, 1964.

Freedman, Ralph. *The Lyrical Novel: Studies in Hermann Hesse, André Gide, and Virginia Woolf.* Princeton: Princeton UP, 1963.

Giddings, Paula. *When and Where I Enter.* New York: Morrow, 1984.

Gilbert, Sandra M., and Susan Gubar. *Madwoman in the Attic: The Woman Writer and the Nineteenth-Century Literary Imagination.* New Haven: Yale UP, 1979.

Lerner, Gerda, ed. *Black Women in White America.* New York: Pantheon, 1972.

Lubiano, Wahneema. "Toni Morrison." *African American Writers.* Ed. Valerie Smith. New York: Scribner's, 1991. 321-333.

Marcus, Jane, ed. *New Feminist Essays on Virginia Woolf.* Lincoln: U of Nebraska P, 1981.

Morrison, Toni. *The Bluest Eye*. New York: Holt, Rinehart, Winston, 1970.

___ . "Interview with Toni Morrison." With Ntozake Shange. *Steve Cannon's House of Magic*. WBAI, New York. Nov. 1977.

___ . *Jazz*. New York: Knopf, 1992.

___ . "The Language Must Not Sweat: A Conversation with Toni Morrison." With Thomas LeClair. *New Republic* 21 March 1981: 25-29.

___ . *Playing in the Dark: Whiteness and the Literary Imagination*. Cambridge: Harvard UP, 1992.

___ . "Rootedness: The Ancestor as Foundation." *Black Women Writers (1950-1980): A Critical Evaluation*. Ed. Mari Evans. Garden City, NY: Anchor-Doubleday, 1983. 339-345.

___ . *Song of Solomon*. New York: New American Library, 1977.

___ . *Sula*. New York: Knopf, 1974.

___ . "Toni Morrison." Interview with Bill Moyers. *A World of Ideas* II. Garden City: Doubleday, 1990. 54-63.

___ . "Toni Morrison." Interview with Claudia Tate. *Black Women Writers at Work*. Ed. Claudia Tate. New York: Continuum, 1983. 117-131.

Spender, Stephen. *The Struggle of the Modern*. Berkeley: U of California P, 1963.

Tate, Claudia. "Allegories of Black Female Desire; or Rereading Nineteenth-Century Sentimental Narratives of Black Female Authority." *Changing Our Own Words*. Ed. Cheryl Wall. New Brunswick: Rutgers UP, 1991. 98-126.

Toni Morrison. Videocassette. Part 3 of *In Black and White: Six Profiles of African American Writers*. Dir. Matteo Bellinelli. Prod. RTSI-Swiss Television. California Newsreel, 1992. 27 min.

Wilson, J. J. "Virginia Woolf." *Dictionary of Literary Biography: British Novelists, 1890-1929: Modernists*. Vol. 36. Ed. Thomas F.

Staley. Detroit: Gale, 1985.

Woolf, Virginia. "How It Strikes A Contemporary." *The Common Reader, First Series*. 1925. New York: Harcourt, Brace, World, 1953. 236-246.

___ . "Modern Fiction." *The Common Reader, First Series*. 1925. New York: Harcourt, Brace, World, 1953. 150-158.

___ . "Nov. 28, 1928." *A Writer's Diary*. London: Hogarth, 1953. 138-139.

___ . *A Room of One's Own*. 1929. New York: Harcourt, Brace, Jovanovich, 1957.

___ . *To the Lighthouse*. 1927. New York: Harcourt, Brace, World, 1955

Shame and Anger in *The Bluest Eye* *

> The trauma of racism is, for the racist and the victim, the severe fragmentation of the self.[1]

Jill Matus

MORRISON has said that what prompted her to begin writing her first novel was a sense of loss, a void. 'Things were moving too fast in the early 1960-70s... it was exciting but it left me bereft.... There were no books about me, I didn't exist in all the literature I had read... this person, this female, this black did not exist center-self.'[2] Responding to a sense of absence and a lack in representations, *The Bluest Eye* (1970) is an imagined history of what it is to grow up black and female in the 1930s and 1940s, but there is another important way in which it responds to contemporary political movements—the way things were moving too fast in the early 1960-70s. However self-affirming assertions such as 'black is beautiful' were in the 1960s and 1970s, they were too simple to redress the complex and long-prepared effects of valuations based on colour. Morrison commented on the movement's assertions of racial beauty: 'If the best thing happened in the world and it all came out perfectly in terms of what the gains and goals of the *Movement* were, nevertheless

* Source: Matus, Jill. *Toni Morrison*. Manchester: Manchester UP, 1998. 37-54. Permission granted.

nobody was going to get away with that; nobody was going to tell me that it had been that easy. That all I needed was a slogan: "Black is Beautiful". Focusing on the complex formations of subjectivity in a racialised country, Morrison's first novel implicitly takes on assertions of racial pride—black is beautiful[3]—and scrutinises the historical backlog of self-devaluation that such assertions cannot magically erase. At a time when the Black Aesthetic movement was calling for positive representations and role models, Morrison created troubled and traumatised characters. Her insistence on making the reader share through Pecola the trauma of racism's effects was a way of signalling the far-reaching range and insidious nature of those effects and their causes.

Perhaps the most telling anecdote concerning the genesis of *The Bluest Eye* is to be found in the 'Afterword' to a recent edition of the novel, where Morrison describes the anger she felt at a schoolfriend's wish for blue eyes: 'The sorrow in her voice is seemed to call for sympathy, and I faked it for her, but, astonished by the desecration she proposed, I "got mad" at her instead.'[4] The sorrow in the other girl's voice may call for sympathy but the wish itself encodes shame. The girl signals that she does not think herself sufficient without blue eyes—a longstanding hallmark of beauty by white Western standards. She conveys her sense of deficiency as a black subject and potentially enlists all black subjects in feeling similarly ashamed. Resisting her own exposure and belittlement as she is pulled into the same shamed category, the younger Morrison, in this brief narrative, responds angrily. The anecdote articulates a relationship between the two main emotions with which Morrison's first novel is concerned—anger and shame.

The novel is built around two young women, Pecola Breedlove and Claudia MacTeer, and their respective families. Many parallels and points of comparison connect Claudia and Pecola: most significantly, Claudia matures to look back on the past and narrate some of the novel through her memories of childhood, while Pecola, in a state of permanent dissociation, is locked in a traumatised childhood and can remember nothing. Claudia's mother may be tough and often angry, but she nevertheless communicates a fierce and protective love; Pecola's mother is more protective of her white charge than her needy daughter. Whereas Claudia's father throws the child-molesting boarder out of their house, Pecola's father is the molester of his own child. Through the stories of Pecola and Claudia, Morrison examines how identity is constructed in young women, scrutinising in the process aspects of commodity and popular culture, pedagogical strategies and the knowledges they produce, and class and labour relations. Through Claudia and Pecola, Morrison attempts to analyse the processes of resistance and submission to a hierarchy of values enshrined in American culture. She does this by exploring the relationship of these girls-becoming-women to the culture and commodities that encode the superiority of whiteness. In the following section, I focus on the narrative's exploration of anger and shame. Anger, Claudia's childhood mode, produces resistance to cultural valuations of blackness; shame, which defines Pecola, ensures submission. Finally, I explore the passage from Claudia's angry younger self to the older, memorialising narrator. It is she who bears witness to Pecola's movement from a continually shamed and diminished self to the lost, traumatised and divided subject we see at the end of the novel.

To feel shame, according to psychological theorists, is to feel a violation of one's sense of dignity, an uncomfortable exposure; it is 'to feel *seen* in a painfully diminished sense'.[5] Profoundly interpersonal, the experience of shame is also therefore social and cultural. Shame is the result of feeling deficient, whether in relation to a parent, an admired school-friend or a more powerful social group. Psychologist Gershen Kaufman summarises: 'The significance of shame lies in its profound impact on personality, psychopathology, and interpersonal relations, as well as its role in minority group relations, minority identity development, national identity development, and international relations.'[6] Any denial of need which leaves the subject feeling belittled, marginalised or inappropriate in its desires is potentially a cause of shame. As Kaufman notes, 'contained in the experience of shame is the piercing awareness of the self as fundamentally deficient in some vital way as a human being ... Shame is an impotence-making experience because *it feels as though* there is no way to relieve the matter, no way to restore the balance of things. One has simply failed as a human being.'[7] This is precisely how Claudia feels when she is ill and her mother is angry:

> She is not talking to me. She is talking to the puke, but she is calling it my name: Claudia. She wipes it up as best as she can and puts a scratchy towel over the large wet place.... My mother's anger humiliates me; her words chafe my cheeks and I am crying. I do not know that she is not angry with me but with my sickness. I believe she despises my weakness for letting the sickness 'take holt.'[8]

Only the narrator's present knowledge, which is implied in the sentence, 'I do not know that she is not angry with me', suggests that one day the young Claudia will understand the memory and offset it against the significant demonstrations of her mother's caring. Angry as Mrs MacTeer usually is, she is also capable of mending the disrupted interpersonal bridge that produces shame and humiliation in her daughters. On one occasion, Claudia's elder sister Frieda is whipped because it appears that she and Pecola are 'playing dirty', whereas Frieda is merely attempting to help Pecola deal with her first experience of menstruation: 'Frieda was destroyed. Whippings wounded and insulted her' (22). Eventually when Mrs MacTeer understands the situation, 'she pulled both of them toward her, their heads against her stomach. Her eyes were sorry. "All right, all right. Now, stop crying. I didn't know"' (22). That their mother is capable of making reparation, however slight, is important in allowing Frieda and Claudia to limit their internalisation of shame and to recover a sense of worth.

But Claudia, whose uninhibited responses to the world around her give her narrative its frankness and freshness of perception, is more often angry than shamed. The first paragraph of the novel introduces us to Claudia and her sister Frieda in the grip of a powerful desire to 'poke the arrogance' out of the eyes of their neighbour Rosemary Villanucci, who is taunting them from within her father's flashy Buick. They inhibit for the moment their urge to 'smash the ownership that curls her chewing mouth', but know that when she comes out of the car, they will beat her up, 'make red marks on her white skin, and she will cry and ask us do we want her to pull her pants down'(5). Rosermary's taunts, as well as her knowledge of self-abasement and submissive behaviour, suggest a familiar world of childish power struggles and retributions that seems to depend more at this point in the narrative on class and wealth than on race, although Morrison will go on to demonstrate the way these categories mutually inflect each other.

There are ample reasons why Claudia might well be angry, not only with Rosemary Villannucci lauding it over her less affluent neighbours, but, on a larger scale, with the pervasive marginalisation and devaluation of black subjects in American culture and society. The novel demonstrates the power of that devaluation in the opening chapter's emphasis on the normative white family of the Dick and Jane reading primer. There are also frequent references to icons of white beauty such as Shirley Temple and Jean Harlow,

Heddy Lamar and Claudette Colbert—the white screen goddesses on whom Pauline and Maureen desire to model themselves—as well as the pretty faces that sell candies like 'Mary Janes'. Everywhere the message resounds in American culture that black cannot be beautiful; indeed, as the Breedloves' self-loathing demonstrates, the blacker, the less beautiful.

When unstifled, Claudia's anger and transgressive urges register a resistance to the indoctrination of the dominant culture's fantasies of beauty and worth. Her anger, however, is readily converted to shame because she does not really understand what makes her feel violent and aggressive.[9] Interested anger, the text implies, is appropriate, legitimate; disinterested anger cannot understand its provocation or bind itself to any rationale. The problem of appropriate anger is articulated as Claudia moves from confessing her destruction and dismembering of white baby dolls to her disturbing desire to perform the same rites of violence on white girls. As far as Claudia is concerned, her motivation is nothing more than curiosity. Like the child who dismantles a fascinating mechanism in order to see how it is put together, she wants to take apart little white girls in order to know the secret of how they work, what makes them beautiful and desirable: 'The indifference with which I could have axed them was shaken only by my desire to do so. To discover what eluded me: the secret of the magic they weaved on others' (15).

Offering curiosity as her motive, Claudia thus never fully confronts her punitive and destructive desires. Though she later refers to her urge for dismemberment as 'pristine sadism', the pleasure of vengeance visited on white baby dolls and little white girls is only implicit in her account of her violent tendencies:

> If I pinched them, their eyes—unlike the crazed glint of the baby doll's eyes—would fold in pain, and their cry would not be the

> sound of an icebox door, but a fascinating cry of pain. When I learned how repulsive this disinterested violence was, that it was repulsive because it was disinterested, my shame floundered about for refuge. (15-16)

The elder Claudia is suggesting that her violence is repulsive because it fails to take in the humanity of the other, for she approaches her subjects with a curiosity that finds even their pain 'fascinating'. Disinterestedness and objectivity are conditions to which the scientific investigator aspires, but in Claudia's case, wanting to know what makes white girls attractive cannot count as a laudatory scientific goal. The text registers some satisfaction, though, in Claudia's pursuits, which suggests that her response is in some ways legitimate, or at least understandable. To the extent that Claudia is disinterested, she might as well be taking a watch apart to see what makes it tick. But the desire to know is not her only motivation.

Disinterestedness suggests also impartiality; one does not stand to gain or lose from the outcome of an act or investigation. Is Claudia's violence interested or disinterested? Though she does not gain anything from the dismemberment of white girls, she would find it of benefit, she thinks, to know the secret of their charms. Is the implication then that, had Claudia been acting openly out of political or other interests, her violence would possibly have been righteous or at least justifiable? Does Claudia's hindsight as she narrates her memories contain the recognition that she would have been less shamed by her impulses had she known that she felt murderous and enraged rather than merely curious? Or perhaps the novel suggests that by confusing curiosity and anger, she displaces the objects of her interested violence. Morrison's text stops short of acknowledging that Claudia may be less disinterested than she protests, but that that interestedness may make her violence less, not more, repulsive.

In her essay on consumer culture in *The Bluest Eye*, Susan Willis reads this passage in the following way: 'By demonstrating that violence against whites runs the risk of being "disinterested violence", Morrison suggests that white people are little more than: abstractions'.[10] The point is surely not so much that whites are 'to some extent reified subjects against which it is impossible to mount passionate, self-affirming resistance or retaliation'.[11] It is rather, as Claudia later understands, that dolls, little white girls, or even 'high yellow' girls in Claudia's community are not the 'Enemy' because they are not the sources of power; they are only vessels into which power flows. No doubt dismembering white girls would have revealed as little of their secret power as had dismembering the dolls that Claudia reduced to their sawdust, gauze and metal constituents. As she admits later, when reflecting on how she hates and envies Maureen Peal, an infuriatingly self-assured, light-skinned schoolmate 'all the time we knew that Maureen Peal was not the Enemy and not worthy of such intense hatred. The *Thing* to fear was the *Thing* that made *her* beautiful, and not us' (58). But if a '*Thing*' is behind the hierarchy of beauty and worth that Claudia is discovering, then in what forms does it manifest itself as an appropriate target for anger? As Claudia and her sister Frieda shout insults at the retreating Maureen Peal, their 'angry faces knotted like dark cauliflowers', they at least keep the 'Thing' outside of themselves. In contrast, Pecola stands apart in pain, folded into herself like a 'pleated wing'. The vulnerability of Pecola provokes Claudia's anger here just as, in the rape scene later, it will enrage her father. Pecola reminds these others of their own vulnerabilities and the perilous weakness of their defences. That perilous weakness is indicated in the incident where Cholly turns his anger on his young girlfriend rather than feel the impotence of anger against the goading white men who interrupt his first sexual experience. So Claudia is irked by Pecola's collapse in the face of Maureen Peal's insults. Whereas she and Frieda maintain a sense of their own worth by conjuring insults and creatively cursing the powerful Peal, Pecola subsides, having absorbed the slurs and teasing. Claudia reacts by wanting 'to open her [Pecola] up, crisp her edges, ram a stick down that hunched and curving spine, stand erect and spit the misery out on the streets. But she held it in where it could lap up into her eyes' (57).

Claudia's anger, directed outward, protects her sense of self. The difference then between Claudia and Pecola is that Pecola internalises the world's actions and judgements, whereas Claudia is able to defend her vulnerability by keeping devaluation external. In so far as it allows her to 'spit the misery out onto the street', her anger is salutory but, as the narrating Claudia will later admit, while anger may protect the self, it may also project itself on to a target selected because it is poorly defended and vulnerable. In that case, anger merely participates in transferring blame—a process that leads to tragic scapegoating.

Pecola's woundability—her tendency to absorb and internalise—is demonstrated in a series of shamings and rejections: the boys' taunting of her at school; the contempt of Geraldine, the mother of one of those boys; her mother's wrath and rejection when Pecola upsets the blueberry cobbler. In each case, Pecola responds to ridicule or castigation in silence, simply absorbing the censure and humiliation. Cholly's rape of his daughter is only the last, and most graphic and literal, instance of the way in which Pecola internalises the incursions of the outside. When Mr Green, the boarder who has been allowed inside the MacTeer's family home, molests Frieda, her parents forcibly expel him from the house as soon as he comes 'up on the porch'. Claudia's father hurls a tricycle at his head and her mother hits him with a broom. In contrast, there is no one to defend the boundaries of Pecola's home (and internal spaces) as her father staggers in drunk and sees her washing dishes.

But while distinctions between inside and outside may tentatively hold in the material cases of the body or the home, they are unstable fictions when negotiating the conceptual boundaries of self and other. As we have seen, Morrison noted that the reclamation of racial beauty in the 1960s made her think about why such slogans as 'black is beautiful' were necessary. Even if reviled by others, why could 'this beauty not be taken for granted within the community?'[12] As *The Bluest Eye* reveals, the community is permeated by standards, aspirations and self valuations derived not only from the commodity culture which it consumes, but inherent in the structuring of labour relations and class positions, both heavily inflected by race. The project of the novel is to reveal the difficulty in maintaining a strong 'inside' whether of self or community against the insidious pervasiveness of racial devaluations.

If anger helps to maintain distinctions between what belongs to the self and what must be kept outside it, shame disturbs those distinctions by distorting responsibility and encouraging self-blame. In so doing it prevents interested and appropriate anger. The culture of shame displaces the focus on external causes or forces. Instead of feeling angry at something, one feels ashamed of the self for something. As a means of producing self-regulating and conforming subjects, the inculcation of shame secures dominant interests, converting and perverting anger in order eventually to breed false loves and desires. So shamed is Claudia by her propensities for violence toward white girls, violence apparently unprovoked and without cause, that she opts for the assuagement of discomforting anger in hypocritical friendships. Her 'shame flounders about for refuge' and finds it in shamming.

Shame displaces anger more thoroughly in Pecola's negotiations with the world. The one occasion in the text during which Pecola experiences feelings of anger is illustrative. Not only is her anger displaced from an appropriate target, but it hardly rises before it subsides under shame. Feeling a storekeeper's distaste for her blackness when she pays him for the precious Mary Jane candies she is buying, Pecola is shamed by his reluctance to touch her hand as he takes her pennies. On leaving the store, she is rouse to a transferred anger as she trips on a sidewalk crack:

> Anger stirs and wakes in her; it opens its mouth, and like a hot-mouthed puppy, laps up the dredges of her shame. Anger is better. There is a sense of being in anger. A reality and presence. An awareness of worth. It is a lovely surging. Her thoughts fall back to Mr. Yacobowski's eyes, his phlegmy voice. The anger will not hold; the puppy is too easily surfeited. Its thirst too quickly quenched, it sleeps. The shame wells up again, its muddy rivulets seeping into her eyes. (38)

The relationship between anger and shame, raised earlier in relation to Claudia's feelings towards white dolls and white girls, is made even clearer, therefore, in the case of Pecola. Anger feels better than shame because it empowers her; shame is a crippling emotion that leaves her merely humiliated, disempowered. But brief 'lovely surges' subside easily not only because the power of the other's distaste is strong, but because the anger itself is displaced. Pecola never actually feels angry with Mr Yacobowski. She is angry because she trips in the sidewalk crack. In both Pecola and Claudia, anger does not identify its appropriate object because neither Pecola nor Claudia is sufficiently aware of what causes their anger in the first place. Claudia implies that the process of growing up has, for her, included a shaming away of anger. Shame swallows anger then itself takes refuge in 'fraudulent love'. As a child, Claudia has hated baths and experienced the absence of dirt as humiliating (22); she suggests further that anger belongs to the dark, unwashed self, but the inevitable effect of being socialised means learning to love Shirley Temple and learning to love cleanliness. The linkage between fraudulent love and cleanliness suggests the sanitising, whitening process of enculturation, experienced in retrospect as a loss, or at best, 'adjustment without improvement'. Pecola's passage in the novel is from repeated shaming and humiliation to dissociation and madness. Claudia's passage is from anger to the fraudulent love which replaces anger and shame, and beyond that, through her memorialising narrative, to a recognition of the community's internalisation of self-hatred and its scapergoating techniques.

Claudia's narrative bears witness not only to the trauma of the incest and rape that Pecola experiences, but to the trauma of pervasive racism. As I outlined in the previous chapter, Laura Brown has recently argued that prevailing definitions of trauma need to be revised to accommodate the trauma that women and girls experience because of their vulnerability to rape and molestation. While trauma is usually defined as an experience of overwhelming or unusual proportions, an event 'outside the range of human experience', the work of Brown suggests that such definitions disqualify those who suffer experiences that are not, statistically speaking, beyond the range of human experience.[13] Brown objects to the way 'normal' traumatic events are defined. 'War and genocide, which are the work of men and male-dominated culture, are agreed-upon traumas; so are natural disasters, vehicle crashes, boats sinking in the freezing ocean.'[14] By defining trauma as the extraordinary, Brown argues, we delude ourselves into believing that ordinary life is safe and manageable. But ordinary life is hardly safe for incest victims or for victims of rape and molestation. She argues that there is a 'constant presence and threat of trauma in the lives of girls and women of all colors, men of color in the United States, lesbian and gay people, people in poverty, and people with disabilities'. What does it mean, she asks 'if we admit that our culture is a factory for the production of so many walking wounded?'[15] Her metaphor—factory and production—does the same work as Claudia's metaphor in the opening chapters of the novel of the unyielding earth and the seeds that fail to come to fruition. Brown's analysis of insidious trauma draws attention to the everyday occurrences that may prove traumatic for marginalised groups in a society. Brown notes too that, while mainstream trauma theory has recognised that post-traumatic symptoms can be inter-generational, as in the case of children of survivors of the Holocaust, it has yet to explore the ways 'trauma can be spread laterally throughout an oppressed social group as well, when membership in that group means a constant lifetime risk of exposure to certain trauma'.[16] Although Brown's analysis focuses largely on gender, it is also clearly applicable to race, and potentially illuminating, therefore, of Morrison's concerns in *The Bluest Eye*, a novel that represents both the traumatogenic effects of living in a racialised society as well the trauma of incest.

Brown's analysis demands that we reconsider the defining condition of Freudian trauma. Do unpreparedness, shock and fright continue to be important elements in insidious trauma? Fright itself, it could be argued, is produced not only in response to cannons firing, ships sinking or natural disasters, but also in response to the quiet opening of the bedroom door or the embrace of a male relative that is sexual under the guise of being protective. Incest may be accompanied by complex feelings that are overwhelming but may go beyond fright, covering a wide range from pain and powerlessness to guilt and pleasure. How are these to be accommodated into traditional definitions of trauma?

Morrison allows Pecola to bear witness to her suffering in her conversations with her imagined friend, but the dialogue of the split self in no way approximates a therapeutic dialogue in which teller and listener share the burden of the sufferer's history. Laub's emphasis on the listener in any testimony to trauma shows the need for sharing, participation and transmission[17] but Pecola's remains a story incapable of transmission; she cannot tell it in the 'real' world. There is, therefore, no reclamation of the past in a way that allows Pecola to assimilate and process what has happened to her.

The function of bearing witness falls to Claudia, who mediates Pecola's story, enlisting the reader as 'listener' and ultimate co-owner of the trauma. When Morrison says in an 'Afterword' that she thinks she failed in the novel because readers pity Pecola rather than find themselves moved by her, she signals her desire to have implicated the reader in Pecola's trauma. Is it possible for Claudia to 'infect' the reader with Pecola's suffering? Can the bearing of witness be delegated, as it were, to an agent?[18] Pecola is almost entirely silent throughout the novel as she sustains blow after blow of rejection and devaluation; her final dialogue as a split self is her most expressive moment. Paradoxically, Morrison articulates Pecola's suffering most powerfully by making her a silent victim.

The nature of Pecola's silence is particularly important in the rape scene, controversially narrated largely from the father-rapist's point of view. In his discussion of the novel, Michael Awkward compares Morrison's handling of this incident to an earlier treatment of rape in the Trueblood episode of Ralph Ellison's *Invisible Man.*[19] Awkward argues that Matty Lou, Trueblood's daughter, is marginalised in a way that Pecola is not. He sees Morrison as rewriting Ellison, taking him to task for the 'phallocentric nature of his representation of incest'.[20] But Ellison's Trueblood episode is surely parodying racist stereotypes of Blacks as lacking in self-control and ruled by animal lust, an aspect of the representation that complicates Awkward's charge of phallocentricism. In his discussion of *Invisible Man*, Awkward claims that 'never in the sharecropper's rendering of the story are Matty Lou's feelings in the foreground or even actually shared with the reader'.[21] In fact, Trueblood does render his daughter's feelings, although the feelings he represents would underscore Awkward's charge of phallocentricism. Truerblood describes her initially as protesting against the rape but then responding to his presence inside her by moving rhythmically: 'Then if that ain' bad enough, Matty Lou can't hold out no longer and gits to movin' herself.... She didn't want me to go then—and to tell the honest-to-God truth I found out that I din't want to go neither.'[22] Trueblood's narrative of his daughter's physical response is admittedly self-serving since it conveniently absolves him from the blame of initiating copulatory movements, but it does go on to include the outrage of his wife and daughter and their banishment of him from the home. In contrast to what he sees as the absence of Matty Lou's feelings from Ellison's text, Awkward finds that Morrison's narrative of Pecola's response to her father's penetration of her body includes her feelings and responses. Though we are following Cholly's thoughts and successive emotional responses to Pecola—rage, revulsion, hate, love, tenderness, lust—Pecola is present through descriptions of her intake of breath—'a hollow suck of air at the back of her throat' (128)—and the description of Cholly's painful attempt to remove himself from her dry vagina. Pecola's feelings are not represented in this scene at all, but the description of her physical state, presumably from the point of view of the omniscient narrator, suggests her feelings through descriprtions of her bodily state. What Awkward does not take into account, however, is that later, in Pecola's dialogue with 'her friend', there is some close questioning about how horrible it was to have Cholly 'coming at her'. The friend quizzes her: 'The second time too?' (159). Pecola's dialogue is an internal debate in which she accuses herself of having in some way enjoyed the attentions of Cholly. Although the incest scenes are narrated very differently, both Ellison and

Morrison raise the question of the daughter's response, both drawing some attention to the horror of possibly pleasurable feelings arising from an illicit and violating source. Furthermore, at the end of her novel, Morrison provocatively has Claudia recognise that Cholly loved his daughter enough to 'touch her, envelop her, give something of himself to her' (163). She recognises too that the love of a 'free man'—a man without self-imposed obligations and responsibilties—is 'never safe. There is no gift for the beloved. The lover alone possesses his gift of love. The loved one is shorn, neutralized, frozen in the glare of the lover's inward eye' (163).

The references to Pecola's rigid, 'shocked body', the silence of her 'stunned throat', the 'hollow suck of air in the back of her throat' may tell us something about her responses to the rape, but such details are signifiers of Pecola's shock, not accounts of her emotions and responses. The narrator observes that Cholly becomes conscious of her wet soapy hands on his wrists, 'but whether her grip was from a hopeless but stubborn struggle to be free, or from some other emotion, he could not tell' (128). Neither can the reader. Morrison does not, it seems, write Pecola's feelings into the scene, but rather represents through their absence the collapse of witnessing that the rape effects. The scene is narrated as if a slow-motion camera were taking in its details. It has been noted that, in moments of disclosure, incest patients are able to recall great detail and deliver accounts of the process as if it took place in slow motion.[23] What is typically absent from narration of the scene is how the victim felt. The trauma is therefore an 'event without a witness', because the witness is blocked from remembering herself or himself as a participant in the event.[24] The collapse of witnessing does not mean that the traumatised subject remembers nothing; on the contrary, what is missing from the remarkable verisimilitude of the account is only the presence of the victim. That is, commonly in trauma cases, the victim can only recount the scene by removing the consciousness or memory of self and participation. This illustrates why trauma precipitates a crisis in witnessing. The witness cannot know herself or himself as a participant in a scene of horror. If trauma occasions the excision of the self from memory, memory of one's participation and feelings, however painful, is presumed to be a sign of health. Either one possesses the past, or one is possessed by it. The emphasis on memory and remembering as a condition of health and growth in *The Bluest Eye* takes on new significance in this light. For as much as the novel is about Pecola, it is also about Claudia, whose ability to remember and bear witness, is its most hopeful aspect.

Indeed, Claudia's narrative relishes and cherishes its capacity to remember. The elder narrating Claudia has a sympathetic connection to and understanding of her younger self, whom she re-experiences as able to discern adult emotions even if she cannot comprehend the actual conversation: 'The edge, the curl, the thrust of their emotions is always clear to Frieda and me. We do not, cannot, know the meanings of all their words, for we are nine and ten years old. So we watch their faces, their hands, their feet, and listen for truth in timbre' (15). Remembering her father, Claudia recalls: 'My Daddy's face is a study. Winter moves into it and presides there. His eyes become a cliff of snow threatening to avalanche... And he will not unrazor his lips until spring' (47). Although this description does not seem to include the feelings of the younger Claudia, they are communicated indirectly in the childlike possessive, 'my daddy', and in the extended simile of his stern, wintry visage. Now Claudia understands the burdens and pressures her parents faced during the Depression; then she simply experienced him as remote and cold. In a Proustian moment, Claudia conveys her reminiscences of summer: 'I have only to break into the tightness of a strawberry and I see summer—its dust and lowering skies'(147). 'But', she continues, self-consciously investigating the nature of memory,

> my memory is uncertain; I recall a summer storm in the town where we lived and imagine a summer my mother knew in 1929. There was a tornado that year, she said that blew away half of south Lorain. I mix up her summer with my own. Biting the strawberry, thinking of storms, I see her. A slim young girl in a pink crepe dress ... So much for memory. Public fact becomes private reality, and the seasons of a Midwestern town become the *Moirai* of our small lives. (147)

Claudia's musings here about the adaptive and absorptive nature of memory signal the difference between the mind that is constantly creative and porous and that which is indelibly imprinted but sealed off from conscious recall. Yet Claudia's reflections seem at first to undercut the power of memory to tell the truth, since memory mixes together imagination, public knowledge, and remembered affective associations. Memory's power to tell the truth, however, goes beyond accuracy of reportage. Its power is to create a past, to make narrative, to put things in time:

> The brain is an enchanted loom where millions of flashing shuttles weave a dissolving pattern. Since the mind recreates reality from the abstractions of sense impressions, it can equally well simulate reality by recall and fantasy. The brain invents stories and runs imagined and remembered events back and forth through time.[25]

Claudia's interrogation of memory late in her narrative brings the recognition that her oppositional stance toward 'everything and everybody' has bred a habit of mind that resists and critiques all around it. On the one hand, this habit of mind, like anger, is a form of salvation; on the other, it has produced an unreal valuation of self-efficacy.

> We remembered Mrs. Breedlove knocking Pecola down and soothing the pink tears of the frozen doll baby that sounded like the door of our icebox. We remembered the knuckled eyes of schoolchildren under the gaze of Meringue Pie and the eyes of these same children when they looked at Pecola. Or maybe we didn't remember; we just knew. We had defended ourselves since memory against everything and everybody, considered all speech a code to be broken by us, and all gestures subject to careful analysis; we had become headstrong, devious, and arrogant. (150)

As Claudia's attention focuses on the state in which Pecola remains frozen, her own narrative becomes more self-conscious about the processes of memory, allowing an interrogation of herself and her own motives in the community's responsibility for Pecola's fate.

When we leave Claudia at the end of her meditation on anger and its accommodation in fraudulent love, we may wonder how she grows from that point to become the mature memorialising narrator who looks back on Pecola's life in the final section of the novel and reflects on Pecola's fate and the way identities are formed relationally. 'The damage done was total', she tells us (162). By this point, Claudia recognises the extent to which Pecola's vulnerability has been exploited by others. We felt 'so wholesome after we cleaned ourselves on her. We were so beautiful when we stood astride her ugliness ... We honed our egos on her, padded our characters with her frailty and yawned in the fantasy of our own strength' (163). Claudia also recognises that strength was really only aggression. Her closing litany of the accommodations and falsifications that she and others have perpetrated articulates an understanding both of why Pecola stepped into madness and the terms on which she, Claudia, survived. The honesty and self-scrutiny of the last paragraphs of the novel suggest a Claudia who can see without fraudulent accommodations, can shoulder responsibility without succumbing to the conformist culture of shame. As Claudia's narrative merges with that of the omniscient narrator, whose voice was previously more markedly distinct from Claudia's at the beginning of each seasonal section, the reader measures the extent of Claudia's growth. Whereas it is the omniscient narrator who recounts the scene of the rape—'So it was on a Saturday afternoon, in the thin light of spring, he staggered home reeling I drunk and saw his daughter in the kitchen' (127)—it is dearly Claudia who comments on the tragic fulfillment of Pecola's desire for blue eyes. 'So it was. A little black girl yearns for the blue eyes of a little white girl, and the horror at the heart of her yearning is exceeded only by the evil of fulfillment' (162). An omniscient narrator is necessary because logically Claudia cannot know and tell of the histories of Cholly and Pauline, Soaphead Church, the three whores and Geraldine; nor is she in a position to describe the rape of Pecola. Yet the closeness of their voices and vision by the end of the novel suggests that the wisdom of this all-knowing narrator is also Claudia's. What defines her, and replaces the anger and aggression of childhood, is ultimately an imaginative understanding, discernible earlier in the quality of her memories and mode of expression, but more explicit in the closing paragraphs of the novel as she comments on the fatal nature of Cholly's love and the sad infertility of the cultural climate for a thriving African American psyche.

The self-recrimination in Claudia's confession of the responsibility she and others bear for Pecola's demise is the cost of her survival. She experiences remorse and self-recrimination; she mourns. The states of emotion that Claudia feels, unpleasant as they may be, underscore the contrast between her and Pecola, who, in her dissociated state, is beyond guilt and grief.

NOTES

1 Toni Morrison, 'Unspeakable Thing Unspoken: The Afro-American Presence in American Literature', in Harold Bloom (ed.), *Toni Morrison; Modern Critical Views* (New York, Chelsea House Publishers 1990), p. 214.

2 Sandi Russell, 'Conversations From Abroad', in Nellie McKay (ed.), Critical Essays on Toni Morrison (Boston, G. K. Hall, 1988), p. 45.

3 Gloria Naylor, 'A Conversation: Toni Morrison and Gloria Naylor' [1985], Conversations, p. 199.

4 Toni Morrison, *The Bluest Eye* (Harmondsworth, Penguin, [1974/ 1994], p. 209.

5 Gershen Kaufman, *Shame: The Power of Caring* 3rd edition, (Rochester, Shenckman Books, 1992), p. xxi, see also Eve Kosofsky Sedgwick and Adam Frank (eds), *Shame and its Sisters: A Silvan Tompkins Reader* (Durham, Duke University Press, 1995).

6 Kaufman, *Shame*, p. xiii.

7 Kaufman, *Shame*, p. 9.

8 Toni Morrison, *The Bluest Eye* (London, Picador, [1970], 1990), pp. 6-7. Further references are to this edition and will be made parenthetically in the text.

9 In this regard, see bell hooks's powerful characterisation of anger against racism as 'killing rage' in *Killing Rage: Ending Racism* (London, Penguin, 1996), pp. 9-20.

10 Susan Willis, 'I Shop Therefore I Am: Is There a Place for Afro-American Culture in Commodity Culture?', in Cheryl Wall (ed.), *Changing Our Own*

Words: Essays on Criticism, Theory and Writing (New Brunswick, Rutgers University Press, 1989), p. 174.

11 Willis, 'I Shop Therefore I Am', p. 174.

12 See Morrison, 'Afterword', *The Bluest Eye*, p. 210.

13 Laura Brown, 'Not Outside the Range: One Feminist Perspective on Psychic Trauma', in Cathy Caruth (ed.) *Trauma: Explorations in Memory* (Baltimore, Johns Hopkins University Press, 1995), p. 100.

14 Brown, 'Not Outside the Range', p. 101.

15 Brown, ''Not Outside the Range', p. 103.

16 Brown, 'Not Outside the Range', p. 108.

17 Shoshona Felman and Dori Laub, *Testimony: Crises of Witnessing in Literature, Psychoanalysis, and History* (London, Routledge, 1992), p. 57.

18 See the discussion of Claudia as a moral agent in Lynne Tirrell, 'Storytelling and Moral Agency', *The Journal of Aesthetics and Art Criticism* 48:2 (1990), 115-26.

19 Michael Awkward, 'Roadblocks and Relatives: Critical Revision in Toni Morrison's *The Bluest Eye*', in McKay, *Critical Essays on Toni Morrison*, p. 63.

20 Awkward, 'Roadblocks and Relatives', p. 66.

21 Awkward, 'Roadblocks and Relatives', p. 64.

22 Ralph Ellison, *Invisible Man* (New York, Vintage, [1947],1995), p. 60.

23 I am grateful to my student, Jennifer Rosenitch, for making this point.

24 Felman and Laub, *Testimony*, p. 75.

25 The quotation is from Edward O. Wilson, On Human Nature (Cambridge, Harvard University Press, 1978); cited in Bessel A. van der Kolk and Onno van der Hart, 'The Intrusive Past: The Flexbility of Memory and the Engraving of Trauma', in Caruth, *Trauma: Explorations in Memory*, pp. 158-82.

이영옥

미국 하와이대학교 미국학 박사
한국영어영문학회 회장
한국현대영미소설학회 회장 역임
현 성균관대학교 영어영문학과 교수

저서
『젠더와 역사 : 미국소수인종문학의 이해』(태학사) 외

역서
『소설과 현대』(D. Daiches저 : 탐구당) 외

최근연구
이창래, 노라 옥자 켈러 등 한국계 미국작가에 대한 논문과
인터뷰를 미국학술지에 게재

손태수

성균관대학교 영어영문학과 졸업
코리아 헤럴드 기자 및 영문 SEOUL지 편집장 역임
성균관대학교 석사, 영문학 박사(과정)
현 성균관대학교 번역-TESOL대학원 겸임 교수

Toni Morrison

The Bluest Eye

가장 파란 눈 – 주석과 작품해설

1판 1쇄 발행 · 2007년 11월 1일
1판 4쇄 발행 · 2020년 4월 5일

편 주 자 · 이영옥 · 손태수
발 행 인 · 정 현 걸
발　 행 · 신 아 사
인　 쇄 · 대명프린팅
주　 소 · 서울특별시 은평구 통일로 59길 4 (2F)
전　 화 · (02) 382–6411 **팩스** · (02) 382–6401
홈페이지 · www.shinasa.co.kr
E-mail · shinasa@daum.net

ISBN: 978-89-8396-580-6 (93840)

정가 14,000원